MEASURING RIPPLES

Most ripple afghans start with a beginning chain.

The first row starts the ripple pattern with evenly spaced increases and decreases. This creates the up and down pattern *(Fig. A)*.

Fig. A

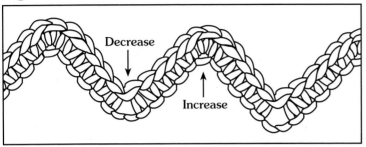

Every row is the same with the increases and decreases "stacked" over each other, with the increases forming the "peaks" of the ripple and the decreases forming the "valleys" of the ripple.

TO MEASURE TH

Lay your gauge swatch c
measure the width.

Measure the height of the gauge swatch by placing the ruler at the bottom of the center stitch of a "peak" increase to the highest point of the swatch.

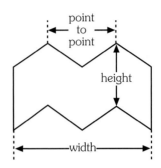

TO MEASURE FROM POINT TO POINT

Lay your piece on a flat, hard surface.

Measure from the center of the "peak" increase to the center of the next "peak" increase.

TO MEASURE THE AFGHAN

Lay your afghan on a flat, hard surface and measure the width.

The height of the afghan is measured from the bottom of the lowest "valley" to the top of the highest "peak".

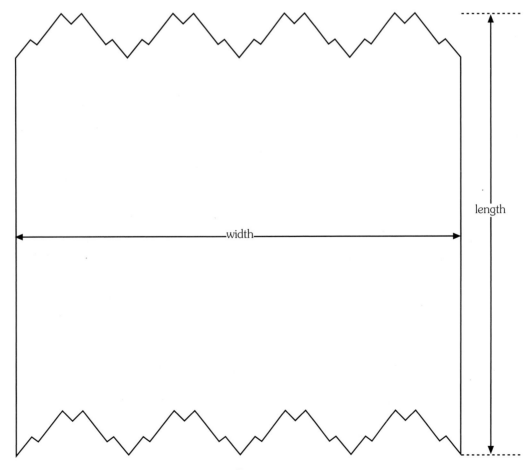

2

JOINING WITH HDC

When instructed to join with hdc, begin with a slip knot on hook. YO, holding loop on hook, insert hook in stitch or space indicated, YO and pull up a loop, YO and draw through all 3 loops on hook.

JOINING WITH DC

When instructed to join with dc, begin with a slip knot on hook. YO, holding loop on hook, insert hook in stitch or space indicated, YO and pull up a loop (3 loops on hook), (YO and draw through 2 loops on hook) twice.

BACK RIDGE

Work only in loops indicated by arrows *(Fig. 1)*.

Fig. 1

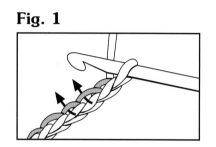

BACK OR FRONT LOOP ONLY

Work only in loop(s) indicated by arrow *(Fig. 2)*.

Fig. 2

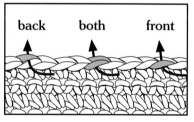

FREE LOOPS

After working in Back or Front Loops Only on a row or round, there will be a ridge of unused loops. These are called the free loops. Later, when instructed to work in the free loops of the same row or round, work in these loops *(Fig. 3a)*.

When instructed to work in free loops of a chain, work in loop indicated by arrow *(Fig. 3b)*.

Fig. 3a

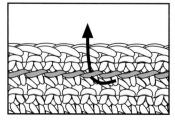

Fig. 3b

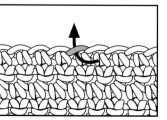

CHANGING COLORS

Work the last stitch to within one step of completion, hook new yarn *(Figs. 4a-d)* and draw through all loops on hook. Cut old yarn and work over both ends unless otherwise indicated.

Fig. 4a

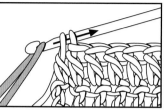

Fig. 4b

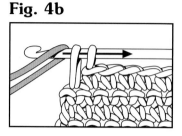

Fig. 4c

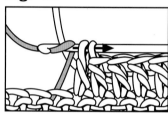

Fig. 4d

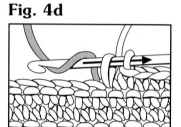

POST STITCH

Work around post of stitch indicated, inserting hook in direction of arrow *(Fig. 5)*.

Fig. 5

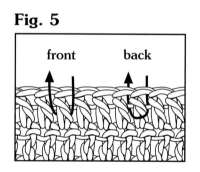

WORKING IN FRONT OF, AROUND, OR BEHIND A STITCH

Work in stitch or space indicated, inserting hook in direction of arrow *(Fig. 6)*.

Fig. 6

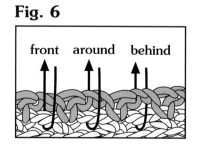

WHIPSTITCH

Place two Strips, Squares, Blocks, or Motifs with **wrong** sides together. Sew through both pieces once to secure the beginning of the seam, leaving an ample yarn end to weave in later. Insert the needle from **front** to **back** through **both** loops on **both** pieces *(Fig. 7a)* or through **inside** loop only of each stitch on **both** pieces *(Fig. 7b)*. Bring the needle around and insert it from **front** to **back** through the next loops of **both** pieces. Continue in this manner across to corner, keeping the sewing yarn fairly loose.

Fig. 7a

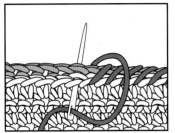

Fig. 7b

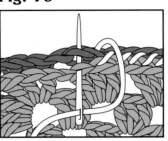

FRINGE

Cut a piece of cardboard 5" (12.5 cm) wide and $1/2$" (1.5 cm) longer than you want your finished fringe to be. Wind the yarn **loosely** and **evenly** around the cardboard until the card is filled, then cut across one end; repeat as needed.

Hold together half as many strands of yarn as desired for the finished fringe; fold in half.

With **wrong** side facing and using a crochet hook, draw the folded end up through a stitch, space, or row and pull the loose ends through the folded end *(Fig. 8a or 8c)*; draw the knot up **tightly** *(Fig. 8b or 8d)*. Repeat, spacing as desired.

Lay flat on a hard surface and trim the ends.

Fig. 8a

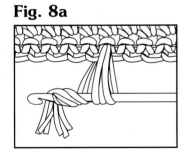

Fig. 8b

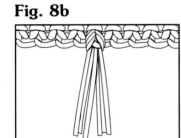

Fig. 8c

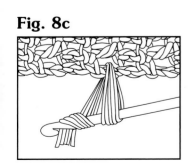

Fig. 8d

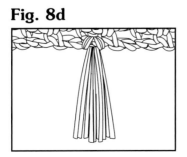

EMBROIDERY
BACKSTITCH

Working from right to left, come up at 1, go down at 2 and come up at 3 *(Fig. 9a)*. The second stitch is made by going down at 1 and coming up at 4 *(Fig. 9b)*. Continue in same manner.

Fig. 9a

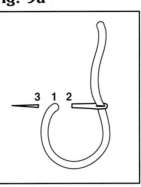

Fig. 9b

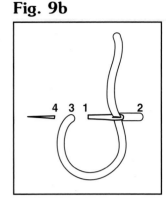

FRENCH KNOT

Bring needle up at 1. Wrap yarn desired number of times around needle and insert needle at 2, holding end of yarn with non-stitching fingers *(Fig. 10)*. Tighten knot; then pull needle through, holding yarn until it must be released.

Fig. 10

We have made every effort to ensure that these instructions are accurate and complete. We cannot, however, be responsible for human error, typographical mistakes, or variations in individual work.

Production Team: Instructional Editor - Susan Ackerman Carter, Technical Editor - Linda Luder; Editorial Editor - Suzie Puckett; Artist - Faith Lloyd; Senior Artist - Diana Sanders; Photo Sylists - Janna Laughlin and Cassie Newsome; and Photographer - Russ Ganser.

Instructions tested and photo models made by Janet Akins, Belinda Baxter, Pam Bland, Mike Cates, Marianna Crowder, Lee Ellis, Freda Gillham, Linda Graves, Raymelle Greening, Vicki Kellogg, Kay Meadors, Dale Potter, Clare Stringer, Margaret Taverner, and Mary Valen.

Wine on the Vine

First Prize

Pat Gibbons

Pat Gibbons of Missouri, our First-Prize winner, accomplished her longtime dream of winning an afghan contest with her Wine on the Vine design. She learned to crochet as a child, taught by her Aunt Bell. "I was amazed at the wonderful doilies she made." Pat's love of designing began at an early age. "I was always making clothes for my dollies. As a teenager, I made a lot of my own clothes and would try my hand at designing them." She says she learned to read patterns with the help of Leisure Arts books. Pat describes Wine on the Vine as an "understated" design, with variations of shades and textures.

Finished Size: 46" x 66$^1/_2$" (117 cm x 169 cm)

MATERIALS
Worsted Weight Yarn:
    Variegated - 27$^1/_2$ ounces, 1,595 yards
      (780 grams, 1,458.5 meters)
    Dk Plum - 17 ounces, 960 yards
      (480 grams, 878 meters)
    Dk Green - 6 ounces, 340 yards
      (170 grams, 311 meters)
    Tan - 4 ounces, 225 yards
      (110 grams, 205.5 meters)
Crochet hook, size G (4 mm) **or** size needed
for gauge

GAUGE: In pattern, one point to point
      repeat (31 sts) = 6$^1/_2$" (16.5 cm);
      Rows 1-16 = 7$^3/_4$" (19.75 cm)

Gauge Swatch: 13"w x 7$^3/_4$"h
               (33 cm x 19.75 cm)
With Variegated, ch 63.
Work same as Afghan Body for 16 rows.
Finish off.

STITCH GUIDE

> **DECREASE** (uses next 2 sc)
> ★ YO, insert hook in **next** sc, YO and pull up a loop, YO and draw through 2 loops on hook; repeat from ★ once **more**, YO and draw through all 3 loops on hook **(counts as one dc)**.
>
> **2-DC CLUSTER**
>   (uses next 2 3-dc Clusters)
> ★ YO, insert hook in free loop of **next** 3-dc Cluster one row **below (Fig. 3a, page 3)**, YO and pull up a loop, YO and draw through 2 loops on hook; repeat from ★ once **more**, YO and draw through all 3 loops on hook.
>
> **3-DC CLUSTER** (uses one sc)
> YO, insert hook in free loop of sc one row **below** next dc **(Fig. 3a, page 3)**, YO and pull up a loop, YO and draw through 2 loops on hook, ★ YO, insert hook in same st, YO and pull up a loop, YO and draw through 2 loops on hook; repeat from ★ once **more**, YO and draw through all 4 loops on hook. Skip dc behind 3-dc Cluster.

Continued on page 14.

Snowman Ridge

Second Prize

Carol Ann Marks

Carol Ann Marks of New Jersey, our Second-Prize winner, enjoys working on novelty crochet projects that capture the attention of her young grandson, Ted. "My grandmother taught me to crochet when I was very young, but I started to crochet more actively after I became a mother just over 35 years ago." Carol Ann says she's never met a crocheter she didn't love. She enjoys working with her local crochet guild on community projects, such as the 750 bookmarks they crocheted for 2nd and 3rd grade students. Her Snowman Ridge *design was inspired by Ted, who waits with great anticipation for the first snow of the season.*

Finished Size: 45" x 57" (114.5 cm x 145 cm)

MATERIALS
Worsted Weight Yarn:
    White - 16 ounces, 905 yards
      (450 grams, 827.5 meters)
    Blue - 16 ounces, 905 yards
      (450 grams, 827.5 meters)
    Dk Blue - 9 ounces, 510 yards
      (260 grams, 466.5 meters)
    Variegated - 1 ounce, 60 yards
      (30 grams, 55 meters)
    Black - small amount (for face and arms)
    Orange - small amount (for nose)
Crochet hook, size I (5.5 mm) **or** size needed
    for gauge
Yarn needle
Tapestry needle

GAUGE: One Block = $6^{1}/_{2}$" (16.5 cm)
      In pattern, one point to point
      repeat (48 sts) = 9" (23 cm);
      10 rows = $3^{3}/_{4}$" (9.5 cm)

Gauge Swatch: $2^{1}/_{8}$" (5.5 cm) square
Work same as Snowman Block, Square A.

STITCH GUIDE

BEGINNING DECREASE
Pull up a loop in first 2 sc, YO and draw through all 3 loops on hook **(counts as one sc)**.

DECREASE (uses next 3 sts)
Insert hook in next sc, YO and pull up a loop, skip next sc or joining, insert hook in next sc, YO and pull up a loop, YO and draw through all 3 loops on hook **(counts as one sc)**.

ENDING DECREASE
Pull up a loop in last 2 sc, YO and draw through all 3 loops on hook **(counts as one sc)**.

SNOWMAN BLOCK (Make 5)
SQUARE A (Make 2 White and 4 Blue)
Rnd 1: Ch 2, 4 sc in second ch from hook; join with slip st to first sc.

Continued on page 9.

Rnd 2 (Right side)**:** Ch 1, turn; skip joining slip st, 3 sc in each sc around; join with slip st to first sc: 12 sc.

Note: Loop a short piece of yarn around any stitch to mark Rnd 2 as **right** side.

Rnd 3: Ch 1, turn; skip joining slip st, sc in next sc, 3 sc in next sc, (sc in next 2 sc, 3 sc in next sc) 3 times, sc in last sc; join with slip st to first sc: 20 sc.

Rnd 4: Ch 1, turn; skip joining slip st, sc in next 2 sc, 3 sc in next sc, (sc in next 4 sc, 3 sc in next sc) 3 times, sc in last 2 sc; join with slip st to first sc, finish off: 28 sc.

SQUARE B (Make 2)
Rnd 1: With White, ch 2, 4 sc in second ch from hook; join with slip st to first sc.

Rnd 2 (Right side)**:** Ch 1, turn; skip joining slip st, 3 sc in each of next 2 sc changing to Blue in last sc made *(Fig. 4d, page 3)* and bringing White to front of work, 3 sc in each of last 2 sc; join with slip st to first sc: 12 sc.

Note: Mark Rnd 2 as **right** side.

Rnd 3: Ch 1, turn; skip joining slip st, 2 sc in next sc, sc in next 2 sc, 3 sc in next sc, sc in next 3 sc changing to White and bringing Blue to front of work, 2 sc in same st, sc in next 2 sc, 3 sc in next sc, sc in last 2 sc and in same st as first sc; join with slip st to first sc: 20 sc.

Rnd 4: Ch 1, turn; sc in same st as joining slip st and in next 4 sc, 3 sc in next sc, sc in next 4 sc, 2 sc in next sc changing to Blue in last sc made, cut White; sc in same st and in next 4 sc, 3 sc in next sc, sc in next 4 sc, 2 sc in same st as first sc; join with slip st to first sc, finish off: 28 sc.

SQUARE C
Rnd 1: With White, ch 2, 4 sc in second ch from hook; join with slip st to first sc.

Rnd 2 (Right side)**:** Ch 1, turn; skip joining slip st, 3 sc in each of next 2 sc changing to Variegated in last sc made and bringing White to front of work, 3 sc in each of last 2 sc; join with slip st to first sc: 12 sc.

Note: Mark Rnd 2 as **right** side.

Rnd 3: Ch 1, turn; skip joining slip st, 2 sc in first sc, sc in next 2 sc, 3 sc in next sc, sc in next 3 sc changing to White and bringing Variegated to front of work, 2 sc in same st, sc in next 2 sc, 3 sc in next sc, sc in last 2 sc and in same st as first sc; join with slip st to first sc: 20 sc.

Rnd 4: Ch 1, turn; sc in same st as joining slip st and in next 4 sc, 3 sc in next sc, sc in next 4 sc, 2 sc in next sc changing to Variegated in last sc made, cut White; sc in same st and in next 4 sc, 3 sc in next sc, sc in next 4 sc, 2 sc in same st as first sc; join with slip st to first sc: 28 sc.

Trim: Do **not** turn; slip st **loosely** diagonally across through center to opposite side forming hat band; finish off.

ASSEMBLY
With matching color and using Placement Diagram as a guide, whipstitch Squares together through **inside** loops *(Fig. 7b, page 4)*, forming 3 strips of 3 Squares each, beginning in center sc of first corner 3-sc group and ending in center sc of next corner 3-sc group; then whipstitch strips together in same manner.

PLACEMENT DIAGRAM

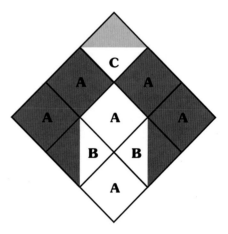

FINISHING
SNOWMAN SCARF
Row 1: With Variegated, ch 4, hdc in third ch from hook **(2 skipped chs count as first hdc)** and in last ch: 3 hdc.

Rows 2-15: Ch 2 **(counts as first hdc, now and throughout)**, turn; hdc in last 2 hdc; at end of Row 15, finish off.

Holding two strands of yarn together, add two fringes to short edges of Scarf *(Figs. 8a & b, page 4)*. Tack to bottom of Square C. Holding two strands of Variegated, add fringe to top of snowman hat. Fray ends of all fringe.

EMBROIDERY
Using photo as a guide for placement:
  With White, backstitch snowflakes in center of Blue Squares *(Figs. 9a & b, page 4)*.
  With Black, backstitch snowman arms.
  Using French knots and Black, add eyes to snowman *(Fig. 10, page 4)*.
  With Black, backstitch snowman mouth.
  With Orange, backstitch snowman nose.

BOTTOM RIPPLE
Row 1: With **right** side facing, holding Snowman Block with Square C at bottom, and working in Back Loops Only *(Fig. 2, page 3)*, join White with

sc in third sc of 3-sc group at Point A *(see Joining With Sc, page 1)*; sc in next 5 sc, ★ † (sc in same st as joining on same Square, skip next joining, sc in same st as joining on next Square and in next 6 sc) twice, 3 sc in next sc, sc in next 6 sc, (sc in same st as joining on same Square, skip next joining, sc in same st as joining on next Square and in next 6 sc) twice †, pull up a loop in next sc, holding next Snowman Block with Square C at bottom, pull up a loop in center sc of 3-sc group at Point A, YO and draw through all 3 loops on hook **(decrease made, counts as one sc)**, sc in next 6 sc; repeat from ★ 3 times **more**, then repeat from † to † once: 239 sc.

Work in Back Loops Only throughout.

Rows 2-9: Ch 1, turn; work beginning decrease, sc in next 21 sc, 3 sc in next sc, ★ sc in next 22 sc, decrease, sc in next 22 sc, 3 sc in next sc; repeat from ★ 3 times **more**, sc in next 21 sc, work ending decrease; at end of Row 9, finish off.

Row 10: With **wrong** side facing, join Blue with slip st in first sc; ch 1, [pull up a loop in same st and in next sc, YO and draw through all 3 loops on hook **(beginning decrease made)**], sc in next 21 sc, 3 sc in next sc, ★ sc in next 22 sc, decrease, sc in next 22 sc, 3 sc in next sc; repeat from ★ 3 times **more**, sc in next 21 sc, work ending decrease.

Rows 11-15: Repeat Row 2, 5 times; at end of Row 15, finish off.

Row 16: With Dk Blue, repeat Row 10.

Rows 17-19: Repeat Row 2, 3 times; at end of Row 19, finish off.

TOP RIPPLE
Row 1: With **right** side facing, holding Snowman Block with Square C at top, and working in Back Loop Only, join Blue with sc in third sc of 3-sc group at Point B; sc in next 5 sc, ★ † (sc in same st as joining on same Square, skip next joining, sc in same st as joining on next Square and in next 6 sc) twice, 3 sc in next sc, sc in next 6 sc, (sc in same st as joining on same Square, skip next joining, sc in same st as joining on next Square and in next 6 sc) twice †, decrease, sc in next 6 sc; repeat from ★ 3 times **more**, then repeat from † to † once: 239 sc.

Work in Back Loops Only throughout.

Rows 2-5: Ch 1, turn; work beginning decrease, sc in next 21 sc, 3 sc in next sc, ★ sc in next 22 sc, decrease, sc in next 22 sc, 3 sc in next sc; repeat from ★ 3 times **more**, sc in next 21 sc, work ending decrease; at end of Row 5, finish off.

Row 6: With **wrong** side facing, join White with slip st in first sc; ch 1, [pull up a loop in same st and in next sc, YO and draw through all 3 loops on hook **(beginning decrease made)**], sc in next 21 sc, 3 sc in next sc, ★ sc in next 22 sc, decrease, sc in next 22 sc, 3 sc in next sc; repeat from ★ 3 times **more**, sc in next 21 sc, work ending decrease.

Rows 7-13: Repeat Row 2, 7 times; at end of Row 13, finish off.

Row 14: With Blue, repeat Row 6.

Rows 15-19: Repeat Row 2, 5 times; at end of Row 19, finish off.

Row 20: With Dk Blue, repeat Row 6.

Rows 21-29: Repeat Row 2, 9 times; at end of last row, finish off.

Row 30: With Blue, repeat Row 6.

Rows 31-35: Repeat Row 2, 5 times; at end of last row, finish off.

Row 36: Repeat Row 6.

Rows 37-43: Repeat Row 2, 7 times; at end of last row, finish off.

Row 44: With Blue, repeat Row 6.

Rows 45-47: Repeat Row 2, 3 times; at end of Row 47, finish off.

Row 48: Repeat Row 6.

Rows 49-55: Repeat Row 2, 7 times; at end of last row, finish off.

Row 56: With Blue, repeat Row 6.

Rows 57-61: Repeat Row 2, 5 times; at end of last row, finish off.

Rows 62-86: Repeat Rows 20-44.

Row 87: Repeat Row 2; finish off.

Rows 88-101: Repeat Rows 48-61.

Row 102: With Dk Blue, repeat Row 6.

Rows 103-109: Repeat Row 2, 7 times; at end of Row 109, do **not** finish off.

TRIM
FIRST SIDE
Ch 1; with **right** side facing and working in end of rows, sc evenly across long edge of Afghan; finish off.

SECOND SIDE
With **right** side facing and working in end of rows, join Dk Blue with sc in last row of Bottom Ripple; sc evenly across long edge of Afghan; finish off.

Embossed Ripple

Third Prize

Marian Meyers

Marian Meyers of Illinois, our Third-Prize winner, has been crocheting since the age of 10. She says her grandmother was a "wonderful teacher." At the age of 44, Marian returned to college to complete her nursing degree. It was during that time that she started crocheting seriously. "Now that school is over and the final child has left home, I don't have time for the 'empty-nest syndrome,' because the dreams of having time to do specific projects are coming true. With a husband who travels all week with his job, I have many uninterrupted hours."

Marian was asked by her son to design a special afghan for his new home and to enter it in our contest. Her Embossed Ripple design was a winner with her son and with us.

Finished Size: $45^1/_2$" x 62"
(115.5 cm x 157.5 cm)

MATERIALS
Worsted Weight Yarn:
Off-White - 24 ounces, 1,575 yards
(680 grams, 1,440 meters)
Blue - $22^1/_2$ ounces, 1,475 yards
(640 grams, 1,348.5 meters)
Crochet hook, size J (6 mm) **or** size needed
for gauge

GAUGE: In pattern, one point to point
repeat (17 sts) = $3^1/_4$" (8.25 cm);
13 rows = $4^1/_2$" (11.5 cm)

Gauge Swatch: $6^1/_2$"w x $2^3/_4$"h
(16.5 cm x 7 cm)
With Off-White, ch 32.
Work same as Afghan Body for 8 rows.

STITCH GUIDE

LONG DOUBLE CROCHET
(abbreviated LDC)
YO, insert hook in st indicated, YO and pull up
a loop even with loop on hook (3 loops on
hook), (YO and draw through 2 loops on hook)
twice. Skip sc behind LDC.

FRONT POST DOUBLE CROCHET
(abbreviated FPdc)
YO, insert hook from **front** to **back** around
post of st indicated **(Fig. 5, page 3)**, YO and
pull up a loop (3 loops on hook), (YO and draw
through 2 loops on hook) twice.

AFGHAN BODY
With Off-White, ch 224.

Row 1 (Right side)**:** Working in back ridges of
beginning ch **(Fig. 1, page 3)**, sc in second ch from
hook and in next 6 chs, 3 sc in next ch, sc in next
7 chs, ★ skip next ch, sc in next 7 chs, 3 sc in next
ch, sc in next 7 chs; repeat from ★ across;
finish off: 238 sc.

Note: Loop a short piece of yarn around any stitch
to mark Row 1 as **right** side.

11

Continued on page 13.

Row 2: With **right** side facing, join Off-White with sc in first sc *(see Joining With Sc, page 1)*; skip next sc, sc in next 6 sc, 3 sc in next sc, ★ sc in next 7 sc, skip next 2 sc, sc in next 7 sc, 3 sc in next sc; repeat from ★ across to last 8 sc, sc in next 6 sc, skip next sc, sc in last sc; finish off.

Row 3: With **right** side facing, join Blue with sc in first sc; skip next sc, sc in next 5 sc, work LDC in same st 2 rows **below** as first 3-sc group worked into (between first and second sc) *(Fig. 11)*, 3 sc in next sc, work LDC in same st as last LDC, ★ sc in next 6 sc, skip next 2 sc, sc in next 6 sc, work LDC in same st 2 rows **below** as next 3-sc group worked into (between first and second sc), 3 sc in next sc, work LDC in same st as last LDC; repeat from ★ 12 times **more**, sc in next 5 sc, skip next sc, sc in last sc; finish off.

Fig. 11

Row 4: With **right** side facing, join Blue with sc in first sc; skip next sc, sc in next 4 sc, work FPdc around next LDC, sc in next sc, 3 sc in next sc, sc in next sc, work FPdc around next LDC, ★ sc in next 5 sc, skip next 2 sc, sc in next 5 sc, work FPdc around next LDC, sc in next sc, 3 sc in next sc, sc in next sc, work FPdc around next LDC; repeat from ★ across to last 6 sc, sc in next 4 sc, skip next sc, sc in last sc; finish off.

Row 5: With **right** side facing, join Blue with sc in first sc; skip next sc, sc in next 3 sc, work FPdc around next FPdc, sc in next 2 sc, 3 sc in next sc, sc in next 2 sc, work FPdc around next FPdc, ★ sc in next 4 sc, skip next 2 sc, sc in next 4 sc, work FPdc around next FPdc, sc in next 2 sc, 3 sc in next sc, sc in next 2 sc, work FPdc around next FPdc; repeat from ★ across to last 5 sc, sc in next 3 sc, skip next sc, sc in last sc; finish off.

Row 6: With **right** side facing, join Blue with sc in first sc; skip next sc, sc in next 2 sc, work FPdc around next FPdc, sc in next 3 sc, 3 sc in next sc, sc in next 3 sc, work FPdc around next FPdc, ★ sc in next 3 sc, skip next 2 sc, sc in next 3 sc, work FPdc around next FPdc, sc in next 3 sc, 3 sc in next sc, sc in next 3 sc, work FPdc around next FPdc; repeat from ★ across to last 4 sc, sc in next 2 sc, skip next sc, sc in last sc; finish off.

Row 7: With **right** side facing, join Blue with sc in first sc; skip next sc, sc in next sc, work FPdc around next FPdc, sc in next 4 sc, 3 sc in next sc, sc in next 4 sc, work FPdc around next FPdc, ★ sc in next 2 sc, skip next 2 sc, sc in next 2 sc, work FPdc around next FPdc, sc in next 4 sc, 3 sc in next sc, sc in next 4 sc, work FPdc around next FPdc; repeat from ★ across to last 3 sc, sc in next sc, skip next sc, sc in last sc; finish off.

Row 8: With **right** side facing, join Blue with sc in first sc; skip next sc, work FPdc around next FPdc, sc in next 5 sc, 3 sc in next sc, sc in next 5 sc, work FPdc around next FPdc, ★ sc in next sc, skip next 2 sc, sc in next sc, work FPdc around next FPdc, sc in next 5 sc, 3 sc in next sc, sc in next 5 sc, work FPdc around next FPdc; repeat from ★ across to last 2 sc, skip next sc, sc in last sc; finish off.

Rows 9-15: With **right** side facing, join Off-White with sc in first sc; skip next st, sc in next 6 sc, 3 sc in next sc, ★ sc in next 7 sts, skip next 2 sc, sc in next 7 sts, 3 sc in next sc; repeat from ★ across to last 8 sts, sc in next 6 sc, skip next st, sc in last sc; finish off.

Row 16: With **right** side facing, join Blue with sc in first sc; skip next sc, sc in next 5 sc, work LDC in same st 2 rows **below** as first 3-sc group worked into (between first and second sc), 3 sc in next sc, work LDC in same st as last LDC, ★ sc in next 6 sc, skip next 2 sc, sc in next 6 sc, work LDC in same st 2 rows **below** as next 3-sc group worked into (between first and second sc), 3 sc in next sc, work LDC in same st as last LDC; repeat from ★ 12 times **more**, sc in next 5 sc, skip next sc, sc in last sc; finish off.

Rows 17-179: Repeat Rows 4-16, 12 times; then repeat Rows 4-10 once **more**; at end of Row 179, do **not** finish off.

TRIM
FIRST SIDE
Ch 1; sc in end of each row across long edge of Afghan; finish off.

SECOND SIDE
With **right** side facing and working in end of rows, join Off-White with sc in first row; sc in each row across; finish off.

13

Wine on the Vine

Continued from page 5.

AFGHAN BODY

With Variegated, ch 223.

Row 1 (Right side)**:** Dc in fourth ch from hook **(3 skipped chs count as first dc)** and in next 12 chs, 3 dc in next ch, dc in next 14 chs, ★ skip next 3 chs, dc in next 14 chs, 3 dc in next ch, dc in next 14 chs; repeat from ★ across; finish off: 217 dc.

Note: Loop a short piece of yarn around any stitch to mark Row 1 as **right** side.

Work in Back Loops Only throughout *(Fig. 2, page 3)*.

Row 2: With **right** side facing, join Dk Plum with sc in first dc *(see Joining With Sc, page 1)*; skip next dc, sc in next 13 dc, 3 sc in next dc, ★ sc in next 14 dc, skip next 2 dc, sc in next 14 dc, 3 sc in next dc; repeat from ★ 5 times **more**, sc in next 13 dc, skip next dc, sc in last dc; finish off.

Row 3: With **right** side facing, join Variegated with dc in first sc *(see Joining With Dc, page 3)*; decrease, dc in next 12 sc, 3 dc in next sc, ★ dc in next 14 dc, skip next 2 sc, dc in next 14 sc, 3 dc in next sc; repeat from ★ 5 times **more**, dc in next 12 sc, decrease, dc in last sc; finish off.

Row 4: With **right** side facing, join Dk Plum with sc in first dc; skip next dc, sc in next 13 dc, 3 sc in next dc, ★ sc in next 5 dc, work 3-dc Cluster, sc in next 8 dc, skip next 2 dc, sc in next 8 dc, work 3-dc Cluster, sc in next 5 dc, 3 sc in next dc; repeat from ★ 5 times **more**, sc in next 13 dc, skip next dc, sc in last dc; finish off.

Row 5: With **right** side facing, join Variegated with dc in first sc; decrease, dc in next 12 sc, 3 dc in next sc, ★ dc in next 14 sts, skip next 2 sc, dc in next 14 sts, 3 dc in next sc; repeat from ★ 5 times **more**, dc in next 12 sc, decrease, dc in last sc; finish off.

Row 6: With **right** side facing, join Dk Plum with sc in first dc; skip next dc, sc in next 13 dc, 3 sc in next dc, ★ sc in next 6 dc, work 3-dc Cluster, sc in next dc, work 3-dc Cluster, sc in next 5 dc, skip next 2 dc, sc in next 5 dc, work 3-dc Cluster, sc in next dc, work 3-dc Cluster, sc in next 6 dc, 3 sc in next dc; repeat from ★ 5 times **more**, sc in next 13 dc, skip next dc, sc in last dc; finish off.

Row 7: Repeat Row 5.

Row 8: With **right** side facing, join Dk Plum with sc in first dc; skip next dc, sc in next 13 dc, 3 sc in next dc, ★ sc in next 7 dc, work 3-dc Cluster, (sc in next dc, work 3-dc Cluster) twice, sc in next 2 dc, skip next 2 dc, sc in next 2 dc, work 3-dc Cluster, (sc in next dc, work 3-dc Cluster) twice, sc in next 7 dc, 3 sc in next dc; repeat from ★ 5 times **more**, sc in next 13 dc, skip next dc, sc in last dc; finish off.

Row 9: Repeat Row 5.

Row 10: With **right** side facing, join Dk Plum with sc in first dc; skip next dc, sc in next 13 dc, 3 sc in next dc, ★ sc in next 10 dc, (work 3-dc Cluster, sc in next dc) twice, skip next 2 dc, (sc in next dc, work 3-dc Cluster) twice, sc in next 10 sc, 3 sc in next dc; repeat from ★ 5 times **more**, sc in next 13 dc, skip next dc, sc in last dc; finish off.

Row 11: Repeat Row 5.

Row 12: With **right** side, join Dk Green with sc in first dc; skip next dc, sc in next 13 dc, 3 sc in next dc, sc in next 13 dc, ★ work 2-dc Cluster twice, skip next 4 dc from last sc worked, sc in next 13 dc, 3 sc in next dc; repeat from ★ 5 times **more**, sc in next 13 dc, skip next dc, sc in last dc; finish off.

Row 13: With **right** side facing, join Tan with dc in first sc; decrease, dc in next 12 sc, 3 dc in next sc, ★ dc in next 14 sc, skip next 2 2-dc Clusters, dc in next 14 sc, 3 dc in next sc; repeat from ★ 5 times **more**, dc in next 12 sc, decrease, dc in last sc; finish off.

Row 14: With **right** side facing, join Dk Green with sc in first dc; skip next dc, sc in next 13 dc, 3 sc in next dc, ★ sc in next 14 dc, skip next 2 dc, sc in next 14 dc, 3 sc in next dc; repeat from ★ 5 times **more**, sc in next 13 dc, skip next dc, sc in last dc; finish off.

Row 15: With **right** side facing, join Variegated with dc in first sc; decrease, dc in next 12 sc, 3 dc in next sc, ★ dc in next 14 sc, skip next 2 sc, dc in next 14 sc, 3 dc in next sc; repeat from ★ 5 times **more**, dc in next 12 sc, decrease, dc in last sc; finish off.

Rows 16-137: Repeat Rows 2-15, 8 times; then repeat Rows 2-11 once **more**.

TRIM

With **right** side facing and working in Back Loops Only, join Dk Green with sc in first dc; skip next dc, sc in next 13 dc, 3 sc in next dc, † sc in next 13 dc, work 2-dc Cluster twice, skip next 4 dc from last sc worked, sc in next 13 dc, 3 sc in next dc †; repeat from † to † 5 times **more**, sc in next 13 dc, skip next dc, sc in last dc; sc evenly across end of rows; working in sps and in free loops across beginning ch *(Fig. 3b, page 3)*, sc in first 13 chs, skip next 3 chs, sc in next 13 chs, ★ 3 sc in next sp, sc in next 13 chs, skip next 3 chs, sc in next 13 chs; repeat from ★ across; sc evenly across end of rows; join with slip st to first sc, finish off.

Romantic Melody

Finished Size: 45" x 50¹/₂"
(114.5 cm x 128.5 cm)

MATERIALS
Worsted Weight Yarn:
  Ecru - 26 ounces, 1,470 yards
    (740 grams, 1,344 meters)
  Rose - 10¹/₂ ounces, 595 yards
    (300 grams, 544 meters)
  Crochet hook, size I (5.5 mm) **or** size needed
  for gauge

GAUGE: In pattern, one point to point
    repeat (17 sts) = 5" (12.75 cm);
    8 rows = 5³/₄" (14.5 cm)

Gauge Swatch: 10"w x 5³/₄"h
    (25.5 cm x 14.5 cm)
With Ecru, ch 34.
Work same as Afghan for 8 rows.

STITCH GUIDE

FRONT POST DOUBLE CROCHET
  (abbreviated FPdc)
YO, insert hook from **front** to **back** around
post of dc indicated *(Fig. 5, page 3)*, YO and
pull up a loop (3 loops on hook), (YO and draw
through 2 loops on hook) twice.

AFGHAN
With Ecru, ch 153.

Row 1 (Wrong side)**:** Dc in fourth ch from hook
(3 skipped chs count as first dc) and in next
5 chs, 3 dc in next ch, dc in next 7 chs, ★ skip next
2 chs, dc in next 7 chs, 3 dc in next ch, dc in next
7 chs; repeat from ★ across: 153 dc.

Note: Loop a short piece of yarn around **back** of
any stitch on Row 1 to mark **right** side.

Rows 2-4: Ch 3 **(counts as first dc, now and
throughout)**, turn; working in Front Loops Only
(Fig. 2, page 3), skip next dc, dc in next 5 sts,
work FPdc around next dc, 3 dc in next dc, work
FPdc around next dc, ★ dc in next 6 sts, skip next
2 dc, dc in next 6 sts, work FPdc around next dc,
3 dc in next dc, work FPdc around next dc; repeat
from ★ across to last 7 sts, dc in next 5 sts, skip
next dc, dc in last dc; at end of Row 4, finish off:
135 dc and 18 FPdc.

Row 5: With **wrong** side facing and working in
Front Loops Only, join Rose with dc in first dc *(see
Joining With Dc, page 3)*; skip next dc, dc in next
5 sts, work FPdc around next dc, 3 dc in next dc,
work FPdc around next dc, ★ dc in next 6 sts, skip
next 2 dc, dc in next 6 sts, work FPdc around next
dc, 3 dc in next dc, work FPdc around next dc;
repeat from ★ across to last 7 sts, dc in next 5 sts,
skip next dc, dc in last dc.

Rows 6-8: Ch 3, turn; working in Front Loops
Only, skip next dc, dc in next 5 sts, work FPdc
around next dc, 3 dc in next dc, work FPdc around
next dc, ★ dc in next 6 sts, skip next 2 dc, dc in
next 6 sts, work FPdc around next dc, 3 dc in next
dc, work FPdc around next dc; repeat from ★ across
to last 7 sts, dc in next 5 sts, skip next dc, dc in last
dc; at end of last row, finish off.

Rows 9-12: With Ecru, repeat Rows 5-8.

Rows 13-25: Repeat Rows 5-12 once, then
repeat Rows 5-9 once **more**.

Rows 26-46: Ch 3, turn; working in Front Loops
Only, skip next dc, dc in next 5 sts, work FPdc
around next dc, 3 dc in next dc, work FPdc around
next dc, ★ dc in next 6 sts, skip next 2 dc, dc in
next 6 sts, work FPdc around next dc, 3 dc in next
dc, work FPdc around next dc; repeat from ★ across
to last 7 sts, dc in next 5 sts, skip next dc, dc in last
dc; at end of Row 46, finish off.

Rows 47-70: Repeat Rows 5-12, 3 times.

Holding 6 strands of Ecru together, each 18"
(45.5 cm) long, add fringe evenly spaced across
short edges of Afghan *(Figs. 8a & b, page 4)*.

Design by Margaret Budnik.

Hugs & Kisses

Finished Size: 45$\frac{1}{2}$" x 65"
        (115.5 cm x 165 cm)

MATERIALS
Worsted Weight Yarn:
    Ecru - 18$\frac{1}{2}$ ounces, 1,215 yards
        (530 grams, 1,111 meters)
    Lt Rose - 10$\frac{1}{2}$ ounces, 690 yards
        (300 grams, 631 meters)
    Rose - 10$\frac{1}{2}$ ounces, 690 yards
        (300 grams, 631 meters)
    Dk Rose - 10$\frac{1}{2}$ ounces, 690 yards
        (300 grams, 631 meters)
  Crochet hook, size H (5 mm) **or** size needed
    for gauge

GAUGE: In pattern, one point to point
        repeat (28 sts) = 5" (12.75 cm)
        Rows 1-4 = 3$\frac{1}{4}$" (8.25 cm)

Gauge Swatch: 10"w x 6"h
        (25.5 cm x 15.25 cm)
With Ecru, ch 59.
Work same as Afghan Body for 8 rows.

STITCH GUIDE

DECREASE (uses next 2 ch-1 sps)
★ YO, insert hook in **next** ch-1 sp, YO and pull up a loop, YO and draw through 2 loops on hook; repeat from ★ once **more**, YO and draw through all 3 loops on hook **(counts as one dc)**.

ENDING DECREASE
  (uses last ch-1 sp and last 2 dc)
YO, insert hook in last ch-1 sp, YO and pull up a loop, YO and draw through 2 loops on hook, YO, skip next dc, insert hook in last dc, YO and pull up a loop, YO and draw through 2 loops on hook, YO and draw through all 3 loops on hook **(counts as one dc)**.

DOUBLE DECREASE (uses next 6 chs)
★ YO, skip **next** ch, insert hook in **next** ch, YO and pull up a loop, YO and draw through 2 loops on hook; repeat from ★ 2 times **more**, YO and draw through all 4 loops on hook **(counts as one dc)**.

CENTER DECREASE (uses next 2 Puff Sts)
★ YO, insert hook in **next** Puff St, YO and pull up a loop, YO and draw through 2 loops on hook; repeat from ★ once **more**, YO and draw through all 3 loops on hook **(counts as one dc)**.

CROSS ST (uses next ch-1 sp and next dc)
Skip next ch-1 sp, dc in next dc, ch 1, working **around** last dc made *(Fig. 6, page 3)*, dc in skipped ch-1 sp.

PUFF ST (uses one ch-1 sp)
★ YO, insert hook in ch-1 sp indicated, YO and pull up a loop even with loop on hook; repeat from ★ 4 times **more**, YO and draw through all 11 loops on hook, ch 1 to close.

AFGHAN BODY
With Ecru, ch 255, place marker in third ch from hook for st placement.

Row 1: Dc in fifth ch from hook, skip next ch, (dc in next ch, ch 1, skip next ch) 5 times, dc in next ch, (ch 1, dc in same st) 3 times, (ch 1, skip next ch, dc in next ch) 5 times, ★ work double decrease, skip next ch, (dc in next ch, ch 1, skip next ch) 5 times, dc in next ch, (ch 1, dc in same st) 3 times, (ch 1, skip next ch, dc in next ch) 5 times; repeat from ★ across to last 4 chs, **[**(YO, skip **next** ch, insert hook in **next** ch, YO and pull up a loop, YO and draw through 2 loops on hook) twice, YO and draw through all 3 loops on hook **(counts as one dc)]**: 136 dc and 117 ch-1 sps.

Continued on page 22.

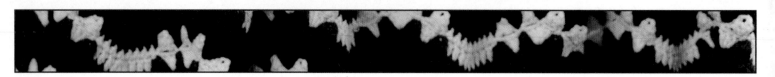

Patriotic Parade

Finished Size: 48" x 60 1/2" (122 cm x 153.5 cm)

MATERIALS
Worsted Weight Yarn:
  Blue - 21 ounces, 1,185 yards
    (600 grams, 1,083.5 meters)
  Red - 17 1/2 ounces, 990 yards
    (500 grams, 905.5 meters)
  Ecru - 15 ounces, 850 yards
    (430 grams, 777 meters)
Crochet hook, size G (4 mm) **or** size needed
  for gauge

GAUGE: In pattern, one repeat = 5 3/4" (14.5 cm);
          8 rows = 3 3/4" (9.5 cm)

Gauge Swatch: 9 3/4"w x 3 3/4"h
                (24.75 cm x 9.5 cm)
Row 1 (Wrong side)**:** With Blue, work Scallop, work
3 Large Scallops, ch 13, 2 dc in fourth ch from
hook **(Scallop made)**, work 3 Large Scallops;
finish off: 8 Scallops.
Note: Loop a short piece of yarn around **back** of
any stitch to mark **right** side.
Rows 2-8: Work same as Afghan Body.
Finish off.

STITCH GUIDE

> **SCALLOP**
> Ch 4, 2 dc in fourth ch from hook.
>
> **SMALL SCALLOP**
> Ch 3, hdc in third ch from hook.
>
> **LARGE SCALLOP**
> Ch 5, 2 dc in fourth ch from hook.
>
> **PICOT SCALLOP**
> (Dc, ch 4, dc in fourth ch from hook, dc) in
> slip st indicated.
>
> **SCALLOP DECREASE**
>   (uses next 2 Scallops)
> Pull up a loop in next ch and in corresponding
> ch of next Scallop, YO and draw through all
> 3 loops on hook.

> **DECREASE** (uses next 3 sts)
> ★ YO, insert hook in **next** st, YO and pull up a
> loop, YO and draw through 2 loops on hook;
> repeat from ★ 2 times **more**, YO and draw
> through all 4 loops on hook **(counts as
> one dc)**.

AFGHAN BODY
Row 1 (Wrong side)**:** With Blue, work Scallop, work
3 Large Scallops, ★ ch 13, 2 dc in fourth ch from
hook **(Scallop made)**, work 3 Large Scallops;
repeat from ★ 6 times **more**; finish off:
32 Scallops.

Note: Loop a short piece of yarn around **back** of
any stitch on Row 1 to mark **right** side.

Row 2: With **right** side facing and being careful
not to twist Row 1, skip first 2 dc and next ch and
join Red with sc in next ch *(see Joining With Sc,
page 1)*; skip next 2 chs, 3 dc in next ch, skip next
2 dc and next ch, sc in next ch, skip next 2 chs,
5 dc in next ch, skip next 2 dc and next ch, sc in
next ch, skip next 2 chs, 3 dc in next ch, skip next
2 dc and next ch, sc in next ch, ★ skip next 2 chs,
dc in next 3 chs, decrease, dc in next 3 chs, skip
next 2 dc and next ch, sc in next ch, skip next
2 chs, 3 dc in next ch, skip next 2 dc and next ch,
sc in next ch, skip next 2 chs, 5 dc in next ch, skip
next 2 dc and next ch, sc in next ch, skip next
2 chs, 3 dc in next ch, skip next 2 dc and next ch,
sc in next ch; repeat from ★ across: 169 sts.

Row 3: Ch 1, turn; sc in first sc, work Scallop, skip
next 3 dc, sc in next sc, (work Scallop, skip next
2 dc, sc in next st) twice, ★ work Scallop, skip next
3 dc, sc in next 9 sts, work Scallop, skip next 3 dc,
sc in next sc, (work Scallop, skip next 2 dc, sc in
next st) twice; repeat from ★ 6 times **more**, work
Scallop, skip next 3 dc, sc in last sc; finish off:
32 Scallops and 89 sc.

Continued on page 21.

Row 4: With **right** side facing, skip first 3 sts and next ch and join Ecru with sc in next ch; 3 dc in next sc, skip next 2 dc and next ch, sc in next ch, 5 dc in next sc, skip next 2 dc and next ch, sc in next ch, 3 dc in next sc, skip next 2 dc and next ch, sc in next ch, ★ dc in next 3 sc, decrease, dc in next 3 sc, skip next 2 dc and next ch, sc in next ch, 3 dc in next sc, skip next 2 dc and next ch, sc in next ch, 5 dc in next sc, skip next 2 dc and next ch, sc in next ch, 3 dc in next sc, skip next 2 dc and next ch, sc in next ch; repeat from ★ across: 169 sts.

Row 5: Ch 1, turn; sc in first sc, work Scallop, skip next 3 dc, sc in next sc, (work Scallop, skip next 2 dc, sc in next st) twice, ★ work Scallop, skip next 3 dc, sc in next 9 sts, work Scallop, skip next 3 dc, sc in next sc, (work Scallop, skip next 2 dc, sc in next st) twice; repeat from ★ 6 times **more**, work Scallop, skip next 3 dc, sc in last sc; finish off: 32 Scallops and 89 sc.

Rows 6 and 7: With Blue, repeat Rows 4 and 5.

Row 8: With Red, repeat Row 4.

Rows 9-119: Repeat Rows 3-8, 18 times; then repeat Rows 3-5 once **more**.

EDGING

Rnd 1: With **right** side facing, skip first 3 sts and next ch on Row 119 and join Blue with sc in next ch; 3 dc in next sc, skip next 2 dc and next ch, sc in next ch, 5 dc in next sc, skip next 2 dc and next ch, sc in next ch, 3 dc in next sc, ★ skip next 2 dc and next ch, sc in next ch, dc in next 3 sc, decrease, dc in next 3 sc, skip next 2 dc and next ch, sc in next ch, 3 dc in next sc, skip next 2 dc and next ch, sc in next ch, 5 dc in next sc, skip next 2 dc and next ch, sc in next ch, 3 dc in next sc; repeat from ★ across to last Scallop, skip next 2 dc and next ch, 3 sc in next ch; work 179 sc evenly spaced across end of rows; working in free loops of beginning ch (*Fig. 3b, page 3*), 3 sc in ch at base of first Scallop and around dc of same Scallop, sc in next ch, (2 sc around dc of next Scallop, sc in next ch) twice, † 3 sc around dc of next Scallop, sc in next 9 chs, 3 sc around dc of next Scallop, sc in next ch, (2 sc around dc of next Scallop, sc in next ch) twice †; repeat from † to † across to last Scallop, 3 sc around dc of last Scallop and in top of same dc; work 179 sc evenly spaced across end of rows, 2 sc in same st as first sc; join with slip st to first sc: 704 sts.

Rnd 2: Do **not** turn; † work Scallop, skip next 3 sts, slip st in next sc, (work Scallop, skip next 2 sts, slip st in next st) twice, ★ (work Scallop, skip next 3 sts, slip st in next sc) 4 times, (work Scallop, skip next 2 sts, slip st in next st) twice; repeat from ★ 6 times **more**, work Scallop, skip next 3 sts, slip st in next sc, work Scallop, skip next sc, slip st in next sc, work Scallop, (skip next 2 sc, slip st in next sc, work Scallop) 60 times, skip next sc †,

slip st in next sc, repeat from † to † once; join with slip st to joining slip st, finish off: 216 Scallops.

Rnd 3: With **right** side facing, join Red with dc in same st as joining (*see Joining With Dc, page 3*); [ch 4, dc in fourth ch from hook and in same st as first dc (**first Picot Scallop made**)], skip next 2 chs, † ★ (slip st in next ch, skip next 2 dc, work Picot Scallop in next slip st, skip next 2 chs) 4 times, work Scallop decrease, skip next 2 dc, work Picot Scallop in next slip st, skip next 2 chs; repeat from ★ 6 times **more** †, (slip st in next ch, skip next 2 dc, work Picot Scallop in next slip st, skip next 2 chs) 9 times, ♥ work Scallop decrease, [skip next 2 dc, work Picot Scallop in next slip st, skip next 2 chs, (slip st in next ch, skip next 2 dc, work Picot Scallop in next slip st, skip next 2 chs) 3 times, work Scallop decrease] 10 times ♥, skip next 2 dc, work Picot Scallop in next slip st, skip next 2 chs, (slip st in next ch, skip next 2 dc, work Picot Scallop in next slip st, skip next 2 chs) 6 times, work Scallop decrease, skip next 2 dc, work Picot Scallop in next slip st, skip next 2 chs, repeat from † to † once, (slip st in next ch, skip next 2 dc, work Picot Scallop in next slip st, skip next 2 chs) 6 times, repeat from ♥ to ♥ once, (skip next 2 dc, work Picot Scallop in next slip st, skip next 2 chs, slip st in next ch) 5 times; join with slip st to first dc, finish off: 179 Picot Scallops.

Rnd 4: With **right** side facing, join Blue with slip st in last slip st made before joining; ch 5, hdc in third ch from hook, slip st in center ch of next Picot Scallop, † ★ (work Small Scallop, skip next 2 dc, hdc in next slip st, work Small Scallop, slip st in center ch of next Picot Scallop) 4 times, skip next 2 dc, hdc in next decrease, slip st in center ch of next Picot Scallop; repeat from ★ 6 times **more** †, (work Small Scallop, skip next 2 dc, hdc in next slip st, work Small Scallop, slip st in center ch of next Picot Scallop) 9 times, ♥ skip next 2 dc, hdc in next decrease, slip st in center ch of next Picot Scallop, [(work Small Scallop, skip next 2 dc, hdc in next slip st, work Small Scallop, slip st in center ch of next Picot Scallop) 3 times, skip next 2 dc, hdc in next decrease, slip st in center ch of next Picot Scallop] 10 times ♥, (work Small Scallop, skip next 2 dc, hdc in next slip st, work Small Scallop, slip st in center ch of next Picot Scallop) 6 times, skip next 2 dc, hdc in next decrease, slip st in center ch of next Picot Scallop, repeat from † to † once, (work Small Scallop, skip next 2 dc, hdc in next slip st, work Small Scallop, slip st in center ch of next Picot Scallop) 6 times, repeat from ♥ to ♥ once, work Small Scallop, skip next 2 dc, (hdc in next slip st, work Small Scallop, slip st in center ch of next Picot Scallop, work Small Scallop, skip next 2 dc) 4 times; join with slip st to second ch of beginning ch-5, finish off.

Design by Rosalie DeVries.

21

Hugs & Kisses

Continued from page 17.

Row 2 (Right side): Ch 2, turn; dc in next ch-1 sp, work 5 Cross Sts, dc in next ch-1 sp, (ch 1, dc in same sp) 3 times, work 5 Cross Sts, ★ decrease, work 5 Cross Sts, dc in next ch-1 sp, (ch 1, dc in same sp) 3 times, work 5 Cross Sts; repeat from ★ across to last ch-1 sp, work ending decrease: 226 dc and 117 ch-1 sps.

Note: Loop a short piece of yarn around any stitch to mark Row 2 as **right** side.

Row 3: Ch 2, turn; dc in each of next 2 ch-1 sps, (ch 1, dc in next ch-1 sp) 5 times, (ch 1, dc in same sp) 3 times, (ch 1, dc in next ch-1 sp) 5 times, ★ decrease, dc in next ch-1 sp, (ch 1, dc in next ch-1 sp) 5 times, (ch 1, dc in same sp) 3 times, (ch 1, dc in next ch-1 sp) 5 times; repeat from ★ across to last ch-1 sp, work ending decrease: 136 dc and 117 ch-1 sps.

Row 4: Ch 2, turn; dc in next ch-1 sp, (work Puff St in next ch-1 sp, ch 1) 5 times, dc in next ch-1 sp, (ch 1, dc in same sp) 3 times, work Puff St in next ch-1 sp, (ch 1, work Puff St in next ch-1 sp) 4 times, ★ decrease, (work Puff St in next ch-1 sp, ch 1) 5 times, dc in next ch-1 sp, (ch 1, dc in same sp) 3 times, work Puff St in next ch-1 sp, (ch 1, work Puff St in next ch-1 sp) 4 times; repeat from ★ across to last ch-1 sp, work ending decrease; finish off: 90 Puff Sts, 46 dc, and 117 ch-1 sps.

When instructed to work into a Puff St, **always** work into the closing ch.

Row 5: With **wrong** side facing, join Lt Rose with slip st in first dc; ch 2, dc in each of next 2 Puff Sts, ch 1, (dc in next Puff St, ch 1) 3 times, dc in next ch-1 sp, ch 1, (dc, ch 1) 4 times in next ch-1 sp, dc in next ch-1 sp, (ch 1, dc in next Puff St) 4 times, ★ work center decrease, (dc in next Puff St, ch 1) 4 times, dc in next ch-1 sp, ch 1, (dc, ch 1) 4 times in next ch-1 sp, dc in next ch-1 sp, (ch 1, dc in next Puff St) 4 times; repeat from ★ across to last Puff St, [YO, insert hook in last Puff St, YO and pull up a loop, YO and draw through 2 loops on hook, YO, insert hook in last dc, YO and pull up a loop, YO and draw through 2 loops on hook, YO and draw through all 3 loops on hook (counts as one dc)]: 136 dc and 117 ch-1 sps.

Row 6: Ch 2, turn; dc in next ch-1 sp, work 5 Cross Sts, dc in next ch-1 sp, (ch 1, dc in same sp) 3 times, work 5 Cross Sts, ★ decrease, work 5 Cross Sts, dc in next ch-1 sp, (ch 1, dc in same sp) 3 times, work 5 Cross Sts; repeat from ★ across to last ch-1 sp, work ending decrease: 226 dc and 117 ch-1 sps.

Row 7: Ch 2, turn; dc in each of next 2 ch-1 sps, (ch 1, dc in next ch-1 sp) 5 times, (ch 1, dc in same sp) 3 times, (ch 1, dc in next ch-1 sp) 5 times, ★ decrease, dc in next ch-1 sp, (ch 1, dc in next ch-1 sp) 5 times, (ch 1, dc in same sp) 3 times, (ch 1, dc in next ch-1 sp) 5 times; repeat from ★ across to last ch-1 sp, work ending decrease: 136 dc and 117 ch-1 sps.

Row 8: Ch 2, turn; dc in next ch-1 sp, (work Puff St in next ch-1 sp, ch 1) 5 times, dc in next ch-1 sp, (ch 1, dc in same sp) 3 times, work Puff St in next ch-1 sp, (ch 1, work Puff St in next ch-1 sp) 4 times, ★ decrease, (work Puff St in next ch-1 sp, ch 1) 5 times, dc in next ch-1 sp, (ch 1, dc in same sp) 3 times, work Puff St in next ch-1 sp, (ch 1, work Puff St in next ch-1 sp) 4 times; repeat from ★ across to last ch-1 sp, work ending decrease; finish off: 90 Puff Sts, 46 dc, and 117 ch-1 sps.

Rows 9-12: With Rose, repeat Rows 5-8.

Rows 13-16: With Dk Rose, repeat Rows 5-8.

Rows 17-20: With Ecru, repeat Row 5-8.

Rows 21-84: Repeat Rows 5-20, 4 times.

TRIM

Top: With **right** side facing, join Ecru with sc in first dc on Row 84 *(see Joining With Sc, page 1)*; skip next Puff St, sc in next ch-1 sp, (sc in next Puff St and in next ch-1 sp) 4 times, sc in next dc, sc in next ch-1 sp and in next dc, 3 sc in next ch-1 sp, sc in next dc, sc in next ch-1 sp and in next dc, (sc in next Puff St and next ch-1 sp) 4 times, ★ skip next 2 Puff Sts, sc in next ch-1 sp, (sc in next Puff St and in next ch-1 sp) 4 times, sc in next dc, sc in next ch-1 sp and in next dc, 3 sc in next ch-1 sp, sc in next dc, sc in next ch-1 sp and in next dc, (sc in next Puff St and next ch-1 sp) 4 times; repeat from ★ across to last Puff St, skip last Puff St, sc in last dc; finish off.

Bottom: With **right** side facing and working in free loops *(Fig. 3b, page 3)* and in sps across beginning ch, join Ecru with sc in marked ch; (sc in next sp and in next ch) 6 times, skip next 3 chs, (sc in next ch and in next sp) 6 times, ★ 3 sc in next ch, (sc in next sp and in next ch) 6 times, skip next 3 chs, (sc in next ch and in next sp) 6 times; repeat from ★ across to last ch, sc in last ch; finish off.

Holding 3 strands of Ecru yarn together, each 17" (43 cm) long, add fringe in every other st across short edges of Afghan *(Figs. 8a & b, page 4)*.

Design by Leana Moon.

Waves of Blue

Finished Size: 47^1/$_2$" x 66"
(120.5 cm x 167.5 cm)

MATERIALS
Worsted Weight Yarn:
White - 20^1/$_2$ ounces, 1,345 yards
(580 grams, 1,230 meters)
Dk Blue - 14^1/$_2$ ounces, 950 yards
(410 grams, 868.5 meters)
Blue - 14 ounces, 920 yards
(400 grams, 841 meters)
Lt Blue - 11^1/$_2$ ounces, 755 yards
(330 grams, 690.5 meters)
Crochet hook, size G (4 mm) **or** size needed
for gauge
Yarn needle

GAUGE: In pattern, one point to point
repeat (17 sts) = 2^1/$_2$" (6.25 cm);
18 rows = 5^3/$_4$" (14.5 cm)

Gauge Swatch: 4" (10 cm) square
With Blue, ch 17.
Row 1: Sc in second ch from hook and in each ch
across: 16 sc.
Rows 2-16: Ch 1, turn; working in Back Loops
Only *(Fig. 2, page 3)*, sc in each sc across.
Finish off.

STITCH GUIDE

LONG DOUBLE CROCHET
(abbreviated LDC)
YO, working in **front** of previous rows *(Fig. 6, page 3)*, insert hook in sc indicated, YO and pull up a loop even with loop on hook (3 loops on hook), (YO and draw through 2 loops on hook) twice. Skip sc behind LDC.

AFGHAN BODY
With Blue, ch 322.

Row 1 (Right side)**:** Working in back ridges of beginning ch *(Fig. 1, page 3)*, sc in second ch from hook and in next 6 chs, 3 sc in next ch, sc in next 7 chs, ★ skip next 2 chs, sc in next 7 chs, 3 sc in next ch, sc in next 7 chs; repeat from ★ across: 323 sc.

Note: Loop a short piece of yarn around any stitch to mark Row 1 as **right** side.

Work in Back Loops Only throughout *(Fig. 2, page 3)*.

Rows 2 and 3: Ch 1, turn; sc in first sc, skip next sc, sc in next 6 sc, 3 sc in next sc, ★ sc in next 7 sc, skip next 2 sc, sc in next 7 sc, 3 sc in next sc; repeat from ★ across to last 8 sc, sc in next 6 sc, skip next sc, sc in last sc.

Row 4: Ch 1, turn; sc in first sc, skip next sc, sc in next 6 sc, 3 sc in next sc, ★ sc in next 7 sc, skip next 2 sc, sc in next 7 sc, 3 sc in next sc; repeat from ★ across to last 8 sc, sc in next 6 sc, skip next sc, sc in last sc changing to White *(Fig. 4b, page 3)*; cut Blue.

Row 5: Ch 1, turn; sc in first sc, skip next sc, sc in next 6 sc, 3 sc in next sc, sc in next 7 sc, ★ † skip next 2 sc, sc in next 3 sc, work LDC in same st as next 3-sc group 4 rows **below** *(Fig. 12)*, sc in next sc, work LDC in same st as last LDC made, sc in next sc, 3 sc in next sc, (sc in next sc, work LDC in same st as last LDC) twice, sc in next 3 sc, skip next 2 sc, sc in next 7 sc, 3 sc in next sc †, sc in next 7 sc; repeat from ★ 7 times **more**, then repeat from † to † once, sc in next 6 sc, skip next sc, sc in last sc.

Fig. 12

Continued on page 28.

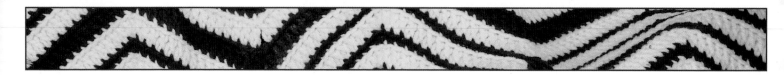

Evergreen Forest

Finished Size: 45" x 60" (114.5 cm x 152.5 cm)

MATERIALS
Worsted Weight Yarn:
Ecru - 21 ounces, 1,185 yards
(600 grams, 1,083.5 meters)
Green - 15¹/₂ ounces, 875 yards
(440 grams, 800 meters)
Crochet hook, size G (4 mm) **or** size needed
for gauge

GAUGE: In pattern, one point to point
repeat (33 sts) = 7¹/₂" (19 cm);
16 sts = 4" (10 cm);
10 rows = 4¹/₄" (10.75 cm)

Gauge Swatch: 4"w x 4¹/₄"h (10 cm x 10.75 cm)
With Green, ch 17.
Row 1 (Right side)**:** Sc in second ch from hook and
in each ch across; finish off: 16 sc.
Work in Back Loops Only throughout **(Fig. 2, page 3)**.
Row 2: With **right** side facing, join Ecru with dc in
first sc **(see Joining With Dc, page 3)**; dc in next
sc and in each sc across; finish off.
Row 3: With **right** side facing, join Green with sc
in first dc **(see Joining With Sc, page 1)**; sc in
next dc and in each dc across; finish off.
Rows 4-10: Repeat Rows 2 and 3, 3 times; then
repeat Row 2 once **more**.

STITCH GUIDE

SC DECREASE
Pull up a loop in next 2 dc, YO and draw
through all 3 loops on hook **(counts as
one sc)**.

DC DECREASE (uses next 2 sts)
★ YO, insert hook in **next** st, YO and pull up a
loop, YO and draw through 2 loops on hook;
repeat from ★ once **more**, YO and draw
through all 3 loops on hook **(counts as
one dc)**.

2-DC CLUSTER
First Leg: YO, insert hook in st indicated, YO
and pull up a loop, YO and draw through
2 loops on hook (2 loops remaining on hook).

Second Leg: YO, insert hook in st indicated,
YO and pull up a loop, YO and draw through
2 loops on hook, YO and draw through all
3 loops on hook.

3-DC CLUSTER
First Leg: YO, insert hook in st indicated, YO
and pull up a loop, YO and draw through
2 loops on hook (2 loops remaining on hook).

Second Leg: YO, insert hook in st indicated,
YO and pull up a loop, YO and draw through
2 loops on hook (3 loops remaining on hook).

Third Leg: YO, insert hook in st indicated, YO
and pull up a loop, YO and draw through
2 loops on hook, YO and draw through all
4 loops on hook.

4-DC CLUSTER (uses next 4 sts)
† YO, insert hook in free loop of **next** sc one
row **below**, YO and pull up a loop, YO and
draw through 2 loops on hook †, ★ YO, insert
hook in Front Loop Only of **next** dc, YO and
pull up a loop, YO and draw through 2 loops on
hook; repeat from ★ once **more**, then repeat
from † to † once, YO and draw through all
5 loops on hook.

AFGHAN
With Green, ch 203.

Row 1 (Right side)**:** Working in back ridges of
beginning ch **(Fig. 1, page 3)**, dc in fourth ch from
hook **(3 skipped chs count as first dc)** and in
next 13 chs, 3 dc in next ch, dc in next 15 chs,
★ skip next 3 chs, dc in next 15 chs, 3 dc in next
ch, dc in next 15 chs; repeat from ★ across;
finish off: 198 dc.

Note: Loop a short piece of yarn around any stitch
to mark Row 1 as **right** side.

Continued on page 27.

Row 2: With **right** side, join Ecru with dc in first dc *(see Joining With Dc, page 3)*; dc decrease, dc in next 13 dc, 3 dc in next dc, ★ dc in next 15 dc, skip next 2 dc, dc in next 15 dc, 3 dc in next dc; repeat from ★ 4 times **more**, dc in next 13 dc, dc decrease, dc in last dc; finish off.

Row 3: With **right** side facing, join Green with sc in first dc *(see Joining With Sc, page 1)*; sc decrease, sc in next 13 dc, 3 sc in next dc, ★ sc in next 15 dc, skip next 2 dc, sc in next 15 dc, 3 sc in next dc; repeat from ★ 4 times **more**, sc in next 13 dc, sc decrease, sc in last dc; finish off.

Row 4: With **right** side facing, join Ecru with dc in first sc; dc decrease, dc in next 13 sc, 3 dc in next sc, ★ dc in next 15 sc, skip next 2 sc, dc in next 15 sc, 3 dc in next sc; repeat from ★ 4 times **more**, dc in next 13 sc, dc decrease, dc in last sc; finish off.

Row 5: With **right** side facing, join Green with sc in first dc; sc decrease, sc in next 13 dc, 3 sc in next dc, ★ sc in next 14 dc, working in **front** of next dc *(Fig. 6, page 3)*, dc in next 2 skipped sc one row **below**, skip next 4 dc on previous row, sc in next 14 dc, 3 sc in next dc; repeat from ★ 4 times **more**, sc in next 13 dc, sc decrease, sc in last dc; finish off.

Row 6: With **right** side facing, join Ecru with dc in first sc; dc decrease, dc in next 13 sc, 3 dc in next sc, ★ dc in next 15 sts, skip next 2 dc, dc in next 15 sts, 3 dc in next sc; repeat from ★ 4 times **more**, dc in next 13 sc, dc decrease, dc in last sc; finish off.

Row 7: With **right** side facing, join Green with sc in first dc; sc decrease, sc in next 13 dc, 3 sc in next dc, ★ sc in next 10 dc, working in **front** of next dc and in free loops of sc one row **below** *(Fig. 3a, page 3)*, dc in next 5 sc, work 4-dc Cluster, dc in next 5 sc, skip next 12 dc on previous row, sc in next 10 dc, 3 sc in next dc; repeat from ★ 4 times **more**, sc in next 13 dc, sc decrease, sc in last dc; finish off: 203 sts.

Row 8: With **right** side facing, join Ecru with dc in first sc; dc decrease, dc in next 13 sc, 3 dc in next sc, ★ dc in next 14 sts, dc decrease, skip next 4-dc Cluster, dc decrease, dc in next 14 sts, 3 dc in next sc; repeat from ★ 4 times **more**, dc in next 13 sc, dc decrease, dc in last sc; finish off: 198 dc.

Row 9: With **right** side facing, join Green with sc in first dc; sc decrease, sc in next 13 dc, 3 sc in next dc, ★ sc in next 13 dc, dc in free loop of dc one row **below** same dc as last sc worked into and in next 3 dc, work 3-dc Cluster working First Leg in free loop of next dc, Second Leg in **both** loops of next 4-dc Cluster, and Third Leg in free loop of next dc, dc in free loops of next 4 dc, skip next 6 dc on previous row from last sc made, sc in next 13 dc, 3 sc in next dc; repeat from ★ 4 times **more**, sc in next 13 dc, sc decrease, sc in last dc; finish off: 223 sts.

Row 10: With **right** side facing, join Ecru with dc in first sc; dc decrease, dc in next 13 sc, 3 dc in next sc, ★ dc in next 15 sts, dc decrease, skip next 3 sts, dc decrease, dc in next 15 sts, 3 dc in next sc; repeat from ★ 4 times **more**, dc in next 13 sc, dc decrease, dc in last sc; finish off: 208 dc.

Row 11: With **right** side facing, join Green with sc in first dc; sc decrease, sc in next 13 dc, 3 sc in next dc, ★ sc in next 15 dc, dc in free loops of next 3 dc one row **below**, work 3-dc Cluster working each leg in **both** loops of next 3 sts, dc in free loops of next 3 dc, skip next 4 dc on previous row from last sc made, sc in next 15 dc, 3 sc in next sc; repeat from ★ 4 times **more**, sc in next 13 dc, sc decrease, sc in last dc; finish off: 233 sts.

Row 12: With **right** side facing, join Ecru with dc in first sc; dc decrease, dc in next 13 sc, 3 dc in next sc, ★ dc in next 15 sc, dc decrease, skip next 5 sts, dc decrease, dc in next 15 sc, 3 dc in next dc; repeat from ★ 4 times **more**, dc in next 13 sc, dc decrease, dc in last sc; finish off: 208 dc.

Row 13: With **right** side facing, join Green with sc in first dc; sc decrease, sc in next 13 dc, 3 sc in next dc, ★ sc in next 15 dc, working in **front** of previous row, skip next 2 dc, work 2-dc Cluster working First Leg in free loop of next dc one row **below** and Second Leg in **both** loops of next dc, work 3-dc Cluster working each leg in **both** loops of next 3 sts, work 2-dc Cluster working First Leg in **both** loops of next dc and Second Leg in free loop of next dc, skip next 4 sts on previous row from last sc made, sc in next 15 dc, 3 sc in next dc; repeat from ★ 4 times **more**, sc in next 13 dc, sc decrease, sc in last dc; finish off: 213 sts.

Row 14: With **right** side facing, join Ecru with dc in first sc; dc decrease, dc in next 13 sc, 3 dc in next sc, ★ dc in next 14 sc, dc decrease, skip next 3 sts, dc decrease, dc in next 14 sc, 3 dc in next sc; repeat from ★ 4 times **more**, dc in next 13 sc, dc decrease, dc in last dc; finish off: 198 dc.

Row 15: With **right** side facing, join Green with sc in first dc; sc decrease, sc in next 13 dc, 3 sc in next dc, ★ sc in next 15 dc, working in **front** of previous row, work 3-dc Cluster working each leg in **both** loops of next 3 Clusters one row **below**, skip next 2 dc on previous row, sc in next 15 dc, 3 sc in next dc; repeat from ★ 4 times **more**, sc in next 13 dc, sc decrease, sc in last dc; finish off: 203 sts.

Row 16: With **right** side facing, join Ecru with dc in first sc; dc decrease, dc in next 13 sc, 3 dc in next sc, ★ dc in next 14 sc, dc decrease, skip next 3-dc Cluster, dc decrease, dc in next 14 sc, 3 dc in next sc; repeat from ★ 4 times **more**, dc in next 13 sc, dc decrease, dc in last dc; finish off: 198 dc.

Row 17: With **right** side facing, join Green with dc in first dc; dc decrease, dc in next 13 dc, 3 dc in next dc, ★ dc in next 15 dc, skip next 2 dc, dc in next 15 dc, 3 dc in next dc; repeat from ★ 4 times **more**, dc in next 13 dc, dc decrease, dc in last dc; finish off.

Rows 18-113: Repeat Rows 2-17, 6 times.

Design by Pat Gibbons.

Waves of Blue
Continued from page 23.

Row 6: Ch 1, turn; sc in first sc, skip next sc, sc in next 6 sc, 3 sc in next sc, ★ sc in next 7 sts, skip next 2 sc, sc in next 7 sts, 3 sc in next sc; repeat from ★ across to last 8 sc, sc in next 6 sc, skip next sc, sc in last sc changing to Lt Blue; cut White.

Rows 7-10: Ch 1, turn; sc in first sc, skip next sc, sc in next 6 sc, 3 sc in next sc, ★ sc in next 7 sc, skip next 2 sc, sc in next 7 sc, 3 sc in next sc; repeat from ★ across to last 8 sc, sc in next 6 sc, skip next sc, sc in last sc; at end of last row, change to White in last sc; cut Lt Blue.

Row 11: Ch 1, turn; sc in first sc, skip next sc, sc in next 6 sc, 3 sc in next sc, sc in next 7 sc, ★ † skip next 2 sc, sc in next 3 sc, work LDC in same st as next 3-sc group 4 rows **below**, sc in next sc, work LDC in same st as last LDC made, sc in next sc, 3 sc in next sc, (sc in next sc, work LDC in same st as last LDC) twice, sc in next 3 sc, skip next 2 sc, sc in next 7 sc, 3 sc in next sc †, sc in next 7 sc; repeat from ★ 7 times **more**, then repeat from † to † once, sc in next 6 sc, skip next sc, sc in last sc.

Row 12: Ch 1, turn; sc in first sc, skip next sc, sc in next 6 sc, 3 sc in next sc, ★ sc in next 7 sts, skip next 2 sc, sc in next 7 sts, 3 sc in next sc; repeat from ★ across to last 8 sc, sc in next 6 sc, skip next sc, sc in last sc changing to Dk Blue; cut White.

Rows 13-16: Ch 1, turn; sc in first sc, skip next sc, sc in next 6 sc, 3 sc in next sc, ★ sc in next 7 sc, skip next 2 sc, sc in next 7 sc, 3 sc in next sc; repeat from ★ across to last 8 sc, sc in next 6 sc, skip next sc, sc in last sc; at end of last row change to White in last sc; cut Dk Blue.

Row 17: Ch 1, turn; sc in first sc, skip next sc, sc in next 6 sc, 3 sc in next sc, sc in next 7 sc, ★ † skip next 2 sc, sc in next 3 sc, work LDC in same st as next 3-sc group 4 rows **below**, sc in next sc, work LDC in same st as last LDC made, sc in next sc, 3 sc in next sc, (sc in next sc, work LDC in same st as last LDC) twice, sc in next 3 sc, skip next 2 sc, sc in next 7 sc, 3 sc in next sc †, sc in next 7 sc; repeat from ★ 5 times **more**, then repeat from † to † once, sc in next 6 sc, skip next sc, sc in last sc.

Row 18: Ch 1, turn; sc in first sc, skip next sc, sc in next 6 sc, 3 sc in next sc, ★ sc in next 7 sts, skip next 2 sc, sc in next 7 sts, 3 sc in next sc; repeat from ★ across to last 8 sc, sc in next 6 sc, skip next sc, sc in last sc changing to Blue; cut White.

Row 19: Ch 1, turn; sc in first sc, skip next sc, sc in next 6 sc, 3 sc in next sc, ★ sc in next 7 sc, skip next 2 sc, sc in next 7 sc, 3 sc in next sc; repeat from ★ across to last 8 sc, sc in next 6 sc, skip next sc, sc in last sc.

Rows 20-204: Repeat Rows 2-19, 10 times; then repeat Rows 2-6 once **more**.

WEAVING
Cut 36 strands of Dk Blue 30" (76 cm) longer than the finished length of Afghan Body.

Thread yarn needle with 4 strands of Dk Blue held together. Using photo as a guide, insert needle down at base of first 4-LDC group on Row 1, (bring needle up between 4-LDC on next row and down between next 2 White rows) across. Continue weaving evenly, pulling yarn gently so Afghan doesn't pucker and leaving excess ends hanging at the top and bottom to be worked into fringe.

Holding 8 strands of Blue together, each 18" (45.5 cm) long, add fringe to both ends of weaving **(Figs. 8a & b, page 4)**.

Holding 8 strands of Lt Blue together, each 18" (45.5 cm) long, add additional fringe to points or valleys between woven fringe on each end.

Design by Pat Gibbons.

28

Lullaby

Finished Size: 33" x 43" (84 cm x 109 cm)

MATERIALS
Worsted Weight Yarn:
   Blue - 8 ounces, 455 yards
      (230 grams, 416 meters)
   Pink - 7 ounces, 395 yards
      (200 grams, 361 meters)
   White - 7 ounces, 395 yards
      (200 grams, 361 meters)
   Crochet hook, size H (5 mm) **or** size needed
      for gauge

GAUGE: In pattern, one point to point repeat
      (28 dc and 5 ch-2 sps) = 8¹/₂" (21.5 cm);
      14 dc = 4" (10 cm);
      8 rows = 5¹/₄" (13.25 cm)

Gauge Swatch: 4"w x 5¹/₄"h (10 cm x 13.25 cm)
With Blue, ch 16.
Row 1: Dc in fourth ch from hook **(3 skipped chs count as first dc)** and in each ch across:
14 dc.
Rows 2-8: Ch 3 **(counts as first dc)**, turn; dc in next dc and in each dc across.
Finish off.

AFGHAN BODY
With Blue, ch 109.

Row 1 (Right side)**:** Working in back ridges of beginning ch *(Fig. 1, page 3)*, dc in fourth ch from hook **(3 skipped chs count as first dc)** and in next 2 chs, ★ † skip next ch, (dc, ch 2, dc) in next ch, skip next ch, dc in next 4 chs, (2 dc, ch 2, 2 dc) in next ch, dc in next 4 chs, skip next ch, (dc, ch 2, dc) in next ch, skip next ch, dc in next 4 chs †, skip next 2 chs, (dc, ch 2, 2 dc, ch 2, dc) in next ch, skip next 2 chs, dc in next 4 chs; repeat from ★ 2 times **more**, then repeat from † to † once: 108 dc and 18 ch-2 sps.

Note: Loop a short piece of yarn around any stitch to mark Row 1 as **right** side.

Row 2: Ch 3 **(counts as first dc, now and throughout)**, turn; skip next dc, dc in next 3 dc, ★ † (dc, ch 2, dc) in next ch-2 sp, skip next 2 dc, dc in next 4 dc, (2 dc, ch 2, 2 dc) in next ch-2 sp, skip next dc, dc in next 4 dc, (dc, ch 2, dc) in next ch-2 sp †, dc in next 4 dc, ch 2, sc in next ch-2 sp, ch 3, sc in next ch-2 sp, ch 2, skip next 2 dc, dc in next 4 dc; repeat from ★ 2 times **more**, then repeat from † to † once, dc in next 3 dc, skip next dc, dc in last dc: 102 sts and 21 sps.

Row 3: Ch 3, turn; skip next dc, dc in next 3 dc, ★ † (dc, ch 2, dc) in next ch-2 sp, skip next 2 dc, dc in next 4 dc, (2 dc, ch 2, 2 dc) in next ch-2 sp, skip next dc, dc in next 4 dc, (dc, ch 2, dc) in next ch-2 sp †, dc in next 4 dc, skip next ch-2 sp, (dc, ch 2, 2 dc, ch 2, dc) in next ch-3 sp, skip next ch-2 sp and next dc, dc in next 4 dc; repeat from ★ 2 times **more**, then repeat from † to † once, dc in next 3 dc, skip next dc, dc in last dc: 108 dc and 18 ch-2 sps.

Row 4: Ch 3, turn; skip next dc, dc in next 3 dc, ★ † (dc, ch 2, dc) in next ch-2 sp, skip next 2 dc, dc in next 4 dc, (2 dc, ch 2, 2 dc) in next ch-2 sp, skip next dc, dc in next 4 dc, (dc, ch 2, dc) in next ch-2 sp †, dc in next 4 dc, ch 2, sc in next ch-2 sp, ch 3, sc in next ch-2 sp, ch 2, skip next 2 dc, dc in next 4 dc; repeat from ★ 2 times **more**, then repeat from † to † once, dc in next 3 dc, skip next dc, dc in last dc; finish off: 102 sts and 21 sps.

Row 5: With **right** side facing, join Pink with dc in first dc *(see Joining With Dc, page 3)*; skip next dc, dc in next 3 dc, ★ † (dc, ch 2, dc) in next ch-2 sp, skip next 2 dc, dc in next 4 dc, (2 dc, ch 2, 2 dc) in next ch-2 sp, skip next dc, dc in next 4 dc, (dc, ch 2, dc) in next ch-2 sp †, dc in next 4 dc, skip next ch-2 sp, (dc, ch 2, 2 dc, ch 2, dc) in next ch-3 sp, skip next ch-2 sp and next dc, dc in next 4 dc; repeat from ★ 2 times **more**, then repeat from † to † once, dc in next 3 dc, skip next dc, dc in last dc: 108 dc and 18 ch-2 sps.

Continued on page 36.

Waves of Grain

Finished Size: 51^1/$_2$" x 66" (131 cm x 167.5 cm)

MATERIALS
Worsted Weight Yarn:
  Ecru - 40^1/$_2$ ounces, 2,655 yards
    (1,150 grams, 2,427.5 meters)
  Tan - 13^1/$_2$ ounces, 885 yards
    (380 grams, 809 meters)
Crochet hook, size G (4 mm) **or** size needed
  for gauge

GAUGE: In pattern, one point to point
    repeat (43 sts) = 8^1/$_2$" (21.5 cm);
    8 rows = 3^1/$_2$" (9 cm)

Gauge Swatch: 17" x 4" (43.25 cm x 10 cm)
With Ecru, ch 87.
Work same as Afghan for 9 rows.

When joining yarn and finishing off, leave an 8"
(20.5 cm) length to be worked into fringe.

STITCH GUIDE

CLUSTER (uses one st)
★ YO, insert hook in free loop of st indicated
(Fig. 3a, page 3), YO and pull up a loop, YO
and draw through 2 loops on hook; repeat from
★ 2 times **more**, YO and draw through all
4 loops on hook.

SC DECREASE
Pull up a loop in next 2 sts, YO and draw
through all 3 loops on hook.

DC DECREASE (uses next 2 sts)
★ YO, insert hook in **next** st, YO and pull up a
loop, YO and draw through 2 loops on hook;
repeat from ★ once **more**, YO and draw
through all 3 loops on hook.

AFGHAN
With Ecru, ch 263.

Row 1 (Right side)**:** Working in back ridges of
beginning ch **(Fig. 1, page 3)**, dc in fourth ch from
hook **(3 skipped chs count as first dc)** and in
next 18 chs, 3 dc in next ch, dc in next 20 chs,
★ skip next 3 chs, dc in next 20 chs, 3 dc in next
ch, dc in next 20 chs; repeat from ★ across;
finish off: 258 dc.

Note: Loop a short piece of yarn around any stitch
to mark Row 1 as **right** side.

Each row is worked in Back Loops Only throughout
(Fig. 2, page 3).

Row 2: With **right** side facing, join Tan with sc in
first dc **(see Joining With Sc, page 1)**;
sc decrease, sc in next 18 dc, 3 sc in next dc, ★ sc
in next 20 dc, skip next 2 dc, sc in next 20 dc, 3 sc
in next sc; repeat from ★ across to last 21 dc, sc in
next 18 dc, sc decrease, sc in last sc; finish off.

Row 3: With **right** side facing, join Ecru with sc in
first sc; sc decrease, sc in next 9 sc, work Cluster in
free loop of dc one row **below** next sc **(Fig. 3a,
page 3)**, skip sc **behind** Cluster, sc in next 8 sc,
3 sc in next sc, sc in next 8 sc, work Cluster in free
loop of dc one row **below** next sc, ★ skip sc
behind Cluster, sc in next 11 sc, skip next 2 sc, sc
in next 11 sc, work Cluster in free loop of dc one
row **below** next sc, skip sc **behind** Cluster, sc in
next 8 sc, 3 sc in next sc, sc in next 8 sc, work
Cluster in free loop of dc one row **below** next sc;
repeat from ★ across to last 13 sc, skip sc **behind**
Cluster, sc in next 9 sc, sc decrease, sc in last sc;
finish off.

Row 4: With **right** side facing, join Tan with sc in
first sc; sc decrease, sc in next 18 sts, 3 sc in next
sc, ★ sc in next 20 sts, skip next 2 sc, sc in next
20 sts, 3 sc in next sc; repeat from ★ across to last
21 sts, sc in next 18 sts, sc decrease, sc in last sc;
finish off.

Continued on page 36.

Daisy Border

Finished Size: 45" x 62" (114.5 cm x 157.5 cm)

MATERIALS
Worsted Weight Yarn:
    Variegated - $12^1/2$ ounces, 725 yards
        (360 grams, 663 meters)
    Ecru - $11^1/2$ ounces, 650 yards
        (330 grams, 594.5 meters)
    Green - $8^1/2$ ounces, 480 yards
        (240 grams, 439 meters)
    Brown - $7^1/2$ ounces, 425 yards
        (210 grams, 388.5 meters)
    Yellow - small amount
Crochet hook, size G (4 mm) **or** size needed
    for gauge
Yarn needle

GAUGE: Each Motif (from straight edge
        to straight edge) = $6^1/4$" (16 cm)
        In pattern, one point to point repeat
        (27 sts) = $6^1/4$" (16 cm);
        6 rows = 3" (7.5 cm)

Gauge Swatch: $6^1/4$" (16 cm) (from
                  straight edge to straight edge)
Work same as Motif.

STITCH GUIDE

BEGINNING CLUSTER (uses one st)
Ch 3, ★ YO twice, insert hook in **same** st, YO
and pull up a loop, (YO and draw through
2 loops on hook) twice; repeat from ★ once
more, YO and draw through all 3 loops on hook.

CLUSTER (uses one sc)
★ YO twice, insert hook in sc indicated, YO and
pull up a loop, (YO and draw through 2 loops
on hook) twice; repeat from ★ 2 times **more**,
YO and draw through all 4 loops on hook.

SC DECREASE
Pull up a loop in next 2 dc, YO and draw
through all 3 loops on hook **(counts as one sc)**.

DC DECREASE (uses next 2 sts)
★ YO, insert hook in **next** st, YO and pull up a
loop, YO and draw through 2 loops on hook;
repeat from ★ once **more**, YO and draw
through all 3 loops on hook **(counts as one dc)**.

MOTIF (Make 7)
Rnd 1 (Right side)**:** With Yellow, ch 2, 6 sc in
second ch from hook; join with slip st to first sc,
finish off.

Note: Loop a short piece of yarn around any stitch
to mark Rnd 1 as **right** side.

Rnd 2: With **right** side facing, join Ecru with slip st
in any sc; work (Beginning Cluster, ch 3, Cluster) in
same st, ch 3, (work Cluster, ch 3) twice in each sc
around; join with slip st to top of Beginning Cluster,
finish off: 12 ch-3 sps.

Rnd 3: With **right** side facing, join Green with sc
in any ch-3 sp *(see Joining With Sc, page 1)*;
ch 3, 3 dc in same sp, (sc, ch 3, 3 dc) in next
ch-3 sp and in each ch-3 sp around; join with slip st
to first sc.

Rnd 4: (Slip st, ch 1, sc) in first ch-3 sp, ch 5, (sc
in next ch-3 sp, ch 5) around; join with slip st to first
sc, finish off.

Rnd 5: With **right** side facing, join Brown with dc
in any ch-5 sp *(see Joining With Dc, page 3)*;
(2 dc, ch 3, 3 dc) in same sp, 5 dc in next ch-5 sp,
★ (3 dc, ch 3, 3 dc) in next ch-5 sp, 5 dc in next
ch-5 sp; repeat from ★ around; join with slip st to
first dc, finish off: 66 dc and 6 ch-3 sps.

Rnd 6: With **right** side facing, join Ecru with sc in
any ch-3 sp; 2 sc in same sp, sc in next 11 dc, (3 sc
in next ch-3 sp, sc in next 11 dc) around; join with
slip st to first sc, finish off: 84 sc.

ASSEMBLY
With Ecru, whipstitch Motifs together to form a strip
(Fig. 7a, page 4), working through **both** loops,
and beginning in center sc of first corner 3-sc group
and ending in center sc of next corner 3-sc group.

Continued on page 35.

BOTTOM RIPPLE

Row 1: With **right** side of long edge facing and working in Back Loops Only *(Fig. 2, page 3)*, join Variegated with dc in center sc of first corner 3-sc group; dc decrease, dc in next 11 sc, 3 dc in next sc, dc in next 11 sc, dc decrease, ★ skip next joining, dc decrease, dc in next 11 sc, 3 dc in next sc, dc in next 11 sc, dc decrease; repeat from ★ 5 times **more**, dc in next dc; finish off: 191 dc.

Row 2: With **right** side facing and working in both loops, join Variegated with dc in first dc; dc decrease, dc in next 11 dc, 3 dc in next dc, dc in next 11 dc, ★ dc decrease twice, dc in next 11 dc, 3 dc in next dc, dc in next 11 dc; repeat from ★ across to last 3 dc, dc decrease, dc in last dc; finish off.

Row 3: With **right** side facing, join Ecru with sc in first dc; sc decrease, sc in next 11 dc, 3 sc in next dc, sc in next 11 dc, ★ sc decrease twice, sc in next 11 dc, 3 sc in next dc, sc in next 11 dc; repeat from ★ across to last 3 dc, sc decrease, sc in last dc; finish off.

Row 4: With **right** side facing and working in Back Loops Only, join Green with dc in first sc; dc decrease, dc in next 11 sc, 3 dc in next sc, dc in next 11 sc, ★ dc decrease twice, dc in next 11 sc, 3 dc in next sc, dc in next 11 sc; repeat from ★ across to last 3 sc, dc decrease, dc in last sc; finish off.

Row 5: With **right** side facing and working in both loops, join Green with dc in first dc; dc decrease, dc in next 11 dc, 3 dc in next dc, dc in next 11 dc, ★ dc decrease twice, dc in next 11 dc, 3 dc in next dc, dc in next 11 dc; repeat from ★ across to last 3 dc, dc decrease, dc in last dc; finish off.

TOP RIPPLE

Rows 1-5: Work same as Bottom Ripple: 191 dc.

Row 6: With **right** side facing, join Ecru with sc in first dc; sc decrease, sc in next 11 dc, 3 sc in next dc, sc in next 11 dc, ★ sc decrease twice, sc in next 11 dc, 3 sc in next dc, sc in next 11 dc; repeat from ★ across to last 3 dc, sc decrease, sc in last dc; finish off.

Row 7: With **right** side facing and working in Back Loops Only, join Variegated with dc in first sc; dc decrease, dc in next 11 sc, 3 dc in next sc, dc in next 11 sc, ★ dc decrease twice, dc in next 11 sc, 3 dc in next sc, dc in next 11 sc; repeat from ★ across to last 3 sc, dc decrease, dc in last sc; finish off.

Row 8: With **right** side facing and working in both loops, join Variegated with dc in first dc; dc decrease, dc in next 11 dc, 3 dc in next dc, dc in next 11 dc, ★ dc decrease twice, dc in next 11 dc, 3 dc in next dc, dc in next 11 dc; repeat from ★ across to last 3 dc, dc decrease, dc in last dc; finish off.

Row 9: Repeat Row 6.

Rows 10 and 11: With Brown, repeat Rows 7 and 8.

Row 12: Repeat Row 6.

Rows 13 and 14: Repeat Rows 7 and 8.

Row 15: Repeat Row 6.

Rows 16 and 17: With Green, repeat Rows 7 and 8.

Rows 18-101: Repeat Rows 6-17, 7 times.

EDGING

Rnd 1: With **right** side facing, and working across Row 101 of Top Ripple, join Ecru with sc in first dc; 2 sc in same st, sc decrease, sc in next 11 dc, 3 sc in next dc, sc in next 11 dc, ★ sc decrease twice, sc in next 11 dc, 3 sc in next dc, sc in next 11 dc; repeat from ★ 5 times **more**, sc decrease, 3 sc in last dc; working across end of rows of Top Ripple, 2 sc in each of first 2 dc rows, (sc in next sc row, 2 sc in each of next 2 dc rows) across to Daisy Motif, sc in next 13 sc, working across end of rows of Bottom Ripple, 2 sc in each of next 2 dc rows, sc in next sc row, 2 sc in each of next 2 dc rows; working across Row 5 of Bottom Ripple, 3 sc in first dc, sc decrease, sc in next 11 dc, 3 sc in next dc, sc in next 11 dc, † sc decrease twice, sc in next 11 dc, 3 sc in next dc, sc in next 11 dc †; repeat from † to † 5 times **more**, sc decrease, 3 sc in last dc; working across end of rows, 2 sc in each of first 2 dc rows, sc in next sc row, 2 sc in each of next 2 dc rows, working across Daisy Motif, sc in next 13 sc, working across end of rows on Top Ripple, 2 sc in each of first 2 rows, (sc in next row, 2 sc in each of next 2 rows) across; join with slip st to first sc: 772 sc.

Rnd 2: Ch 1, sc in same st, (sc, ch 3, sc) in next sc, ★ sc in next sc, (sc, ch 3, sc) in next sc; repeat from ★ around; join with slip st to first sc, finish off.

Design by Pat Gibbons.

Lullaby
Continued from page 29.

Row 6: Ch 3, turn; skip next dc, dc in next 3 dc, ★ † (dc, ch 2, dc) in next ch-2 sp, skip next 2 dc, dc in next 4 dc, (2 dc, ch 2, 2 dc) in next ch-2 sp, skip next dc, dc in next 4 dc, (dc, ch 2, dc) in next ch-2 sp †, dc in next 4 dc, ch 2, sc in next ch-2 sp, ch 3, sc in next ch-2 sp, ch 2, skip next 2 dc, dc in next 4 dc; repeat from ★ 2 times **more**, then repeat from † to † once, dc in next 3 dc, skip next dc, dc in last dc: 102 sts and 21 sps.

Row 7: Ch 3, turn; skip next dc, dc in next 3 dc, ★ † (dc, ch 2, dc) in next ch-2 sp, skip next 2 dc, dc in next 4 dc, (2 dc, ch 2, 2 dc) in next ch-2 sp, skip next dc, dc in next 4 dc, (dc, ch 2, dc) in next ch-2 sp †, dc in next 4 dc, skip next ch-2 sp, (dc, ch 2, 2 dc, ch 2, dc) in next ch-3 sp, skip next ch-2 sp and next dc, dc in next 4 dc; repeat from ★ 2 times **more**, then repeat from † to † once, dc in next 3 dc, skip next dc, dc in last dc: 108 dc and 18 ch-2 sps.

Row 8: Ch 3, turn; skip next dc, dc in next 3 dc, ★ † (dc, ch 2, dc) in next ch-2 sp, skip next 2 dc, dc in next 4 dc, (2 dc, ch 2, 2 dc) in next ch-2 sp, skip next dc, dc in next 4 dc, (dc, ch 2, dc) in next ch-2 sp †, dc in next 4 dc, ch 2, sc in next ch-2 sp, ch 3, sc in next ch-2 sp, ch 2, skip next 2 dc, dc in next 4 dc; repeat from ★ 2 times **more**, then repeat from † to † once, dc in next 3 dc, skip next dc, dc in last dc; finish off: 102 sts and 21 sps.

Rows 9-12: With White, Repeat Rows 5-8.

Rows 13-16: With Blue, Repeat Rows 5-8.

Rows 17-64: Repeat Rows 5-16, 4 times.

TRIM
FIRST SIDE
With **right** side facing and working in end of rows, join White with sc in first row *(see Joining With Sc, page 1)*; ch 2, sc in same row, (sc, ch 2, sc) in next row and in each row across; finish off.

SECOND SIDE
Work same as First Side.

Design by Roseanna E. Beck.

Waves of Grain
Continued from page 31.

Row 5: With **right** side facing, join Ecru with sc in first sc; sc decrease, sc in next 5 sc, ★ † work Cluster in free loop of sc one row **below** next sc, skip sc **behind** Cluster, sc in next 3 sc, work Cluster in free loop of sc one row **below** next sc, skip sc **behind** Cluster, sc in next 8 sc, 3 sc in next sc, sc in next 8 sc, work Cluster in free loop of sc one row **below** next sc, skip sc **behind** Cluster, sc in next 3 sc, work Cluster in free loop of sc one row **below** next sc, skip sc **behind** Cluster †, sc in next 7 sc, skip next 2 sc, sc in next 7 sc; repeat from ★ 4 times **more**, then repeat from † to † once, sc in next 5 sc, sc decrease, sc in last sc; finish off.

Row 6: With **right** side facing, join Tan with sc in first sc; sc decrease, sc in next 18 sts, 3 sc in next sc, ★ sc in next 20 sts, skip next 2 sc, sc in next 20 sts, 3 sc in next sc; repeat from ★ across to last 21 sts, sc in next 18 sts, sc decrease, sc in last sc; finish off.

Row 7: With **right** side facing, join Ecru with sc in first sc; sc decrease, sc in next 5 sc, work Cluster in free loop of sc one row **below** next sc, skip sc **behind** Cluster, sc in next 12 sc, 3 sc in next sc, sc in next 12 sc, work Cluster in free loop of sc one row **below** next sc, ★ skip sc **behind** Cluster, sc in next 7 sc, skip next 2 sc, sc in next 7 sc, work Cluster in free loop of sc one row **below** next sc, skip sc **behind** Cluster, sc in next 12 sc, 3 sc in next sc, sc in next 12 sc, work Cluster in free loop of sc one row **below** next sc; repeat from ★ across to last 9 sc, skip sc **behind** Cluster, sc in next 5 sc, sc decrease, sc in last sc; finish off.

Rows 8 and 9: With **right** side facing, join Ecru with dc in first st *(see Joining With Dc, page 3)*; dc decrease, dc in next 18 sts, 3 dc in next st, ★ dc in next 20 sts, skip next 2 sts, dc in next 20 sts, 3 dc in next st; repeat from ★ across to last 21 sts, dc in next 18 sts, dc decrease, dc in last st; finish off.

Rows 10-144: Repeat Rows 2-9, 16 times; then repeat Rows 2-8 once **more**.

Holding 2 strands of corresponding color yarn together, each 17" (43 cm) long, add additional fringe across long edges of Afghan *(Figs. 8c & d, page 4)*.

Design by Pat Gibbons.

Blue Skies

Finished Size: 48¹/₂" x 61¹/₂"
(123 cm x 156 cm)

MATERIALS

Worsted Weight Yarn:
White - 30 ounces, 1,695 yards
(850 grams, 1,550 meters)
Lt Blue - 9¹/₂ ounces, 535 yards
(270 grams, 489 meters)
Blue and Dk Blue - 5¹/₂ ounces, 310 yards
(160 grams, 283.5 meters) **each**
Crochet hook, size H (5 mm) **or** size needed
for gauge

GAUGE: In pattern, one point to point repeat
(26 sts) = 4¹/₄" (10.75 cm);
5 rows = 4" (10 cm)

Gauge Swatch: 8¹/₂"w x 4"h (21.5 cm x 10 cm)
With White, ch 59.
Work same as Afghan Body for 5 rows.

STITCH GUIDE

V-ST
(Dc, ch 1, dc) in st or sp indicated.

PUFF ST
(YO, insert hook in st or sp indicated, YO and
pull up a loop even with loop on hook) 5 times,
YO and draw through all 11 loops on hook.

DOUBLE DECREASE (uses next 7 chs)
YO, skip next 2 chs, insert hook in next ch, YO
and pull up a loop, YO and draw through
2 loops on hook, ★ YO, skip next ch, insert
hook in next ch, YO and pull up a loop, YO and
draw through 2 loops on hook; repeat from ★
once **more**, YO and draw through all 4 loops
on hook **(counts as one dc)**.

BEGINNING DECREASE
(uses next dc and next ch-1 sp)
YO, insert hook in next dc, YO and pull up a
loop, YO and draw through 2 loops on hook,
YO, insert hook in next ch-1 sp, YO and pull up
a loop, YO and draw through 2 loops on hook,
YO and draw through all 3 loops on hook
(counts as one dc).

DECREASE
(uses next 2 ch-1 sps and next 3 dc)
YO, insert hook in next ch-1 sp, YO and pull up
a loop, YO and draw through 2 loops on hook,
YO, skip next 3 dc, insert hook in next ch-1 sp,
YO and pull up a loop, YO and draw through
2 loops on hook, YO and draw through all
3 loops on hook **(counts as one dc)**.

ENDING DECREASE
(uses last ch-1 sp and last 2 dc)
YO, insert hook in last ch-1 sp, YO and pull up
a loop, YO and draw through 2 loops on hook,
★ YO, insert hook in **next** dc, YO and pull up a
loop, YO and draw through 2 loops on hook;
repeat from ★ once **more**, YO and draw
through all 4 loops on hook **(counts as
one dc)**.

RIGHT DECREASE (uses first 3 sts)
YO, skip same st as joining, insert hook in next
ch, YO and pull up a loop, YO and draw
through 2 loops on hook, YO, insert hook in
next Puff St, YO and pull up a loop, YO and
draw through 2 loops on hook, YO and draw
through all 3 loops on hook **(counts as
one dc)**.

LEFT DECREASE (uses last 6 sts)
YO, skip next Puff St and next 2 chs, insert
hook in next ch, YO and pull up a loop, YO and
draw through 2 loops on hook, YO, insert hook
in next Puff St, YO and pull up a loop, YO and
draw through 2 loops on hook, YO, insert hook
in last dc, YO and pull up a loop, YO and draw
through 2 loops on hook, YO and draw through
all 4 loops on hook **(counts as one dc)**.

CENTER DECREASE (uses next 7 sts)
YO, skip next Puff St and next 2 chs, insert
hook in next ch, YO and pull up a loop, YO and
draw through 2 loops on hook, YO, skip next
Puff St and next dc, insert hook in next ch, YO
and pull up a loop, YO and draw through
2 loops on hook, YO and draw through all
3 loops on hook **(counts as one dc)**.

Continued on page 39.

AFGHAN BODY

With White, ch 311, place marker in third ch from hook for st placement.

Row 1 (Right side): [YO, insert hook in fourth ch from hook, YO and pull up a loop, YO and draw through 2 loops on hook, YO, insert hook in next ch, YO and pull up a loop, YO and draw through 2 loops on hook, YO and draw through all 3 loops on hook **(counts as first dc)**], (skip next 2 chs, work V-St in next ch) 3 times, skip next 2 chs, work (V-St, ch 1, V-St) in next ch, (skip next 2 chs, work V-St in next ch) 3 times, ★ double decrease, (skip next 2 chs, work V-St in next ch) 3 times, skip next 2 chs, work (V-St, ch 1, V-St) in next ch, (skip next 2 chs, work V-St in next ch) 3 times; repeat from ★ across to last 5 chs, [YO, skip next 2 chs, insert hook in next ch, YO and pull up a loop, YO and draw through 2 loops on hook, (YO, insert hook in **next** ch, YO and pull up a loop, YO and draw through 2 loops on hook) twice, YO and draw through all 4 loops on hook **(counts as one dc)**]: 188 dc and 99 ch-1 sps.

Note: Loop a short piece of yarn around any stitch to mark Row 1 as **right** side.

Row 2: Ch 2, turn; work beginning decrease, work V-St in next 3 ch-1 sps, work (V-St, ch 1, V-St) in next ch-1 sp, work V-St in next 3 ch-1 sps, ★ decrease, work V-St in next 3 ch-1 sps, work (V-St, ch 1, V-St) in next ch-1 sp, work V-St in next 3 ch-1 sps; repeat from ★ across to last ch-1 sp, work ending decrease; finish off.

Row 3: With **right** side facing, join Lt Blue with slip st in first dc; ch 2, work beginning decrease, work Puff St in next ch-1 sp, (ch 3, work Puff St in next ch-1 sp) twice, ch 1, work (V-St, ch 1, V-St) in next ch-1 sp, work Puff St in next ch-1 sp, (ch 3, work Puff St in next ch-1 sp) twice, ch 1, ★ decrease, work Puff St in next ch-1 sp, (ch 3, work Puff St in next ch-1 sp) twice, ch 1, work (V-St, ch 1, V-St) in next ch-1 sp, work Puff St in next ch-1 sp, (ch 3, work Puff St in next ch-1 sp) twice, ch 1; repeat from ★ across to last ch-1 sp, work ending decrease; finish off: 66 Puff Sts, 56 dc, and 99 sps.

Row 4: With **wrong** side facing, join White with slip st in first dc; ch 2, work right decrease, skip next 2 chs, work V-St in next ch, skip next Puff St and next 2 chs, work V-St in next ch, skip next Puff St and next dc, work V-St in next ch-1 sp, work (V-St, ch 1, V-St) in next ch-1 sp, work V-St in next ch-1 sp, skip next dc, work V-St in next ch, skip next Puff St and next 2 chs, work V-St in next ch, ★ work center decrease, (skip next Puff St and next 2 chs, work V-St in next ch) twice, skip next Puff St and next dc, work V-St in next ch-1 sp, work (V-St, ch 1, V-St) in next ch-1 sp, work V-St in next

ch-1 sp, skip next dc, work V-St in next ch, skip next Puff St and next 2 chs, work V-St in next ch; repeat from ★ across to last 6 sts, work left decrease: 188 dc and 99 ch-1 sps.

Row 5: Ch 2, turn; work beginning decrease, work V-St in next 3 ch-1 sps, work (V-St, ch 1, V-St) in next ch-1 sp, work V-St in next 3 ch-1 sps, ★ decrease, work V-St in next 3 ch-1 sps, work (V-St, ch 1, V-St) in next ch-1 sp, work V-St in next 3 ch-1 sps; repeat from ★ across to last ch-1 sp, work ending decrease; finish off.

Row 6: With **wrong** side facing, join Lt Blue with slip st in first dc; ch 2, work beginning decrease, work V-St in next 3 ch-1 sps, work (V-St, ch 1, V-St) in next ch-1 sp, work V-St in next 3 ch-1 sps, ★ decrease, work V-St in next 3 ch-1 sps, work (V-St, ch 1, V-St) in next ch-1 sp, work V-St in next 3 ch-1 sps; repeat from ★ across to last ch-1 sp, work ending decrease.

Row 7: Ch 2, turn; work beginning decrease, work V-St in next 3 ch-1 sps, work (V-St, ch 1, V-St) in next ch-1 sp, work V-St in next 3 ch-1 sps, ★ decrease, work V-St in next 3 ch-1 sps, work (V-St, ch 1, V-St) in next ch-1 sp, work V-St in next 3 ch-1 sps; repeat from ★ across to last ch-1 sp, work ending decrease; finish off.

Row 8: With **wrong** side facing, join White with slip st in first dc; ch 2, work beginning decrease, work Puff St in next ch-1 sp, (ch 3, work Puff St in next ch-1 sp) twice, ch 1, work (V-St, ch 1, V-St) in next ch-1 sp, work Puff St in next ch-1 sp, (ch 3, work Puff St in next ch-1 sp) twice, ch 1, ★ decrease, work Puff St in next ch-1 sp, (ch 3, work Puff St in next ch-1 sp) twice, ch 1, work (V-St, ch 1, V-St) in next ch-1 sp, work Puff St in next ch-1 sp, (ch 3, work Puff St in next ch-1 sp) twice, ch 1; repeat from ★ across to last ch-1 sp, work ending decrease; finish off: 66 Puff Sts, 56 dc, and 99 sps.

Row 9: With **right** side facing, join Lt Blue with slip st in first dc; ch 2, work right decrease, skip next 2 chs, work V-St in next ch, skip next Puff St and next 2 chs, work V-St in next ch, skip next Puff St and next dc, work V-St in next ch-1 sp, work (V-St, ch 1, V-St) in next ch-1 sp, work V-St in next ch-1 sp, skip next dc, work V-St in next ch, skip next Puff St and next 2 chs, work V-St in next ch, ★ work center decrease, (skip next Puff St and next 2 chs, work V-St in next ch) twice, skip next Puff St and next dc, work V-St in next ch-1 sp, work (V-St, ch 1, V-St) in next ch-1 sp, work V-St in next ch-1 sp, skip next dc, work V-St in next ch, skip next Puff St and next 2 chs, work V-St in next ch; repeat from ★ across to last 6 sts, work left decrease: 188 dc and 99 ch-1 sps.

Row 10: Ch 2, turn; work beginning decrease, work V-St in next 3 ch-1 sps, work (V-St, ch 1, V-St) in next ch-1 sp, work V-St in next 3 ch-1 sps, ★ decrease, work V-St in next 3 ch-1 sps, work (V-St, ch 1, V-St) in next ch-1 sp, work V-St in next 3 ch-1 sps; repeat from ★ across to last ch-1 sp, work ending decrease; finish off.

Row 11: With **right** side facing, join White with slip st in first dc; ch 2, work beginning decrease, work V-St in next 3 ch-1 sps, work (V-St, ch 1, V-St) in next ch-1 sp, work V-St in next 3 ch-1 sps, ★ decrease, work V-St in next 3 ch-1 sps, work (V-St, ch 1, V-St) in next ch-1 sp, work V-St in next 3 ch-1 sps; repeat from ★ across to last ch-1 sp, work ending decrease.

Row 12: Ch 2, turn; work beginning decrease, work V-St in next 3 ch-1 sps, work (V-St, ch 1, V-St) in next ch-1 sp, work V-St in next 3 ch-1 sps, ★ decrease, work V-St in next 3 ch-1 sps, work (V-St, ch 1, V-St) in next ch-1 sp, work V-St in next 3 ch-1 sps; repeat from ★ across to last ch-1 sp, work ending decrease; finish off.

Row 13: With Blue, repeat Row 3.

Rows 14 and 15: Repeat Rows 4 and 5.

Rows 16 and 17: With Blue, repeat Rows 6 and 7.

Row 18: Repeat Row 8.

Rows 19 and 20: With Blue, repeat Rows 9 and 10.

Rows 21 and 22: Repeat Rows 11 and 12.

Row 23: With Dk Blue, repeat Row 3.

Rows 24 and 25: Repeat Rows 4 and 5.

Rows 26 and 27: With Dk Blue, repeat Rows 6 and 7.

Row 28: Repeat Row 8.

Rows 29 and 30: With Dk Blue, repeat Rows 9 and 10.

Rows 31 and 32: Repeat Rows 11 and 12.

Rows 33-72: Repeat Rows 3-32 once, then repeat Rows 3-12 once **more**; at end of Row 72, do **not** finish off.

EDGING

Rnd 1: Ch 1, turn; sc in first dc and in next ch-1 sp, (sc in next 2 dc and in next ch-1 sp) 3 times, (sc in next dc and in next ch-1 sp) twice, (sc in next 2 dc and in next ch-1 sp) 3 times, ★ sc in next dc, skip next dc, sc in next dc and in next ch-1 sp, (sc in next 2 dc and in next ch-1 sp) 3 times, (sc in next dc and in next ch-1 sp) twice, (sc in next 2 dc and in next ch-1 sp) 3 times; repeat from ★ across to last 2 dc, skip next dc, sc in last dc; working in end of rows, 2 sc in each of first 2 rows, (3 sc in next row, 2 sc in next row) across; working in free loops *(Fig. 3b, page 3)* and in sps across beginning ch, sc in first ch, place marker in sc just made for st placement, sc in next 2 chs, (2 sc in next sp, sc in next ch) 3 times, sc in next 2 sps, † sc in next ch, (2 sc in next sp, sc in next ch) 8 times, sc in next 2 sps †; repeat from † to † 9 times **more**, (sc in next ch, 2 sc in next sp) 3 times, sc in next 2 chs and in marked ch, place marker in last sc made for st placement; working in end of rows, 2 sc in each of first 2 rows, (3 sc in next row, 2 sc in next row) across; join with slip st to first sc: 929 sc.

Rnd 2: Ch 1, do **not** turn; work Puff St in same st, ★ (ch 3, skip next 2 sc, work Puff St in next sc) 8 times, work Puff St in next sc; repeat from ★ 9 times **more**, ch 3, (skip next 2 sc, work Puff St in next sc, ch 3) around to within 2 sc of marked sc, skip next 2 sc, work Puff St in marked sc, ch 3, skip next sc, work Puff St in next sc, (ch 3, skip next 2 sc, work Puff St in next sc) 3 times, skip next 2 sc, work Puff St in next sc, † (ch 3, skip next 2 sc, work Puff St in next sc) 8 times, skip next 2 sc, work Puff St in next sc †; repeat from † to † 9 times **more**, ch 3, (skip next 2 sc, work Puff St in next sc, ch 3) 3 times, skip next sc, work Puff St in marked sc, ch 3, skip next 2 sc, (work Puff St in next sc, ch 3, skip next 2 sc) across; join with slip st to top of first Puff St.

Rnd 3: (Slip st, ch 1, 3 sc) in first ch-3 sp, 3 sc in next ch-3 sp and in each ch-3 sp around; join with slip st to first sc, finish off.

Design by Leana Moon.

Impressive Plaid

Finished Size: 45 $1/2$" x 60 $1/2$"
(115.5 cm x 153.5 cm)

MATERIALS
Worsted Weight Yarn:
Black - 23 ounces, 1,300 yards
(650 grams, 1,188.5 meters)
Red - 6 ounces, 340 yards
(170 grams, 311 meters)
Grey - 5 $1/2$ ounces, 310 yards
(160 grams, 283.5 meters)
Crochet hook, size H (5 mm) **or** size needed
for gauge
Yarn needle

GAUGE: In pattern, one point to point repeat
(12 dc and one ch-2 sp) = 3 $1/2$" (9 cm);
14 rows = 7 $1/2$" (19 cm)

Gauge Swatch: 7"w x 3 $3/4$"h (17.75 cm x 9.5 cm)
With Black, ch 26.
Work same as Afghan Body for 7 rows.

AFGHAN BODY
With Black, ch 169.

Row 1 (Right side)**:** Working in back ridges of
beginning ch **(Fig. 1, page 3)**, dc in fourth ch from
hook **(3 skipped chs count as first dc)** and in
next 3 chs, (dc, ch 2, dc) in next ch, dc in next
5 chs, ★ skip next 2 chs, dc in next 5 chs, (dc, ch 2,
dc) in next ch, dc in next 5 chs; repeat from ★
across: 156 dc and 13 ch-2 sps.

Note: Loop a short piece of yarn around any stitch
to mark Row 1 as **right** side.

Rows 2-4: Ch 3 **(counts as first dc, now and
throughout)**, turn; skip next dc, dc in next 4 dc,
(dc, ch 2, dc) in next ch-2 sp, ★ dc in next 5 dc,
skip next 2 dc, dc in next 5 dc, (dc, ch 2, dc) in next
ch-2 sp; repeat from ★ across to last 6 dc, dc in
next 4 dc, skip next dc, dc in last dc; at end of
Row 4, finish off.

Row 5: With **right** side facing, join Grey with dc in
first dc **(see Joining With Dc, page 3)**; skip next
dc, dc in next 4 dc, (dc, ch 2, dc) in next ch-2 sp,
★ dc in next 5 dc, skip next 2 dc, dc in next 5 dc,
(dc, ch 2, dc) in next ch-2 sp; repeat from ★ across
to last 6 dc, dc in next 4 dc, skip next dc, dc in last
dc.

Row 6: Ch 3, turn; skip next dc, dc in next 4 dc,
(dc, ch 2, dc) in next ch-2 sp, ★ dc in next 5 dc,
skip next 2 dc, dc in next 5 dc, (dc, ch 2, dc) in next
ch-2 sp; repeat from ★ across to last 6 dc, dc in
next 4 dc, skip next dc, dc in last dc; finish off.

Row 7: With **right** side facing, join Red with sc in
first dc **(see Joining With Sc, page 1)**; skip next
dc, sc in next 4 dc, (sc, ch 2, sc) in next ch-2 sp,
★ sc in next 5 dc, skip next 2 dc, sc in next 5 dc,
(sc, ch 2, sc) in next ch-2 sp; repeat from ★ across
to last 6 dc, sc in next 4 dc, skip next dc, sc in last
dc; finish off: 156 sc and 26 chs.

Row 8: With **wrong** side facing and working in
Front Loops Only **(Fig. 2, page 3)**, join Grey with
dc in first sc; skip next sc, dc in next 4 sc and in
next ch, ch 2, ★ dc in next ch and in next 5 sc, skip
next 2 sc, dc in next 5 sc and in next ch, ch 2;
repeat from ★ across to last 7 sts, dc in next ch and
in next 4 sc, skip next sc, dc in last sc: 156 dc and
13 ch-2 sps.

Row 9: Ch 3, turn; working in **both** loops, skip
next dc, dc in next 4 dc, (dc, ch 2, dc) in next
ch-2 sp, ★ dc in next 5 dc, skip next 2 dc, dc in
next 5 dc, (dc, ch 2, dc) in next ch-2 sp; repeat from
★ across to last 6 dc, dc in next 4 dc, skip next dc,
dc in last dc; finish off.

Row 10: With **wrong** side facing, join Black with
dc in first dc; skip next dc, dc in next 4 dc, (dc,
ch 2, dc) in next ch-2 sp, ★ dc in next 5 dc, skip
next 2 dc, dc in next 5 dc, (dc, ch 2, dc) in next
ch-2 sp; repeat from ★ across to last 6 dc, dc in
next 4 dc, skip next dc, dc in last dc.

Rows 11-13: Ch 3, turn; skip next dc, dc in next
4 dc, (dc, ch 2, dc) in next ch-2 sp, ★ dc in next
5 dc, skip next 2 dc, dc in next 5 dc, (dc, ch 2, dc)
in next ch-2 sp; repeat from ★ across to last 6 dc,
dc in next 4 dc, skip next dc, dc in last dc; at end of
last row, finish off.

Continued on page 48.

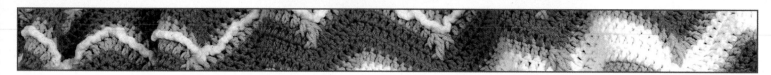

Ruffled Intrigue

Finished Size: 48" x 64½" (122 cm x 164 cm)

MATERIALS
Worsted Weight Yarn:
  Purple - 15 ounces, 850 yards
    (430 grams, 777 meters)
  Lt Purple - 11 ounces, 620 yards
    (310 grams, 567 meters)
  White - 8½ ounces, 480 yards
    (240 grams, 439 meters)
Crochet hook, size K (6.5 mm) **or** size needed
  for gauge

GAUGE: In pattern, one large point to large
          point repeat (36 sts) = 11" (28 cm);
          Rows 1-8 = 4" (10 cm)
          12 dc and 8 rows = 4" (10 cm)

Gauge Swatch: 15"w x 4"h (38 cm x 10 cm)
With Purple, ch 54.
Work same as Afghan for 8 rows.
Finish off.

STITCH GUIDE

DECREASE (uses next 3 sts)
★ YO, insert hook in **next** st, YO and pull up a
loop, YO and draw through 2 loops on hook;
repeat from ★ 2 times **more**, YO and draw
through all 4 loops on hook **(counts as
one dc)**.

FRONT POST CLUSTER
  (abbreviated FP Cluster (uses next 3 dc)
† YO, insert hook from **front** to **back** around
post of **next** dc *(Fig. 5, page 3)*, YO and pull
up a loop, YO and draw through 2 loops on
hook †, YO twice, insert hook from **front** to
back around post of dc one row **below** next dc,
YO and pull up a loop, (YO and draw through
2 loops on hook) twice, repeat from † to † once,
YO and draw through all 4 loops on hook.

AFGHAN
With Purple, ch 162.

Row 1 (Right side)**:** Working in back ridges of
beginning ch *(Fig. 1, page 3)*, dc in fourth ch from
hook **(3 skipped chs count as first dc)** and in
next 5 chs, decrease, dc in next 5 chs, ★ 3 dc in
next ch, dc in next 9 chs, decrease, dc in next
9 chs, 3 dc in next ch, dc in next 5 chs, decrease,
dc in next 5 chs; repeat from ★ across to last ch,
2 dc in last ch: 159 sts.

Note: Loop a short piece of yarn around any stitch
to mark Row 1 as **right** side.

Row 2: Ch 3 **(counts as first dc, now and
throughout)**, turn; dc in same st and in next 5 dc,
decrease, dc in next 5 dc, ★ 3 dc in next dc, dc in
next 9 dc, decrease, dc in next 9 dc, 3 dc in next
dc, dc in next 5 dc, decrease, dc in next 5 dc; repeat
from ★ across to last dc, 2 dc in last dc changing to
Lt Purple in last dc *(Fig. 4a, page 3)*.

Continue to change colors in same manner.

Row 3: With Lt Purple, ch 3, turn; dc in same st
and in next 5 dc, work FP Cluster, dc in next 5 dc,
★ 3 dc in next dc, dc in next 9 dc, work FP Cluster,
dc in next 9 dc, 3 dc in next dc, dc in next 5 dc,
work FP Cluster, dc in next 5 dc; repeat from ★
across to last dc, 2 dc in last dc.

Row 4: With White, ch 1, turn; (sc, ch 1, sc) in first
7 dc, ★ skip next FP Cluster, (sc, ch 1, sc) in next
17 dc; repeat from ★ across to last 7 sts, skip next
FP Cluster, (sc, ch 1, sc) in last 7 dc.

Row 5: With Lt Purple, ch 3, turn; working
behind Row 4 **and** in dc on Row 3 (between sc),
dc in same st and in next 5 dc, decrease, dc in next
5 dc, ★ 3 dc in next dc, dc in next 9 dc, decrease,
dc in next 9 dc, 3 dc in next dc, dc in next 5 dc,
decrease, dc in next 5 dc; repeat from ★ across to
last dc, 2 dc in last dc.

Rows 6-8: With Purple, ch 3, turn; dc in same st
and in next 5 dc, decrease, dc in next 5 dc, ★ 3 dc
in next dc, dc in next 9 dc, decrease, dc in next
9 dc, 3 dc in next dc, dc in next 5 dc, decrease, dc
in next 5 dc; repeat from ★ across to last dc, 2 dc in
last dc.

Continued on page 48.

American Waves

Finished Size: 46" x 60" (117 cm x 152.5 cm)

MATERIALS
Worsted Weight Yarn:
Red - 29 ounces, 1,640 yards
(820 grams, 1,499.5 meters)
White - 21^1/$_2$ ounces, 1,215 yards
(610 grams, 1,111 meters)
Blue - 4^1/$_2$ ounces, 255 yards
(130 grams, 233 meters)
Crochet hooks, sizes G (4 mm) **and**
H (5.00 mm) **or** sizes needed for gauge
Yarn needle

GAUGE: Each Square = 3^1/$_2$" (9 cm);
In pattern, one point to point
repeat (25 sts) = 4^1/$_2$" (11.5 cm);
10 rows = 3^1/$_4$" (8.25 cm);
16 sc = 4" (10 cm)

Gauge Swatch #1: 3^1/$_2$" (9 cm) square
Work same as Square.

Gauge Swatch #2: 9"w x 3^1/$_4$"h
(22.75 cm x 8.25 cm)
With Red and using larger size hook, ch 51.
Work same as Bottom Ripple for 10 rows.

STAR STRIP (Make 2)
SQUARE (Make 19)
With White and using smaller size hook, ch 5; join
with slip st to form a ring.

Rnd 1 (Right side)**:** Ch 1, 10 sc in ring; join with
slip st to first sc.

Note: Loop a short piece of yarn around any stitch
to mark Rnd 1 as **right** side.

Rnd 2: Ch 1, sc in same st, (2 dc, ch 5, 2 dc) in
next sc, ★ sc in next sc, (2 dc, ch 5, 2 dc) in next
sc; repeat from ★ around; join with slip st to first sc,
finish off: 5 ch-5 sps.

Rnd 3: With **right** side facing and using smaller
size hook, join Blue with sc in center ch of any ch-5
(see Joining With Sc, page 1); ch 7, (sc in center
ch of next ch-5, ch 7) around; join with slip st to
first sc: 5 sc and 5 ch-7 sps.

Rnd 4: Ch 5 **(counts as first dc plus ch 2,
now and throughout)**, dc in same st and in next
ch, hdc in next ch, sc in next 5 chs, hdc in next sc,
dc in next ch, ★ (dc, ch 2, dc) in next ch, dc in next
ch, hdc in next st, sc in next 5 sts, hdc in next ch,
dc in next ch; repeat from ★ 2 times **more**; join
with slip st to first dc, finish off: 44 sts and
4 ch-2 sps.

HALF SQUARE (Make 2)
With White and using smaller size hook, ch 5; join
with slip st to form a ring.

Row 1: Ch 1, 6 sc in ring; do **not** join.

Row 2 (Right side)**:** Ch 3 **(counts as first dc)**,
turn; (dc, ch 5, 2 dc) in same st, sc in next sc,
★ (2 dc, ch 5, 2 dc) in next sc, sc in next sc; repeat
from ★ once **more**; finish off: 3 ch-5 sps.

Note: Mark Row 2 as **right** side.

Row 3: With **wrong** side facing and using smaller
size hook, join Blue with slip st in first sc; (ch 7, sc
in center ch of next ch-5) 3 times, leave last 2 dc
unworked: 3 sc and 3 ch-7 sps.

Row 4: Ch 5, turn; dc in same st and in next ch,
† hdc in next ch, sc in next 5 sts, hdc in next st, dc
in next ch, (dc, ch 2, dc) in next ch †, dc in next ch,
repeat from † to † once, leave last 3 chs unworked;
finish off: 24 sts and 3 ch-2 sps.

ASSEMBLY
With Blue, using Placement Diagram as a guide, and
working through **inside** loops *(Fig. 7b, page 4)*,
whipstitch 19 Squares and 2 Half Squares together
to form one Strip, beginning in second ch of first
corner ch-2 and ending in first ch of next corner
ch-2.

PLACEMENT DIAGRAM

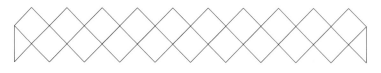

Continued on page 47.

TRIM

With **right** side facing and using larger size hook, skip first dc and next ch on first Half Square and join Red with sc in next ch; sc in next 11 sts, pull up a loop in next dc and in next ch, YO and draw through all 3 loops on hook, skip next joining, pull up a loop in next ch on next Square and in next dc, YO and draw through all 3 loops on hook, ★ sc in next 10 sts, 3 sc in next corner ch-2 sp, sc in next 10 sts, pull up a loop in next dc and in next ch, YO and draw through all 3 loops on hook, skip next joining, pull up a loop in next ch on next Square and in next dc, YO and draw through all 3 loops on hook; repeat from ★ 8 times **more**, sc in next 12 sts, leave last dc unworked; finish off: 251 sts.

BOTTOM RIPPLE

With Red and using larger size hook, ch 251.

Row 1 (Wrong side)**:** Sc in second ch from hook, skip next ch, sc in next 10 chs, 3 sc in next ch, ★ sc in next 11 chs, skip next 2 chs, sc in next 11 chs, 3 sc in next ch; repeat from ★ across to last 12 chs, sc in next 10 chs, skip next ch, sc in last ch: 250 sc.

Note: Mark the **back** of any stitch on Row 1 as **right** side and bottom edge.

Rows 2-10: Ch 1, turn; sc in both loops of first sc, skip next sc, working in Back Loops Only *(Fig. 2, page 3)*, sc in next 10 sc, 3 sc in next sc, ★ sc in next 11 sc, skip next 2 sc, sc in next 11 sc, 3 sc in next sc; repeat from ★ across to last 12 sc, sc in next 10 sc, skip next sc, sc in **both** loops of last sc; at end of last row, finish off.

Row 11: With **wrong** side facing and using larger size hook, join White with sc in both loops of first sc; skip next sc, working in Back Loops Only, sc in next 10 sc, 3 sc in next sc, ★ sc in next 11 sc, skip next 2 sc, sc in next 11 sc, 3 sc in next sc; repeat from ★ across to last 12 sc, sc in next 10 sc, skip next sc, sc in **both** loops of last sc.

Rows 12-20: Repeat Rows 2-10.

Rows 21-30: With Red, repeat Rows 11-20.

Rows 31-49: Repeat Rows 11-29; at end of last row, finish off.

ASSEMBLY

With **right** sides facing, place Trim of one Star Strip adjacent to Row 49 of Bottom Ripple, matching stitches. With Red and working through **inside** loops only, whipstitch pieces together.

CENTER RIPPLE

Row 1: With **wrong** side facing, join Red with sc in corner sp at top of first Half Square on Star Border; skip next joining and next ch and dc on next Square, working in Back Loops Only, sc in next 10 sts, 3 sc in next ch-2 sp, ★ sc in next 10 sts, pull up a loop in next dc and in next ch, YO and draw through all 3 loops on hook, skip next joining, pull up a loop in next ch on next Square and in next dc, YO and draw through all 3 loops on hook, sc in next 10 sts, 3 sc in next ch-2 sp; repeat from ★ 8 times **more**, sc in next 10 sts, skip next dc, next ch, and next joining, sc in corner sp at top of next Half Square: 250 sts.

Rows 2-49: Work same as Bottom Ripple.

ASSEMBLY

With **right** sides facing, place Trim of remaining Star Strip adjacent to Row 49 of Center Ripple, matching stitches. With Red and working through **inside** loops only, whipstitch pieces together.

TOP RIPPLE

Rows 1-41: Work same as Center Ripple.

Rows 42-50: Ch 1, turn; sc in both loops of first sc, skip next sc, working in Back Loops Only, sc in next 10 sc, 3 sc in next sc, ★ sc in next 11 sc, skip next 2 sc, sc in next 11 sc, 3 sc in next sc; repeat from ★ across to last 12 sc, sc in next 10 sc, skip next sc, sc in **both** loops of last sc; do **not** finish off.

EDGING

Ch 1, do **not** turn; sc evenly across end of rows; working in free loops *(Fig. 3b, page 3)* and in sps across beginning ch, 3 sc in ch at base of first sc, sc in next 10 chs, ★ skip next ch, sc in next 11 chs, 3 sc in next sp, sc in next 11 chs; repeat from ★ 8 times **more**, skip next ch, sc in next 10 chs, skip next ch, 3 sc in last ch; sc evenly across end of rows; working in **both** loops across Row 50 of Top Ripple, 3 sc in first sc, skip next sc, sc in next 10 sc, 3 sc in next sc, (sc in next 11 sc, skip next 2 sc, sc in next 11 sc, 3 sc in next sc) 9 times, sc in next 10 sc, skip next sc, 3 sc in last sc; join with slip st to first sc, finish off.

Design by Laurie Halama.

Impressive Plaid
Continued from page 41.

Row 14: With **wrong** side facing, join Red with sc in first dc; skip next dc, sc in next 4 dc, (sc, ch 2, sc) in next ch-2 sp, ★ sc in next 5 dc, skip next 2 dc, sc in next 5 dc, (sc, ch 2, sc) in next ch-2 sp; repeat from ★ across to last 6 dc, sc in next 4 dc, skip next dc, sc in last dc; finish off: 156 sc and 26 chs.

Row 15: With **right** side facing and working in Back Loops Only, join Black with dc in first sc; skip next sc, dc in next 4 sc and in next ch, ch 2, ★ dc in next ch and in next 5 sc, skip next 2 sc, dc in next 5 sc and in next ch, ch 2; repeat from ★ across to last 7 sts, dc in next ch and in next 4 sc, skip next sc, dc in last sc: 156 dc and 13 ch-2 sps.

Rows 16-18: Ch 3, turn; working in **both** loops, skip next dc, dc in next 4 dc, (dc, ch 2, dc) in next ch-2 sp, ★ dc in next 5 dc, skip next 2 dc, dc in next 5 dc, (dc, ch 2, dc) in next ch-2 sp; repeat from ★ across to last 6 dc, dc in next 4 dc, skip next dc, dc in last dc; at end of last row, finish off.

Rows 19-111: Repeat Rows 5-18, 6 times; then repeat Rows 5-13 once **more**.

WEAVING
CHAIN (Make 25)
With Red and leaving a 6" (15 cm) end for sewing, make a chain 10" (25.5 cm) longer than finished length of Afghan; finish off leaving a 6" (15 cm) end for sewing.

FIRST ROW
Thread yarn needle with 6" (15 cm) end at top of any Chain. Holding Afghan Body with beginning ch at your right, insert needle down through ch below first ch-2 sp on first row. Working toward last row (left), bring needle up in ch-2 sp of first row and down in ch-2 sp of next row. Continue weaving in same manner in each ch-2 sp across. Pull row of weaving evenly so Afghan does not pucker. Wrap top of Chain over last ch-2 and weave 6" (15 cm) end back through Chain. Thread yarn needle with remaining 6" (15 cm) end; wrap bottom of Chain over ch below first ch-2 sp and weave 6" (15 cm) end back through Chain.

SECOND ROW
Thread yarn needle with 6" (15 cm) end at top of any Chain. Holding Afghan Body with beginning ch at your right, insert needle down through sp on first row above 2 skipped chs. Working toward last row (left), bring needle up in sp between 2 skipped dc on second row and down in sp between 2 skipped dc on next row. Continue weaving in same manner in each sp between 2 skipped sts across. Pull row of weaving evenly so Afghan does not pucker. Wrap top of Chain over end of last row and weave 6" (15 cm) end back through Chain. Thread yarn needle with remaining 6" (15 cm) end; wrap bottom of Chain over 2 skipped chs and weave 6" (15 cm) end back through Chain.

REMAINING 23 ROWS
Weave remaining Chains in same manner, alternately working through rows of ch-2 sps and rows of sps between skipped sts.

Design by Joyce L. Rodriguez.

Ruffled Intrigue
Continued from page 43.

Row 9: With Lt Purple, ch 3, turn; dc in same st and in next 5 dc, work FP Cluster, dc in next 5 dc, ★ 3 dc in next dc, dc in next 9 dc, work FP Cluster, dc in next 9 dc, 3 dc in next dc, dc in next 5 dc, work FP Cluster, dc in next 5 dc; repeat from ★ across to last dc, 2 dc in last dc.

Rows 10-15: Repeat Rows 4-9.

Rows 16-18: With White, ch 3, turn; dc in same st and in next 5 dc, decrease, dc in next 5 dc, ★ 3 dc in next dc, dc in next 9 dc, decrease, dc in next 9 dc, 3 dc in next dc, dc in next 5 dc, decrease, dc in next 5 dc; repeat from ★ across to last dc, 2 dc in last dc.

Row 19: With Lt Purple, ch 3, turn; dc in same st and in next 5 dc, work FP Cluster, dc in next 5 dc, ★ 3 dc in next dc, dc in next 9 dc, work FP Cluster, dc in next 9 dc, 3 dc in next dc, dc in next 5 dc, work FP Cluster, dc in next 5 dc; repeat from ★ across to last dc, 2 dc in last dc.

Rows 20-22: With Purple, ch 3, turn; dc in same st and in next 5 dc, decrease, dc in next 5 dc, ★ 3 dc in next dc, dc in next 9 dc, decrease, dc in next 9 dc, 3 dc in next dc, dc in next 5 dc, decrease, dc in next 5 dc; repeat from ★ across to last dc, 2 dc in last dc.

Rows 23-36: Repeat Rows 9-22.

Rows 37-115: Repeat Rows 3-36 twice, then repeat Rows 3-13 once **more**.

Finish off.

Design by Michelle Higley.

Lady's Choice

Finished Size: 45¹/₂" x 62"
(115.5 cm x 157.5 cm)

MATERIALS
Worsted Weight Yarn:
Lt Green - 24¹/₂ ounces, 1,385 yards
(700 grams, 1,266.5 meters)
Ecru - 19 ounces, 1,075 yards
(540 grams, 983 meters)
Red - 6¹/₂ ounces, 370 yards
(180 grams, 338.5 meters)
Green - 3¹/₂ ounces, 200 yards
(100 grams, 183 meters)
Crochet hooks, sizes G (4 mm) **and** H (5 mm)
or sizes needed for gauge

GAUGE: With smaller size hook,
in pattern, one point to point
repeat (27 sts) = 4¹/₄" (10.75 cm)
With larger size hook,
in pattern, one point to point repeat
(16 sts and 7 sps) = 5" (12.75 cm)
Rows 1-7 = 4" (10 cm)

Gauge Swatch: 10"w x 4"h (25.5 cm x 10 cm)
With larger size hook and Lt Green, ch 56.
Work same as Afghan Body for 7 rows.
Finish off.

AFGHAN BODY
With Lt Green and using larger size hook, ch 245,
place marker in third ch from hook for st placement.

Row 1 (Right side)**:** Dc in fourth ch from hook
(3 skipped chs count as first dc), ch 2, skip
next 3 chs, (2 dc in next ch, ch 2, skip next 3 chs)
twice, (2 dc, ch 2) twice in next ch, ★ skip next
3 chs, 2 dc in next ch, (ch 2, skip next 3 chs, 2 dc
in next ch) twice, skip next 2 chs, (2 dc in next ch,
ch 2, skip next 3 chs) 3 times, (2 dc, ch 2) twice in
next ch; repeat from ★ 7 times **more**, skip next
3 chs, (2 dc in next ch, ch 2, skip next 3 chs) twice,
dc in last 2 chs: 63 ch-2 sps.

Note: Loop a short piece of yarn around any stitch
to mark Row 1 as **right** side.

Row 2: Ch 3 **(counts as first dc, now and
throughout)**, turn; working **around** next ch-2
(Fig. 6, page 3) and in skipped chs on beginning
ch, dc in center ch of next 3 skipped chs, ch 2,
(working **around** next ch-2, 2 dc in center ch of
next 3 skipped chs, ch 2) twice, (2 dc, ch 2) twice in
next ch-2 sp, working **around** next ch-2, 2 dc in
center ch of 3 skipped chs, ★ (ch 2, working
around next ch-2, 2 dc in center ch of next
3 skipped chs) twice, skip next 4 dc, working
around next ch-2, 2 dc in center ch of next
3 skipped chs, ch 2, (working **around** next ch-2,
2 dc in center ch of next 3 skipped chs, ch 2) twice,
(2 dc, ch 2) twice in next ch-2 sp, working **around**
next ch-2, 2 dc in center ch of next 3 skipped chs;
repeat from ★ across to last 2 ch-2 sps, ch 2,
working **around** next ch-2, 2 dc in center ch of
next 3 skipped chs, ch 2, working **around** next
ch-2, dc in center ch of next 3 skipped chs, skip
next dc, dc in last dc.

Rows 3-7: Ch 3, turn; working **around** next ch-2,
dc in sp **between** next 2-dc group one row **below**,
ch 2, (working **around** next ch-2, 2 dc in sp
between next 2-dc group one row **below**, ch 2)
twice, (2 dc, ch 2) twice in next ch-2 sp, working
around next ch-2, 2 dc in sp **between** next
2-dc group one row **below**, ★ (ch 2, working
around next ch-2, 2 dc in sp **between** next
2-dc group one row **below**) twice, skip next 4 dc,
(working **around** next ch-2, 2 dc in sp **between**
next 2-dc group one row **below**, ch 2) 3 times,
(2 dc, ch 2) twice in next ch-2 sp, working **around**
next ch-2, 2 dc in sp **between** next 2-dc group one
row **below**; repeat from ★ across to last 2 ch-2 sps,
ch 2, working **around** next ch-2, 2 dc in sp
between next 2-dc group one row **below**, ch 2,
working **around** next ch-2, dc in sp **between** next
2-dc group one row **below**, skip next dc, dc in last
dc; at end of Row 7, change to Ecru in last dc made
(Fig. 4a, page 3).

Rows 8-10: Repeat Row 3, 3 times; at end of last
row, change to Green.

Continued on page 56.

Aztec Sun

Finished Size: 60" (152.5 cm) diameter

MATERIALS

Worsted Weight Yarn:
Red - 19 ounces, 1,075 yards
(540 grams, 983 meters)
Yellow - 14 ounces, 790 yards
(400 grams, 722.5 meters)
Orange - 14 ounces, 790 yards
(400 grams, 722.5 meters)
Crochet hook, size J (6 mm) **or** size needed
for gauge

GAUGE: 8 dc and 4 rows = 2" (5 cm)

Gauge Swatch: $3^1/4$" (8.25 cm) (from
straight edge to straight edge)
Work same as Afghan through Rnd 3.

STITCH GUIDE

DC DECREASE (uses next 2 sts)
★ YO, insert hook in **next** st, YO and pull up a
loop, YO and draw through 2 loops on hook;
repeat from ★ once **more**, YO and draw
through all 3 loops on hook **(counts as
one dc)**.

CENTER RIPPLE

With Yellow, ch 4; join with slip st to form a ring.

Rnd 1 (Right side)**:** Ch 3 **(counts as first dc,
now and throughout)**, 11 dc in ring; join with
slip st to first dc: 12 dc.

Note: Loop a short piece of yarn around any stitch
to mark Rnd 1 as **right** side.

Rnd 2: Ch 3, dc in same st, 2 dc in next dc and in
each dc around; join with slip st to first dc: 24 dc.

Rnd 3: Ch 3, dc in same st and in next 2 dc, (3 dc
in next dc, dc in next 2 dc) around, dc in same st as
first dc; join with slip st to first dc: 40 dc.

Rnd 4: Ch 3, dc in same st and in next 4 dc, (3 dc
in next dc, dc in next 4 dc) around, dc in same st as
first dc; join with slip st to first dc: 56 dc.

Rnd 5: Ch 3, dc in same st and in next 6 dc, (3 dc
in next dc, dc in next 6 dc) around, dc in same st as
first dc; join with slip st to first dc: 72 dc.

Rnd 6: Ch 3, dc in same st and in next 8 dc, (3 dc
in next dc, dc in next 8 dc) around, dc in same st as
first dc; join with slip st to first dc: 88 dc.

Rnd 7: Ch 3, dc in same st, hdc in next 2 dc, sc in
next 2 dc, slip st in next 2 dc, sc in next 2 dc, hdc
in next 2 dc, ★ 3 dc in next dc, hdc in next 2 dc, sc
in next 2 dc, slip st in next 2 dc, sc in next 2 dc,
hdc in next 2 dc; repeat from ★ around, dc in same
st as first dc; join with slip st to first dc: 104 sts.

Rnd 8: Ch 3, 2 dc in same st, dc in next dc, hdc in
next 2 hdc, sc in next 2 sc, skip next 2 slip sts, sc in
next 2 sc, hdc in next 2 hdc, dc in next dc, ★ 5 dc
in next dc, dc in next dc, hdc in next 2 hdc, sc in
next 2 sc, skip next 2 slip sts, sc in next 2 sc, hdc in
next 2 hdc, dc in next dc; repeat from ★ around,
2 dc in same st as first dc; join with slip st to first dc:
120 sts.

Rnd 9: Ch 3, 2 dc in same st, dc in next 3 dc, hdc
in next 2 sts, sc in next sc, skip next 2 sc, sc in next
sc, hdc in next 2 sts, dc in next 3 dc, ★ 5 dc in next
dc, dc in next 3 dc, hdc in next 2 sts, sc in next sc,
skip next 2 sc, sc in next sc, hdc in next 2 sts, dc in
next 3 dc; repeat from ★ around, 2 dc in same st as
first dc; join with slip st to first dc, finish off:
136 sts.

Rnd 10: With **right** side facing, join Orange with
dc in center dc of any 5-dc group *(see Joining
With Dc, page 3)*; 2 dc in same st, dc in next 4 dc,
hdc in next 2 sts, sc in next hdc, skip next 2 sc, sc
in next hdc, hdc in next 2 sts, dc in next 4 dc,
★ 5 dc in next dc, dc in next 4 dc, hdc in next 2 sts,
sc in next hdc, skip next 2 sc, sc in next hdc, hdc in
next 2 sts, dc in next 4 dc; repeat from ★ around,
2 dc in same st as first dc; join with slip st to first dc:
152 sts.

Rnd 11: Ch 3, 2 dc in same st, dc in next 5 dc,
hdc in next 2 sts, sc in next hdc, skip next 2 sc, sc
in next hdc, hdc in next 2 sts, dc in next 5 dc,
★ 5 dc in next dc, dc in next 5 dc, hdc in next 2 sts,
sc in next hdc, skip next 2 sc, sc in next hdc, hdc in
next 2 sts, dc in next 5 dc; repeat from ★ around,
2 dc in same st as first dc; join with slip st to first dc:
168 sts.

Continued on page 53.

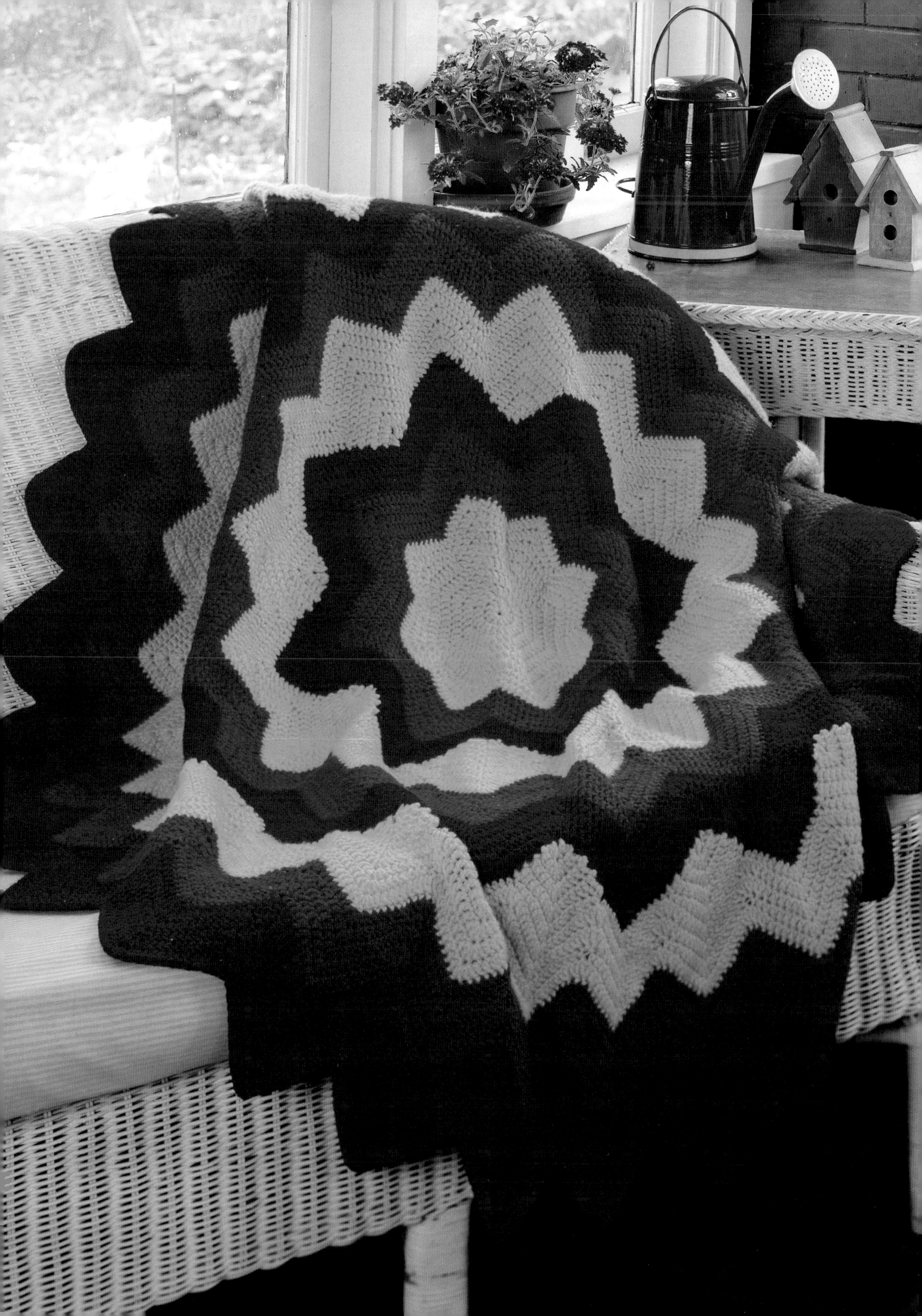

Rnd 12: Ch 3, 2 dc in same st, dc in next 6 dc, hdc in next 2 sts, sc in next hdc, skip next 2 sc, sc in next hdc, hdc in next 2 sts, dc in next 6 dc, ★ 5 dc in next dc, dc in next 6 dc, hdc in next 2 sts, sc in next hdc, skip next 2 sc, sc in next hdc, hdc in next 2 sts, dc in next 6 dc; repeat from ★ around, 2 dc in same st as first dc; join with slip st to first dc: 184 sts.

Rnd 13: Ch 3, 2 dc in same st, dc in next 7 dc, hdc in next 2 sts, sc in next hdc, skip next 2 sc, sc in next hdc, hdc in next 2 sts, dc in next 7 dc, ★ 5 dc in next dc, dc in next 7 dc, hdc in next 2 sts, sc in next hdc, skip next 2 sc, sc in next hdc, hdc in next 2 sts, dc in next 7 dc; repeat from ★ around, 2 dc in same st as first dc; join with slip st to first dc: 200 sts.

Rnd 14: Ch 3, 2 dc in same st, dc in next 8 dc, hdc in next 2 sts, sc in next hdc, skip next 2 sc, sc in next hdc, hdc in next 2 sts, dc in next 8 dc, ★ 5 dc in next dc, dc in next 8 dc, hdc in next 2 sts, sc in next hdc, skip next 2 sc, sc in next hdc, hdc in next 2 sts, dc in next 8 dc; repeat from ★ around, 2 dc in same st as first dc; join with slip st to first dc, finish off: 216 sts.

Rnd 15: With **right** side facing, join Red with dc in center dc of any 5-dc group; 2 dc in same st, dc in next 9 dc, hdc in next 2 sts, sc in next hdc, skip next 2 sc, sc in next hdc, hdc in next 2 sts, dc in next 9 dc, ★ 5 dc in next dc, dc in next 9 dc, hdc in next 2 sts, sc in next hdc, skip next 2 sc, sc in next hdc, hdc in next 2 sts, dc in next 9 dc; repeat from ★ around, 2 dc in same st as first dc; join with slip st to first dc: 232 sts.

Rnd 16: Ch 3, 2 dc in same st, dc in next 10 dc, hdc in next 2 sts, sc in next hdc, skip next 2 sc, sc in next hdc, hdc in next 2 sts, dc in next 10 dc, ★ 5 dc in next dc, dc in next 10 dc, hdc in next 2 sts, sc in next hdc, skip next 2 sc, sc in next hdc, hdc in next 2 sts, dc in next 10 dc; repeat from ★ around, 2 dc in same st as first dc; join with slip st to first dc: 248 sts.

Rnd 17: Ch 3, 2 dc in same st, dc in next 11 dc, hdc in next 2 sts, sc in next hdc, skip next 2 sc, sc in next hdc, hdc in next 2 sts, dc in next 11 dc, ★ 5 dc in next dc, dc in next 11 dc, hdc in next 2 sts, sc in next hdc, skip next 2 sc, sc in next hdc, hdc in next 2 sts, dc in next 11 dc; repeat from ★ around, 2 dc in same st as first dc; join with slip st to first dc: 264 sts.

Rnd 18: Ch 3, 2 dc in same st, dc in next 12 dc, hdc in next 2 sts, sc in next hdc, skip next 2 sc, sc in next hdc, hdc in next 2 sts, dc in next 12 dc, ★ 5 dc in next dc, dc in next 12 dc, hdc in next 2 sts, sc in next hdc, skip next 2 sc, sc in next hdc, hdc in next 2 sts, dc in next 12 dc; repeat from ★ around, 2 dc in same st as first dc; join with slip st to first dc: 280 sts.

Rnd 19: Ch 3, 2 dc in same st, dc in next 13 dc, hdc in next 2 sts, sc in next hdc, skip next 2 sc, sc in next hdc, hdc in next 2 sts, dc in next 13 dc, ★ 5 dc in next dc, dc in next 13 dc, hdc in next 2 sts, sc in next hdc, skip next 2 sc, sc in next hdc, hdc in next 2 sts, dc in next 13 dc; repeat from ★ around, 2 dc in same st as first dc; join with slip st to first dc, finish off: 296 sts.

FIRST FILL-IN POINT
Row 1: With **right** side facing, skip next 15 dc from joining and join Yellow with slip st in next hdc; skip next hdc, 2 dc in next sc, ch 1, 2 dc in next sc, skip next hdc, slip st in next hdc; finish off: 4 dc and one ch-1 sp.

Row 2: With **right** side facing, join Yellow with slip st in second dc **before** joining on Row 1 (on Rnd 19 of Center Ripple); dc in next 2 dc on Row 1, 5 dc in next ch-1 sp, dc in next 2 dc, skip next dc on Rnd 19 of Center Ripple, slip st in next dc; finish off: 9 dc.

Row 3: With **right** side facing, join Yellow with slip st in second dc **before** joining on Row 2; dc in next 4 dc on Row 2, 5 dc in next dc, dc in next 4 dc, skip next dc on Rnd 19 of Center Ripple, slip st in next dc; finish off: 13 dc.

Row 4: With **right** side facing, join Yellow with slip st in second dc **before** joining on Row 3; dc in next 6 dc on Row 3, 5 dc in next dc, dc in next 6 dc, skip next dc on Rnd 19 of Center Ripple, slip st in next dc; finish off: 17 dc.

REMAINING 7 FILL-IN POINTS
Row 1: With **right** side facing, skip next 25 dc on Rnd 19 of Center Ripple and join Yellow with slip st in next hdc; skip next hdc, 2 dc in next sc, ch 1, 2 dc in next sc, skip next hdc, slip st in next hdc; finish off: 4 dc and one ch-1 sp.

Rows 2-4: Work same as First Fill-In Point.

MIDDLE RIPPLE
Rnd 1: With **right** side facing, join Yellow with dc in center dc of any 5-dc group on Rnd 19 of Center Ripple; 2 dc in same st, ★ ✝ dc in next 5 dc, hdc in next 2 dc, sc in next dc, skip next dc, sc in first dc on Row 4 of next Fill-In Point, hdc in next 2 dc, dc in next 5 dc, 5 dc in next dc, dc in next 5 dc, hdc in next 2 dc, sc in next dc, skip next dc on Rnd 19 of Center Ripple, sc in next dc, hdc in next 2 dc, dc in next 5 dc ✝, 5 dc in next dc; repeat from ★ 6 times **more**, then repeat from ✝ to ✝ once, 2 dc in same st as first dc; join with slip st to first dc: 336 sts.

Rnd 2: Ch 3, 2 dc in same st, dc in next 6 dc, dc decrease 4 times, dc in next 6 dc, ★ 5 dc in next dc, dc in next 6 dc, dc decrease 4 times, dc in next 6 dc; repeat from ★ around, 2 dc in same st as first dc; join with slip st to first dc.

Rnd 3: Ch 3, 2 dc in same st, dc in next 6 dc, hdc in next 2 dc, sc in next dc, skip next 2 dc, sc in next dc, hdc in next 2 dc, dc in next 6 dc, ★ 5 dc in next dc, dc in next 6 dc, hdc in next 2 dc, sc in next dc, skip next 2 dc, sc in next dc, hdc in next 2 dc, dc in next 6 dc; repeat from ★ around, 2 dc in same st as first dc; join with slip st to first dc: 368 sts.

Rnd 4: Ch 3, 2 dc in same st, dc in next 7 dc, dc decrease 4 times, dc in next 7 dc, ★ 5 dc in next dc, dc in next 7 dc, dc decrease 4 times, dc in next 7 dc; repeat from ★ around, 2 dc in same st as first dc; join with slip st to first dc.

Rnd 5: Ch 3, 2 dc in same st, dc in next 7 dc, hdc in next 2 dc, sc in next dc, skip next 2 dc, sc in next dc, hdc in next 2 dc, dc in next 7 dc, ★ 5 dc in next dc, dc in next 7 dc, hdc in next 2 dc, sc in next dc, skip next 2 dc, sc in next dc, hdc in next 2 dc, dc in next 7 dc; repeat from ★ around, 2 dc in same st as first dc; join with slip st to first dc, finish off: 400 sts.

Rnd 6: With **right** side facing, join Orange with dc in center dc of any 5-dc group; 2 dc in same st, dc in next 8 dc, dc decrease 4 times, dc in next 8 dc, ★ 5 dc in next dc, dc in next 8 dc, dc decrease 4 times, dc in next 8 dc; repeat from ★ around, 2 dc in same st as first dc; join with slip st to first dc.

Rnd 7: Ch 3, 2 dc in same st, dc in next 8 dc, hdc in next 2 dc, sc in next dc, skip next 2 dc, sc in next dc, hdc in next 2 dc, dc in next 8 dc, ★ 5 dc in next dc, dc in next 8 dc, hdc in next 2 dc, sc in next dc, skip next 2 dc, sc in next dc, hdc in next 2 dc, dc in next 8 dc; repeat from ★ around, 2 dc in same st as first dc; join with slip st to first dc: 432 sts.

Rnd 8: Ch 3, 2 dc in same st, dc in next 9 dc, dc decrease 4 times, dc in next 9 dc, ★ 5 dc in next dc, dc in next 9 dc, dc decrease 4 times, dc in next 9 dc; repeat from ★ around, 2 dc in same st as first dc; join with slip st to first dc.

Rnd 9: Ch 3, 2 dc in same st, dc in next 9 dc, hdc in next 2 dc, sc in next dc, skip next 2 dc, sc in next dc, hdc in next 2 dc, dc in next 9 dc, ★ 5 dc in next dc, dc in next 9 dc, hdc in next 2 dc, sc in next dc, skip next 2 dc, sc in next dc, hdc in next 2 dc, dc in next 9 dc; repeat from ★ around, 2 dc in same st as first dc; join with slip st to first dc: 464 sts.

Rnd 10: Ch 3, 2 dc in same st, dc in next 10 dc, dc decrease 4 times, dc in next 10 dc, ★ 5 dc in next dc, dc in next 10 dc, dc decrease 4 times, dc in next 10 dc; repeat from ★ around, 2 dc in same st as first dc; join with slip st to first dc, finish off.

Rnd 11: With **right** side facing, join Red with dc in center dc of any 5-dc group; 2 dc in same st, dc in next 10 dc, hdc in next 2 dc, sc in next dc, skip next 2 dc, sc in next dc, hdc in next 2 dc, dc in next 10 dc, ★ 5 dc in next dc, dc in next 10 dc, hdc in next 2 dc, sc in next dc, skip next 2 dc, sc in next dc, hdc in next 2 dc, dc in next 10 dc; repeat from ★ around, 2 dc in same st as first dc; join with slip st to first dc: 496 sts.

Rnd 12: Ch 3, 2 dc in same st, dc in next 11 dc, dc decrease 4 times, dc in next 11 dc, ★ 5 dc in next dc, dc in next 11 dc, dc decrease 4 times, dc in next 11 dc; repeat from ★ around, 2 dc in same st as first dc; join with slip st to first dc.

Rnd 13: Ch 3, 2 dc in same st, dc in next 11 dc, hdc in next 2 dc, sc in next dc, skip next 2 dc, sc in next dc, hdc in next 2 dc, dc in next 11 dc, ★ 5 dc in next dc, dc in next 11 dc, hdc in next 2 dc, sc in next dc, skip next 2 dc, sc in next dc, hdc in next 2 dc, dc in next 11 dc; repeat from ★ around, 2 dc in same st as first dc; join with slip st to first dc: 528 sts.

Rnd 14: Ch 3, 2 dc in same st, dc in next 12 dc, dc decrease 4 times, dc in next 12 dc, ★ 5 dc in next dc, dc in next 12 dc, dc decrease 4 times, dc in next 12 dc; repeat from ★ around, 2 dc in same st as first dc; join with slip st to first dc.

Rnd 15: Ch 3, 2 dc in same st, dc in next 12 dc, hdc in next 2 dc, sc in next dc, skip next 2 dc, sc in next dc, hdc in next 2 dc, dc in next 12 dc, ★ 5 dc in next dc, dc in next 12 dc, hdc in next 2 dc, sc in next dc, skip next 2 dc, sc in next dc, hdc in next 2 dc, dc in next 12 dc; repeat from ★ around, 2 dc in same st as first dc; join with slip st to first dc, finish off: 560 sts.

FIRST FILL-IN POINT

Row 1: With **right** side facing, skip next 14 dc from joining and join Yellow with slip st in next hdc; skip next hdc, 2 dc in next sc, ch 1, 2 dc in next sc, skip next hdc, slip st in next hdc; finish off: 4 dc and one ch-1 sp.

Row 2: With **right** side facing, join Yellow with slip st in second dc **before** joining on Row 1 (on Rnd 15 of Middle Ripple); dc in next 2 dc on Row 1, 5 dc in next ch-1 sp, dc in next 2 dc, skip next dc on Rnd 15 of Middle Ripple, slip st in next dc; finish off: 9 dc.

Continued on page 55.

Row 3: With **right** side facing, join Yellow with slip st in second dc **before** joining on Row 2; dc in next 4 dc on Row 2, 5 dc in next dc, dc in next 4 dc, skip next dc on Rnd 15 of Middle Ripple, slip st in next dc; finish off: 13 dc.

Row 4: With **right** side facing, join Yellow with slip st in second dc **before** joining on Row 3; dc in next 6 dc on Row 3, 5 dc in next dc, dc in next 6 dc, skip next dc on Rnd 15 of Middle Ripple, slip st in next dc; finish off: 17 dc.

REMAINING 15 FILL-IN POINTS

Row 1: With **right** side facing, skip next 23 dc on Rnd 15 of Middle Ripple and join Yellow with slip st in next hdc; skip next hdc, 2 dc in next sc, ch 1, 2 dc in next sc, skip next hdc, slip st in next hdc; finish off: 4 dc and one ch-1 sp.

Rows 2-4: Work same as First Fill-In Point.

OUTER RIPPLE

Rnd 1: With **right** side facing, join Yellow with dc in center dc of any 5-dc group on Rnd 15 of Middle Ripple; 2 dc in same st, ★ † dc in next 4 dc, hdc in next 2 dc, sc in next dc, skip next dc on Middle Ripple and first dc on Rnd 4 of next Fill-In Point, sc in next dc, hdc in next 2 dc, dc in next 4 dc, 5 dc in next dc, dc in next 4 dc, hdc in next 2 dc, sc in next dc, skip last dc on Fill-In Point and next dc on Rnd 15 of Middle Ripple, sc in next dc, hdc in next 2 dc, dc in next 4 dc †, 5 dc in next dc; repeat from ★ 14 times **more**, then repeat from † to † once, 2 dc in same st as first dc; join with slip st to first dc: 608 sts.

Rnds 2 and 3: Ch 3, 2 dc in same st, dc in next 5 dc, dc decrease 4 times, dc in next 5 dc, ★ 5 dc in next dc, dc in next 5 dc, dc decrease 4 times, dc in next 5 dc; repeat from ★ around, 2 dc in same st as first dc; join with slip st to first dc.

Rnd 4: Ch 3, 2 dc in same st, dc in next 5 dc, hdc in next 2 dc, sc in next dc, skip next 2 dc, sc in next dc, hdc in next 2 dc, dc in next 5 dc, ★ 5 dc in next dc, dc in next 5 dc, hdc in next 2 dc, sc in next dc, skip next 2 dc, sc in next dc, hdc in next 2 dc, dc in next 5 dc; repeat from ★ around, 2 dc in same st as first dc; join with slip st to first dc: 672 sts.

Rnd 5: Ch 3, 2 dc in same st, dc in next 6 dc, dc decrease 4 times, dc in next 6 dc, ★ 5 dc in next dc, dc in next 6 dc, dc decrease 4 times, dc in next 6 dc; repeat from ★ around, 2 dc in same st as first dc; join with slip st to first dc, finish off.

Rnd 6: With **right** side facing, join Orange with dc in center dc of any 5-dc group; 2 dc in same st, dc in next 6 dc, dc decrease 4 times, dc in next 6 dc, ★ 5 dc in next dc, dc in next 6 dc, dc decrease 4 times, dc in next 6 dc; repeat from ★ around, 2 dc in same st as first dc; join with slip st to first dc.

Rnd 7: Ch 3, 2 dc in same st, dc in next 6 dc, hdc in next 2 dc, sc in next dc, skip next 2 dc, sc in next dc, hdc in next 2 dc, dc in next 6 dc, ★ 5 dc in next dc, dc in next 6 dc, hdc in next 2 dc, sc in next dc, skip next 2 dc, sc in next dc, hdc in next 2 dc, dc in next 6 dc; repeat from ★ around, 2 dc in same st as first dc; join with slip st to first dc: 736 sts.

Rnds 8 and 9: Ch 3, 2 dc in same st, dc in next 7 dc, dc decrease 4 times, dc in next 7 dc, ★ 5 dc in next dc, dc in next 7 dc, dc decrease 4 times, dc in next 7 dc; repeat from ★ around, 2 dc in same st as first dc; join with slip st to first dc.

Rnd 10: Ch 3, 2 dc in same st, dc in next 7 dc, hdc in next 2 dc, sc in next dc, skip next 2 dc, sc in next dc, hdc in next 2 dc, dc in next 7 dc, ★ 5 dc in next dc, dc in next 7 dc, hdc in next 2 dc, sc in next dc, skip next 2 dc, sc in next dc, hdc in next 2 dc, dc in next 7 dc; repeat from ★ around, 2 dc in same st as first dc; join with slip st to first dc, finish off: 800 sts.

Rnd 11: With **right** side facing, join Red with dc in center dc of any 5-dc group; 2 dc in same st, dc in next 8 dc, dc decrease 4 times, dc in next 8 dc, ★ 5 dc in next dc, dc in next 8 dc, dc decrease 4 times, dc in next 8 dc; repeat from ★ around, 2 dc in same st as first dc; join with slip st to first dc.

Rnd 12: Ch 3, 2 dc in same st, dc in next 8 dc, dc decrease 4 times, dc in next 8 dc, ★ 5 dc in next dc, dc in next 8 dc, dc decrease 4 times, dc in next 8 dc; repeat from ★ around, 2 dc in same st as first dc; join with slip st to first dc.

Rnd 13: Ch 3, 2 dc in same st, dc in next 8 dc, hdc in next 2 dc, sc in next dc, skip next 2 dc, sc in next dc, hdc in next 2 dc, dc in next 8 dc, ★ 5 dc in next dc, dc in next 8 dc, hdc in next 2 dc, sc in next dc, skip next 2 dc, sc in next dc, hdc in next 2 dc, dc in next 8 dc; repeat from ★ around, 2 dc in same st as first dc; join with slip st to first dc: 864 sts.

Rnds 14 and 15: Ch 3, 2 dc in same st, dc in next 9 dc, dc decrease 4 times, dc in next 9 dc, ★ 5 dc in next dc, dc in next 9 dc, dc decrease 4 times, dc in next 9 dc; repeat from ★ around, 2 dc in same st as first dc; join with slip st to first dc.

Rnd 16: Ch 3, 4 dc in same st, dc in next 9 dc, hdc in next 2 dc, sc in next dc, skip next 2 dc, sc in next dc, hdc in next 2 dc, dc in next 9 dc, ★ 5 dc in next dc, dc in next 9 dc, hdc in next 2 dc, sc in next dc, skip next 2 dc, sc in next dc, hdc in next 2 dc, dc in next 9 dc; repeat from ★ around; join with slip st to first dc, finish off.

Design by Julene S. Watson.

55

Lady's Choice

Continued from page 49.

Row 11: With smaller size hook, ch 3, turn; working **around** next ch-2, dc in sp **between** next 2-dc group one row **below**, [working **around** next ch-2, (dc, ch 2, dc) in sp **between** next 2-dc group one row **below**] twice, (dc, ch 5, dc) in next ch-2 sp, [working **around** next ch-2, (dc, ch 2, dc) in sp **between** next 2-dc group one row **below**] twice, ★ working **around** next ch-2, (dc, ch 3, dc) in sp **between** next 2-dc group one row **below**, skip next 4 dc, working **around** next ch-2, (dc, ch 3, dc) in sp **between** next 2-dc group one row **below**, [working **around** next ch-2, (dc, ch 2, dc) in sp **between** next 2-dc group one row **below**] twice, (dc, ch 5, dc) in next ch-2 sp, [working **around** next ch-2, (dc, ch 2, dc) in sp **between** next 2-dc group one row **below**] twice; repeat from ★ across to last ch-2 sp, working **around** last ch-2, dc in sp **between** next 2-dc group one row **below**, skip next dc, dc in last dc changing to Red.

Row 12: Ch 3, turn; (4 dc in next ch-2 sp, ch 1) twice, 5 dc in next ch-5 sp, (ch 1, 4 dc in next ch-2 sp) twice, ★ dc in next 2 ch-3 sps, (4 dc in next ch-2 sp, ch 1) twice, 5 dc in next ch-5 sp, (ch 1, 4 dc in next ch-2 sp) twice; repeat from ★ across to last 3 dc, skip next 2 dc, dc in last dc changing to Ecru: 36 ch-1 sps.

Row 13: Ch 1, turn; working in each dc and in each ch, skip first dc, sc in next 12 sts, (sc, ch 2, sc) in next dc, sc in next 12 sts, ★ skip next 2 dc, sc in next 12 sts, (sc, ch 2, sc) in next dc, sc in next 12 sts; repeat from ★ across to last dc, leave last dc unworked: 234 sc and 9 ch-1 sps.

Row 14: Ch 3, turn; dc in next sc, ch 2, skip next 3 sc, (2 dc in next sc, ch 2, skip next 3 sc) twice, (2 dc, ch 2) twice in next ch-2 sp, ★ skip next 3 sc, 2 dc in next sc, (ch 2, skip next 3 sc, 2 dc in next sc) twice, skip next 2 sc, (2 dc in next sc, ch 2, skip next 3 sc) 3 times, (2 dc, ch 2) twice in next ch-1 sp; repeat from ★ across to last 13 sc, (skip next 3 sc, 2 dc in next sc, ch 2) twice, skip next 3 sc, dc in last 2 sc: 63 ch-2 sps.

Row 15: Ch 3, turn; working **around** next ch-2, dc in center sc of next skipped 3 sc one row **below**, ch 2, (working **around** next ch-2, 2 dc in center sc of 3 skipped sc one row **below**, ch 2) twice, (2 dc, ch 2) twice in next ch-2 sp, working **around** next ch-2, 2 dc in center sc of 3 skipped sc one row **below**, ★ (ch 2, working **around** next ch-2, 2 dc in center sc of 3 skipped sc one row **below**) twice, skip next 4 dc, (working **around** next ch-2, 2 dc in center sc of 3 skipped sc one row **below**, ch 2) 3 times, (2 dc, ch 2) twice in next ch-2 sp, working **around** next ch-2, 2 dc in center sc of 3 skipped sc one row **below**; repeat from ★ across to last 2 ch-2 sps, (ch 2, working **around** next ch-2, dc in center sc of next skipped 3 sc one row **below**) twice, skip next dc, dc in last dc changing to Lt Green.

Rows 16-29: With larger size hook, repeat Row 3, 14 times; at end of last row, change to Ecru.

Rows 30-88: Repeat Rows 8-29 twice, then repeat Rows 8-22 once **more**; at end of Row 88, do **not** change colors and do **not** finish off.

EDGING

With Lt Green and using smaller size hook, ch 1, turn; 2 sc in first dc, working **around** next ch-2, dc in sp **between** 2-dc group one row **below**, sc in next 2 dc, (working **around** next ch-2, 2 dc in sp **between** 2-dc group one row **below**, sc in next 2 dc) twice, (2 sc, ch 2, 2 sc) in next ch-2 sp, ★ (sc in next 2 dc, working **around** next ch-2, 2 dc in sp **between** 2-dc group one row **below**) 3 times, skip next 4 dc, (working **around** next ch-2, 2 dc in sp **between** 2-dc group one row **below**, sc in next 2 dc) 3 times, (2 sc, ch 2, 2 sc) in next ch-2 sp; repeat from ★ across to last 3 ch-2 sps, sc in next 2 dc, (working **around** next ch-2, 2 dc in sp **between** 2-dc group one row **below**, sc in next 2 dc) twice, working **around** next ch-2, dc in sp **between** 2-dc group one row **below**, sc in next dc, 2 sc in last dc; sc evenly across end of rows; working in free loops *(Fig. 3b, page 3)* and in sps of beginning ch, 2 sc in ch at base of first dc, sc in next ch, (sc in next sp and in next ch) 5 times, skip next 3 chs, sc in next ch, (sc in next sp and in next ch) 5 times, † (2 sc, ch 2, 2 sc) in next sp, sc in next ch, (sc in next sp and in next ch) 5 times, skip next 3 chs, sc in next ch, (sc in next sp and in next ch) 5 times †; repeat from † to † across to marked ch, 2 sc in marked ch; sc evenly across end of rows; join with slip st to first sc, finish off.

Design by Kathleen Stuart.

56

Candy Stripe

Finished Size: 35" x 41¹/₂" (89 cm x 105.5 cm)

MATERIALS
Worsted Weight Yarn:
- White - 7 ounces, 395 yards
  (200 grams, 361 meters)
- Pink - 3¹/₂ ounces, 200 yards
  (100 grams, 183 meters)
- Blue - 3 ounces, 170 yards
  (90 grams, 155.5 meters)
- Yellow - 3 ounces, 170 yards
  (90 grams, 155.5 meters)
- Green - 3 ounces, 170 yards
  (90 grams, 155.5 meters)

Crochet hook, size H (5 mm) **or** size needed
for gauge

GAUGE: In pattern, one point to point repeat
(26 dc and 3 ch-2 sps) = 7¹/₄" (18.5 cm);
8 rows = 5" (12.75 cm)
14 dc and 8 rows = 4" (10 cm)

Gauge Swatch: 4" (10 cm) square
With Pink, ch 16.
Row 1: Dc in fourth ch from hook **(3 skipped
chs count as first dc)** and in each ch across:
14 dc.
Rows 2-8: Ch 3 **(counts as first dc)**, turn; dc in
next dc and in each dc across.
Finish off.

AFGHAN BODY
With Pink, ch 117.

Row 1 (Right side)**:** Working in back ridges of
beginning ch **(Fig. 1, page 3)**, dc in fourth ch from
hook **(3 skipped chs count as first dc)** and in
next 7 chs, (2 dc, ch 2, 2 dc) in next ch, dc in next
9 chs, ★ skip next 2 chs, (dc, ch 2, 2 dc, ch 2, dc)
in next ch, skip next 2 chs, dc in next 9 chs, (2 dc,
ch 2, 2 dc) in next ch, dc in next 9 chs; repeat from
★ across; finish off: 126 dc and 13 ch-2 sps.

Note: Loop a short piece of yarn around any stitch
to mark Row 1 as **right** side.

Row 2: With **wrong** side facing, join White with dc
in first dc **(see Joining With Dc, page 3)**; ch 1,
skip next 2 dc, (dc in next dc, ch 1, skip next dc) 4
times, (2 dc, ch 2, 2 dc) in next ch-2 sp, ★ (ch 1,
skip next dc, dc in next dc) 5 times, ch 2, sc in next
ch-2 sp, ch 3, sc in next ch-2 sp, ch 2, skip next
2 dc, (dc in next dc, ch 1, skip next dc) 5 times,
(2 dc, ch 2, 2 dc) in next ch-2 sp; repeat from ★
3 times **more**, ch 1, (skip next dc, dc in next dc,
ch 1) 4 times, skip next 2 dc, dc in last dc; finish off:
78 sts and 67 sps.

Row 3: With **right** side facing, join Blue with dc in
first dc; skip next ch, dc in next dc, [dc in top
2 loops of next ch **(Fig. 13)**, dc in next dc] 3 times,
★ † skip next ch, dc in next dc, (2 dc, ch 2, 2 dc) in
next ch-2 sp, skip next dc, dc in next dc, skip next
ch †, (dc in next dc and in top 2 loops of next ch) 4
times, skip next ch-2 sp, (dc, ch 2, 2 dc, ch 2, dc) in
next ch-3 sp, skip next ch-2 sp and next dc, (dc in
top 2 loops of next ch and in next dc) 4 times;
repeat from ★ 3 times **more**, then repeat from
† to † once, dc in next dc, (dc in top 2 loops of next
ch and in next dc) 3 times, skip next ch, dc in last
dc; finish off: 126 dc and 13 ch-2 sps.

Fig. 13

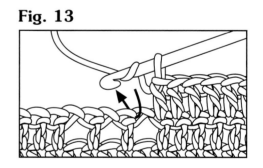

Row 4: With **wrong** side facing, join White with dc
in first dc; ch 1, skip next 2 dc, (dc in next dc, ch 1,
skip next dc) 4 times, (2 dc, ch 2, 2 dc) in next
ch-2 sp, ★ (ch 1, skip next dc, dc in next dc) 5
times, ch 2, sc in next ch-2 sp, ch 3, sc in next
ch-2 sp, ch 2, skip next 2 dc, (dc in next dc, ch 1,
skip next dc) 5 times, (2 dc, ch 2, 2 dc) in next
ch-2 sp; repeat from ★ 3 times **more**, ch 1, (skip
next dc, dc in next dc, ch 1) 4 times, skip next 2 dc,
dc in last dc; finish off: 78 sts and 67 sps.

Continued on page 67.

Rippling Ribbons

Finished Size: 47" x 58" (119.5 cm x 147.5 cm)

MATERIALS
Worsted Weight Yarn:
Blue - 19^1/$_2$ ounces, 1,135 yards
(550 grams, 1,038 meters)
Dk Blue - 17^1/$_2$ ounces, 1,020 yards
(500 grams, 932.5 meters)
Cream - 12 ounces, 700 yards
(340 grams, 640 meters)
Crochet hook, size J (6 mm) **or** size needed
for gauge

GAUGE: In pattern, one point to point
repeat (13 sts) = 3^5/$_8$" (9.25 cm);
8 rows = 4^1/$_2$" (11.5 cm)

Gauge Swatch: 7^1/$_4$"w x 4^1/$_2$"h
(18.5 cm x 11.5 cm)
With Blue, ch 25.
Work same as Afghan Body for 8 rows.

Each row is worked across length of Afghan Body.
When joining yarn and finishing off, leave a 9"
(23 cm) length to be worked into fringe.

STITCH GUIDE

PUFF ST
★ YO, insert hook in hdc indicated, YO and pull
up a loop even with loop on hook; repeat from
★ 2 times **more**, YO and draw through all
7 loops on hook.

AFGHAN BODY
With Blue, ch 207, place marker in second ch from
hook to mark st placement.

Row 1: Hdc in third ch from hook **(2 skipped
chs counts as first hdc)** and in next 3 chs, 3 hdc
in next ch, hdc in next 5 chs, ★ skip next 2 chs, hdc
in next 5 chs, 3 hdc in next ch, hdc in next 5 chs;
repeat from ★ across: 208 hdc.

Row 2 (Right side)**:** Turn; skip first hdc, slip st in
next hdc, ch 3 **(counts as first hdc plus ch 1,
now and throughout)**, skip next hdc, work Puff St
in next hdc, ch 1, skip next hdc, (work Puff St in
next hdc, ch 1) 3 times, skip next hdc, work Puff St
in next hdc, ch 1, ★ skip next hdc, work Puff St in
next hdc, skip next 2 hdc, work Puff St in next hdc,
ch 1, skip next hdc, work Puff St in next hdc, ch 1,
skip next hdc, (work Puff St in next hdc, ch 1) 3
times, skip next hdc, work Puff St in next hdc, ch 1;
repeat from ★ across to last 3 hdc, skip next hdc,
hdc in next hdc, leave last hdc unworked:
110 Puff Sts and 96 ch-1 sps.

Note: Loop a short piece of yarn around any stitch
to mark Row 1 as **right** side.

Row 3: Turn; slip st in first ch-1 sp, ch 2 **(counts
as first hdc, now and throughout)**, (hdc in next
Puff St and in next ch-1 sp) twice, 3 hdc in next
Puff St, hdc in next ch-1 sp, (hdc in next Puff St and
in next ch-1 sp) twice, ★ skip next 2 Puff Sts, hdc in
next ch-1 sp, (hdc in next Puff St and in next
ch-1 sp) twice, 3 hdc in next Puff St, hdc in next
ch-1 sp, (hdc in next Puff St and in next ch-1 sp)
twice; repeat from ★ across to last hdc, leave last
hdc unworked; finish off: 208 hdc.

Row 4: With **right** side facing and working in Back
Loops Only **(Fig. 2, page 3)**, skip first hdc and join
Cream with hdc in next hdc **(see Joining With
Hdc, page 3)**; hdc in next 4 hdc, 3 hdc in next
hdc, hdc in next 5 hdc, ★ skip next 2 hdc, hdc in
next 5 hdc, 3 hdc in next hdc, hdc in next 5 hdc;
repeat from ★ across to last hdc, leave last hdc
unworked; finish off.

Row 5: With **wrong** side facing and working in
both loops, skip first hdc and join Dk Blue with hdc
in next hdc; hdc in next 4 hdc, 3 hdc in next hdc,
hdc in next 5 hdc, ★ skip next 2 hdc, hdc in next
5 hdc, 3 hdc in next hdc, hdc in next 5 hdc; repeat
from ★ across to last hdc, leave last hdc unworked.

Row 6: Turn; skip first hdc, slip st in next hdc,
ch 3, skip next hdc, work Puff St in next hdc, ch 1,
skip next hdc, (work Puff St in next hdc, ch 1) 3
times, skip next hdc, work Puff St in next hdc, ch 1,
★ skip next hdc, work Puff St in next hdc, skip next
2 hdc, (work Puff St in next hdc, ch 1, skip next
hdc) twice, (work Puff St in next hdc, ch 1) 3 times,
skip next hdc, work Puff St in next hdc, ch 1; repeat
from ★ across to last 3 hdc, skip next hdc, hdc in
next hdc, leave last hdc unworked: 110 Puff Sts and
96 ch-1 sps.

Continued on page 68.

Rosebud

Finished Size: 38$\frac{1}{2}$" x 58" (98 cm x 147.5 cm)

MATERIALS
Worsted Weight Yarn:
Green - 21$\frac{1}{2}$ ounces, 1,410 yards
(610 grams, 1,289.5 meters)
Pink - 7$\frac{1}{2}$ ounces, 490 yards
(210 grams, 448 meters)
Lt Green - 4 ounces, 260 yards
(110 grams, 237.5 meters)
Crochet hook, size K (10.5 mm) **or** size needed for gauge

GAUGE: In pattern, one point to point
repeat (24 sts) = 6$\frac{1}{4}$" (16 cm);
8 pattern rows = 6$\frac{1}{4}$" (16 cm);
Rows 1-5 = 3$\frac{1}{2}$" (9 cm)

Gauge Swatch: 12$\frac{1}{2}$"w x 3$\frac{1}{2}$"h
(31.75 cm x 9 cm)
With Green, ch 52.
Work same as Afghan Body for 5 rows.
Finish off.

STITCH GUIDE

TREBLE CROCHET (abbreviated tr)
YO twice, insert hook in slip st indicated, YO and pull up a loop (4 loops on hook), (YO and draw through 2 loops on hook) 3 times.

DECREASE (uses next 5 sts)
★ YO, insert hook in **next** st, YO and pull up a loop, YO and draw through 2 loops on hook; repeat from ★ 4 times **more**, YO and draw through all 6 loops on hook.

CLUSTER (uses one st)
★ YO twice, insert hook in st indicated, YO and pull up a loop, (YO and draw through 2 loops on hook) twice; repeat from ★ once **more**, YO and draw through all 3 loops on hook.

BEGINNING POPCORN
Ch 4 **(counts as first tr)**, 3 tr in slip st indicated, drop loop from hook, insert hook from **back** to **front** in first tr, hook dropped loop and draw through.

POPCORN
4 Tr in slip st indicated, drop loop from hook, insert hook from **back** to **front** in first tr, hook dropped loop and draw through.

AFGHAN BODY
With Green, ch 148, place marker in fourth ch from hook for st placement.

Row 1 (Right side)**:** 2 Dc in fourth ch from hook **(3 skipped chs count as first dc)**, dc in next 9 chs, decrease, dc in next 9 chs, ★ 5 dc in next ch, dc in next 9 chs, decrease, dc in next 9 chs; repeat from ★ across to last ch, 3 dc in last ch: 145 sts.

Note: Loop a short piece of yarn around any stitch to mark Row 1 as **right** side.

Row 2: Ch 3 **(counts as first dc, now and throughout)**, turn; working in back ridges of each st **(Fig. 14)**, 2 dc in same st, dc in next 9 dc, decrease, dc in next 9 dc, ★ 5 dc in next dc, dc in next 9 dc, decrease, dc in next 9 dc; repeat from ★ across to last dc, 3 dc in last dc; finish off.

Fig. 14

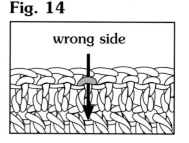

Row 3: With **right** side facing and working in **both** loops, join Lt Green with slip st in first dc; ch 3, work Cluster in same st as joining, ★ skip next 2 dc, (slip st, ch 3, work Cluster) in next st; repeat from ★ across to last 3 dc, skip next 2 dc, slip st in last dc; finish off: 49 slip sts and 48 Clusters.

Row 4: With **wrong** side facing, join Pink with slip st in first slip st; work Beginning Popcorn in same st, ★ ch 3, skip next Cluster, work Popcorn in next slip st; repeat from ★ across, ch 1; finish off.

Continued on page 68.

Granny's Ripple

Finished Size: 46" x 62" (117 cm x 157.5 cm)

MATERIALS
Worsted Weight Yarn:
  Dk Purple - 12$^1/_2$ ounces, 705 yards
    (360 grams, 644.5 meters)
  Lt Purple - 12$^1/_2$ ounces, 705 yards
    (360 grams, 644.5 meters)
  Purple - 8 ounces, 450 yards
    (230 grams, 411.5 meters)
  Yellow - 2$^1/_2$ ounces, 140 yards
    (70 grams, 128 meters)
Crochet hook, size J (6 mm) **or** size needed
  for gauge
Yarn needle

GAUGE: Each Square = 4$^3/_4$" (12 cm);
    from point to opposite
    point = 6$^1/_2$" (16.5 cm)

Gauge Swatch: 2$^3/_4$" (7 cm) square
Work same as Bottom Panel Square through Rnd 2.

STITCH GUIDE

SQUARE JOINING (uses 2 ch-2 sps)
Pull up a loop in next ch-2 sp on same Square,
with **right** side of next Square facing, pull up a
loop in corner ch-2 sp, YO and draw through all
3 loops on hook **(counts as one sc)**.

BEGINNING DECREASE
Pull up a loop in first or same st **and** in next sc,
YO and draw through all 3 loops on hook
(counts as one sc).

DECREASE
Pull up a loop in next 2 sc, YO and draw
through all 3 loops on hook **(counts as
one sc)**.

BOTTOM PANEL
SQUARE (Make 7)
Rnd 1 (Right side)**:** With Dk Purple, ch 4, 2 dc in
fourth ch from hook **(3 skipped chs count as
first dc, now and throughout)**, ch 1, (3 dc in
same ch, ch 1) 3 times; join with slip st to first dc:
12 dc and 4 ch-1 sps.

Note: Loop a short piece of yarn around any stitch
to mark Rnd 1 as **right** side.

Rnd 2: Ch 3 **(counts as first dc, now and
throughout)**, turn; (2 dc, ch 1, 3 dc) in first
ch-1 sp, (3 dc, ch 1, 3 dc) in next 3 ch-1 sps; join
with slip st to first dc, finish off: 24 dc and
4 ch-1 sps.

Rnd 3: With **right** side facing, join Purple with dc
in any corner ch-1 sp *(see Joining With Dc,
page 3)*; 2 dc in same sp, skip next 3 dc, 3 dc in sp
before next dc, ★ (3 dc, ch 1, 3 dc) in next corner
ch-1 sp, skip next 3 dc, 3 dc in sp **before** next dc;
repeat from ★ 2 times **more**, 3 dc in same sp as
first dc, ch 1; join with slip st to first dc: 36 dc and
4 ch-1 sps.

Rnd 4: Ch 3, turn; (2 dc, ch 2, 3 dc) in first corner
ch-1 sp, (skip next 3 dc, 3 dc in sp **before** next dc)
twice, ★ (3 dc, ch 2, 3 dc) in next corner ch-1 sp,
(skip next 3 dc, 3 dc in sp **before** next dc) twice;
repeat from ★ 2 times **more**; join with slip st to first
dc, finish off: 48 dc and 4 ch-2 sps.

BORDER
FIRST SIDE
Row 1 (Joining row)**:** With **right** side facing and
working in Back Loops Only *(Fig. 2, page 3)*, join
Lt Purple with sc in first dc **after** any corner ch-2 sp
on first Square *(see Joining With Sc, page 1)*; sc
in next 11 dc, (sc, ch 2, sc) in next corner ch-2 sp,
sc in next 12 dc, ★ work Square Joining, sc in next
12 dc, (sc, ch 2, sc) in next corner ch-2 sp, sc in
next 12 dc; repeat from ★ 5 times **more**; finish off:
188 sc and 14 chs.

Continued on page 65.

Row 2: With **right** side facing and working in Back Loops Only, join Lt Purple with slip st in first sc; ch 1, work beginning decrease, sc in next 11 sc and in next ch, ch 2, sc in next ch and in next 11 sc, decrease, ★ skip next sc, decrease, sc in next 11 sc and in next ch, ch 2, sc in next ch and in next 11 sc, decrease; repeat from ★ across; finish off: 182 sc and 14 chs.

Row 3: With **wrong** side facing and working in Front Loops Only *(Fig. 2, page 3)*, join Yellow with slip st in first sc; ch 1, work beginning decrease, sc in next 11 sc and in next ch, ch 2, sc in next ch, ★ sc in next 12 sc, skip next 2 sc, sc in next 12 sc and in next ch, ch 2, sc in next ch; repeat from ★ across to last 13 sc, sc in next 11 sc, decrease; finish off.

Row 4: With **right** side facing and working in Back Loops Only, join Dk Purple with slip st in first sc; ch 1, work beginning decrease, sc in next 11 sc, (sc, ch 2, sc) in next ch-2 sp, ★ sc in next 12 sc, skip next 2 sc, sc in next 12 sc, (sc, ch 2, sc) in next ch-2 sp; repeat from ★ across to last 13 sc, sc in next 11 sc, decrease; finish off.

Row 5: With **right** side facing and working through Back Loop **and** back ridge of each sc *(Fig. 15)*, join Lt Purple with slip st in first sc; ch 1, work beginning decrease, sc in next 11 sc and in next ch, ch 2, sc in next ch, ★ sc in next 12 sc, skip next 2 sc, sc in next 12 sc and in next ch, ch 2, sc in next ch; repeat from ★ across to last 13 sc, sc in next 11 sc, decrease; do **not** finish off.

Fig. 15

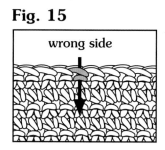

Row 6: Ch 1, turn; working in Front Loops Only, work beginning decrease, sc in next 11 sc and in next ch, ch 2, sc in next ch, ★ sc in next 12 sc, skip next 2 sc, sc in next 12 sc and in next ch, ch 2, sc in next ch; repeat from ★ across to last 13 sc, sc in next 11 sc, decrease.

Row 7: Ch 1, turn; working in **both** loops, work beginning decrease, sc in next 11 sc, (sc, ch 2, sc) in next ch-2 sp, ★ sc in next 12 sc, skip next 2 sc, sc in next 12 sc, (sc, ch 2, sc) in next ch-2 sp; repeat from ★ across to last 13 sc, sc in next 11 sc, decrease; finish off.

Row 8: With **right** side facing and working through Back Loop **and** back ridge of each sc, join Purple with slip st in first sc; ch 1, work beginning decrease, sc in next 11 sc and in next ch, ch 2, sc in next ch, ★ sc in next 12 sc, skip next 2 sc, sc in next 12 sc and in next ch, ch 2, sc in next ch; repeat from ★ across to last 13 sc, sc in next 11 sc, decrease; do **not** finish off.

Row 9: Ch 1, turn; working in Front Loops Only, work beginning decrease, sc in next 11 sc and in next ch, ch 2, sc in next ch, ★ sc in next 12 sc, skip next 2 sc, sc in next 12 sc and in next ch, ch 2, sc in next ch; repeat from ★ across to last 13 sc, sc in next 11 sc, decrease.

Rows 10-12: Ch 1, turn; working in **both** loops, work beginning decrease, sc in next 11 sc, (sc, ch 2, sc) in next ch-2 sp, ★ sc in next 12 sc, skip next 2 sc, sc in next 12 sc, (sc, ch 2, sc) in next ch-2 sp; repeat from ★ across to last 13 sc, sc in next 11 sc, decrease.

Finish off.

Row 13: With **right** side facing and working through Back Loop **and** back ridge of each sc, join Dk Purple with slip st in first sc; ch 1, work beginning decrease, sc in next 11 sc and in next ch, ch 2, sc in next ch, ★ sc in next 12 sc, skip next 2 sc, sc in next 12 sc and in next ch, ch 2, sc in next ch; repeat from ★ across to last 13 sc, sc in next 11 sc, decrease; do **not** finish off.

Row 14: Ch 1, turn; working in Front Loops Only, work beginning decrease, sc in next 11 sc and in next ch, ch 2, sc in next ch, ★ sc in next 12 sc, skip next 2 sc, sc in next 12 sc and in next ch, ch 2, sc in next ch; repeat from ★ across to last 13 sc, sc in next 11 sc, decrease.

Rows 15 and 16: Ch 1, turn; working in **both** loops, work beginning decrease, sc in next 11 sc, (sc, ch 2, sc) in next ch-2 sp, ★ sc in next 12 sc, skip next 2 sc, sc in next 12 sc, (sc, ch 2, sc) in next ch-2 sp; repeat from ★ across to last 13 sc, sc in next 11 sc, decrease.

Finish off.

SECOND SIDE

Row 1 (Joining row)**:** With **right** side facing and working in Back Loops Only across opposite side of Squares, skip next corner ch-2 sp from First Side and join Lt Purple with sc in first dc; sc in next 11 dc, (sc, ch 2, sc) in next corner ch-2 sp, sc in next 12 dc, ★ work Square Joining, sc in next 12 dc, (sc, ch 2, sc) in next corner ch-2 sp, sc in next 12 dc; repeat from ★ 5 times **more**; finish off: 188 sc and 14 chs.

Complete same as First Side.

TOP PANEL
Work same as Bottom Panel.

CENTER PANEL
SQUARE (Make 6)
Rnd 1 (Right side): With Yellow, ch 4, 2 dc in fourth ch from hook, ch 1, (3 dc in same ch, ch 1) 3 times; join with slip st to first dc, finish off: 12 dc and 4 ch-1 sps.

Note: Mark Rnd 1 as **right** side.

Rnd 2: With **wrong** side facing, join Purple with dc in any ch-1 sp; 2 dc in same sp, (3 dc, ch 1, 3 dc) in next 3 ch-1 sps, 3 dc in same sp as first dc, ch 1; join with slip st to first dc: 24 dc and 4 ch-1 sps.

Rnd 3: Ch 3, turn; (2 dc, ch 1, 3 dc) in first corner ch-1 sp, skip next 3 dc, 3 dc in sp **before** next dc, ★ (3 dc, ch 1, 3 dc) in next corner ch-1 sp, skip next 3 dc, 3 dc in sp **before** next dc; repeat from ★ 2 times **more**; join with slip st to first dc, finish off: 36 dc and 4 ch-1 sps.

Rnd 4: With **wrong** side facing, join Dk Purple with dc in any corner ch-1 sp; (2 dc, ch 2, 3 dc) in same sp, (skip next 3 dc, 3 dc in sp **before** next dc) twice, ★ (3 dc, ch 2, 3 dc) in next corner ch-1 sp, (skip next 3 dc, 3 dc in sp **before** next dc) twice; repeat from ★ 2 times **more**; join with slip st to first dc, finish off: 48 dc and 4 ch-2 sps.

HALF SQUARE (Make 2)
Row 1 (Right side): With Yellow, ch 4, (3 dc, ch 1, 4 dc) in fourth ch from hook; finish off: 8 dc and one ch-1 sp.

Note: Mark Row 1 as **right** side.

Row 2: With **wrong** side facing, join Purple with dc in first dc; 3 dc in sp **before** next dc, (3 dc, ch 1, 3 dc) in next ch-1 sp, skip next 3 dc, 3 dc in sp **before** last dc, dc in last dc: 14 dc and one ch-1 sp.

Row 3: Ch 3, turn; 3 dc in sp **before** next dc, skip next 3 dc, 3 dc in sp **before** next dc, (3 dc, ch 1, 3 dc) in next corner ch-1 sp, (skip next 3 dc, 3 dc in sp **before** next dc) twice, dc in last dc; finish off: 20 dc and one ch-1 sp.

Row 4: With **wrong** side facing, join Dk Purple with dc in first dc; 3 dc in sp **before** next dc, (skip next 3 dc, 3 dc in sp **before** next dc) twice, (3 dc, ch 2, 3 dc) in next corner ch-1 sp, (skip next 3 dc, 3 dc in sp **before** next dc) 3 times, dc in last dc; finish off: 26 dc and one ch-2 sp.

BORDER
FIRST SIDE
Join Squares together in the following order: One Half Square, 6 Squares, one Half Square.

Row 1 (Joining row): With **right** side facing and working in Back Loops Only, join Lt Purple with sc in first dc on first Half Square; sc in same st and in next 12 dc, work Square Joining, sc in next 12 dc, ★ (sc, ch 2, sc) in next ch-2 sp, sc in next 12 dc, work Square Joining, sc in next 12 dc; repeat from ★ 5 times **more**, 2 sc in last dc; finish off: 191 sc and 12 chs.

Row 2: With **right** side facing and working in Back Loops Only, join Lt Purple with sc in first sc; sc in same st and in next 11 sc, decrease, skip next sc, decrease, sc in next 11 sc, ★ sc in next ch, ch 2, sc in next ch and in next 11 sc, decrease, skip next sc, decrease, sc in next 11 sc; repeat from ★ across to last sc, 2 sc in last sc; finish off: 184 sc and 12 chs.

Row 3: With **wrong** side facing and working in Front Loops Only, join Yellow with sc in first sc; sc in same st and in next 12 sc, skip next 2 sc, sc in next 12 sc, ★ sc in next ch, ch 2, sc in next ch and in next 12 sc, skip next 2 sc, sc in next 12 sc; repeat from ★ across to last sc, 2 sc in last sc; finish off.

Row 4: With **right** side facing and working in Back Loops Only, join Dk Purple with sc in first sc; sc in same st and in next 12 sc, skip next 2 sc, sc in next 12 sc, ★ (sc, ch 2, sc) in next ch-2 sp, sc in next 12 sc, skip next 2 sc, sc in next 12 sc; repeat from ★ across to last sc, 2 sc in last sc; finish off.

Row 5: With **right** side facing and working through Back Loop **and** back ridge of each sc, join Lt Purple with sc in first sc; sc in same st and in next 12 sc, skip next 2 sc, sc in next 12 sc, ★ sc in next ch, ch 2, sc in next ch and in next 12 sc, skip next 2 sc, sc in next 12 sc; repeat from ★ across to last sc, 2 sc in last sc; do **not** finish off.

Row 6: Ch 1, turn; working in Front Loops Only, 2 sc in first sc, sc in next 12 sc, skip next 2 sc, sc in next 12 sc, ★ sc in next ch, ch 2, sc in next ch and in next 12 sc, skip next 2 sc, sc in next 12 sc; repeat from ★ across to last sc, 2 sc in last sc.

Row 7: Ch 1, turn; working in **both** loops, 2 sc in first sc, sc in next 12 sc, skip next 2 sc, sc in next 12 sc, ★ (sc, ch 2, sc) in next ch-2 sp, sc in next 12 sc, skip next 2 sc, sc in next 12 sc; repeat from ★ across to last sc, 2 sc in last sc; finish off.

Continued on page 67.

Row 8: With **right** side facing and working through Back Loop **and** back ridge of each sc, join Purple with sc in first sc; sc in same st and in next 12 sc, skip next 2 sc, sc in next 12 sc, ★ sc in next ch, ch 2, sc in next ch and in next 12 sc, skip next 2 sc, sc in next 12 sc; repeat from ★ across to last sc, 2 sc in last sc; do **not** finish off.

Row 9: Ch 1, turn; working in Front Loops Only, 2 sc in first sc, sc in next 12 sc, skip next 2 sc, sc in next 12 sc, ★ sc in next ch, ch 2, sc in next ch and in next 12 sc, skip next 2 sc, sc in next 12 sc; repeat from ★ across to last sc, 2 sc in last sc.

Rows 10-12: Ch 1, turn; working in **both** loops, 2 sc in first sc, sc in next 12 sc, skip next 2 sc, sc in next 12 sc, ★ (sc, ch 2, sc) in next ch-2 sp, sc in next 12 sc, skip next 2 sc, sc in next 12 sc; repeat from ★ across to last sc, 2 sc in last sc.

Finish off.

Row 13: With **right** side facing and working through Back Loop **and** back ridge of each sc, join Dk Purple with sc in first sc; sc in same st and in next 12 sc, skip next 2 sc, sc in next 12 sc, ★ sc in next ch, ch 2, sc in next ch and in next 12 sc, skip next 2 sc, sc in next 12 sc; repeat from ★ across to last sc, 2 sc in last sc; do **not** finish off.

Row 14: Ch 1, turn; working in Front Loops Only, 2 sc in first sc, sc in next 12 sc, skip next 2 sc, sc in next 12 sc, ★ sc in next ch, ch 2, sc in next ch and in next 12 sc, skip next 2 sc, sc in next 12 sc; repeat from ★ across to last sc, 2 sc in last sc.

Rows 15-17: Ch 1, turn; working in **both** loops, 2 sc in first sc, sc in next 12 sc, skip next 2 sc, sc in next 12 sc, ★ (sc, ch 2, sc) in next ch-2 sp, sc in next 12 sc, skip next 2 sc, sc in next 12 sc; repeat from ★ across to last sc, 2 sc in last sc.

Finish off.

SECOND SIDE
Row 1 (Joining row)**:** With **right** side facing and working in Back Loops Only across opposite side of Squares, join Lt Purple with sc in first dc on first Half Square; sc in same st and in next 12 dc, work Square Joining, sc in next 12 dc, ★ (sc, ch 2, sc) in next ch-2 sp, sc in next 12 dc, work Square Joining, sc in next 12 dc; repeat from ★ 5 times **more**, 2 sc in last dc; finish off: 191 sc and 12 chs.

Complete same as First Side.

ASSEMBLY
Working through **both** loops, whipstitch Center Panel between Top and Bottom Panels *(Fig. 7a, page 4)*.

EDGING
Rnd 1: With **right** side facing, join Dk Purple with sc in first sc on Top Panel; sc evenly around entire Afghan increasing and decreasing as necessary to keep piece laying flat; join with slip st to first sc.

Rnd 2: Slip st **loosely** in Back Loop Only of each st around; join with slip st to **both** loops of joining slip st, finish off.

Design by Diana May.

Candy Stripes
Continued from page 57.

Row 5: With **right** side facing, join Yellow with dc in first dc; skip next ch, dc in next dc, (dc in top 2 loops of next ch, dc in next dc) 3 times, ★ † skip next ch, dc in next dc, (2 dc, ch 2, 2 dc) in next ch-2 sp, skip next dc, dc in next dc, skip next ch †, (dc in next dc and in top 2 loops of next ch) 4 times, skip next ch-2 sp, (dc, ch 2, 2 dc, ch 2, dc) in next ch-3 sp, skip next ch-2 sp and next dc, (dc in top 2 loops of next ch and in next dc) 4 times; repeat from ★ 3 times **more**, then repeat from † to † once, dc in next dc, (dc in top 2 loops of next ch and in next dc) 3 times, skip next ch, dc in last dc; finish off: 126 dc and 13 ch-2 sps.

Row 6: Repeat Row 4.

Row 7: With Green, repeat Row 5.

Row 8: Repeat Row 4.

Row 9: With Pink, repeat Row 5.

Rows 10-65: Repeat Rows 2-9, 7 times.

TRIM
FIRST SIDE
With **right** side facing and working in end of rows, join White with sc in first row *(see Joining With Sc, page 1)*; ch 2, dc in same row, (sc, ch 2, dc) in next row and in each row across to last row, slip st in last row; finish off.

SECOND SIDE
Work same as First Side.

Design by Roseanna E. Beck.

Rippling Ribbons
Continued from page 59.

Row 7: Turn; slip st in first ch-1 sp, ch 2, (hdc in next Puff St and in next ch-1 sp) twice, 3 hdc in next Puff St, hdc in next ch-1 sp, (hdc in next Puff St and in next ch-1 sp) twice, ★ skip next 2 Puff Sts, hdc in next ch-1 sp, (hdc in next Puff St and in next ch-1 sp) twice, 3 hdc in next Puff St, hdc in next ch-1 sp, (hdc in next Puff St and in next ch-1 sp) twice; repeat from ★ across to last hdc, leave last hdc unworked; finish off: 208 hdc.

Row 8: With **right** side facing and working in Back Loops Only, skip first hdc and join Cream with hdc in next hdc; hdc in next 4 hdc, 3 hdc in next hdc, hdc in next 5 hdc, ★ skip next 2 hdc, hdc in next 5 hdc, 3 hdc in next hdc, hdc in next 5 hdc; repeat from ★ across to last hdc, leave last hdc unworked; finish off.

Row 9: With **wrong** side facing and working in **both** loops, skip first hdc and join Blue with hdc in next hdc; hdc in next 4 hdc, 3 hdc in next hdc, hdc in next 5 hdc, ★ skip next 2 hdc, hdc in next 5 hdc, 3 hdc in next hdc, hdc in next 5 hdc; repeat from ★ across to last hdc, leave last hdc unworked.

Rows 10-83: Repeat Rows 2-9, 9 times; then repeat Rows 2 and 3 once **more**.

TRIM
FIRST SIDE
With **right** side facing and working across Row 83, skip first hdc and join Cream with sc in next hdc *(see Joining With Sc, page 1)*; sc in next 4 hdc, 3 sc in next hdc, sc in next 5 hdc, ★ skip next 2 hdc, sc in next 5 hdc, 3 sc in next hdc, sc in next 5 hdc; repeat from ★ across to last hdc, leave last hdc unworked; finish off.

SECOND SIDE
With **right** side facing and working in sps and in free loops of beginning ch *(Fig. 3b, page 3)*, join Cream with sc in marked ch; sc in next 4 chs, ★ skip next ch, sc in next 5 chs, 3 sc in next sp, sc in next 5 chs; repeat from ★ across to last 6 chs, skip next ch, sc in next 5 chs; finish off.

Holding 4 strands of corresponding color together, each 18" (45.5 cm) long, add additional fringe across short edges of Afghan *(Figs. 8c & d, page 4)*.

Design by Kathryn A. Clark.

Rosebud
Continued from page 61.

Row 5: With **right** side facing, join Green with dc in first Popcorn *(see Joining With Dc, page 3)*; 2 dc in same st, ★ ♥ 3 dc in each of next 3 ch-3 sps, [† YO, insert hook in **next** ch-3 sp, YO and pull up a loop, YO and draw through 2 loops on hook, YO, insert hook in **same** sp, YO and pull up a loop, YO and draw through 2 loops on hook †, YO, insert hook in next Popcorn, YO and pull up a loop, YO and draw through 2 loops on hook, repeat from † to † once, YO and draw through all 6 loops on hook **(decrease made)]**, 3 dc in each of next 3 ch-3 sps ♥, 5 dc in next Popcorn; repeat from ★ 4 times **more**, then repeat from ♥ to ♥ once, 3 dc in last Popcorn; do **not** finish off: 145 sts.

Rows 6-10: Ch 3, turn; working in back ridges of each st, 2 dc in same st, dc in next 9 dc, decrease, dc in next 9 dc, ★ 5 dc in next dc, dc in next 9 dc, decrease, dc in next 9 dc; repeat from ★ across to last dc, 3 dc in last dc; at end of last row, finish off.

Rows 11-70: Repeat Rows 3-10, 7 times; then repeat Rows 3-6 once **more**; at end of Row 70, do **not** finish off.

EDGING
Ch 1, turn; (slip st, ch 3, work Cluster) in first dc, ★ skip next 2 dc, (slip st, ch 3, work Cluster) in next st; repeat from ★ across; working in end of rows, skip first row, (slip st, ch 3, work Cluster) in top of next row, [skip next row, (slip st, ch 3, work Cluster) in top of next row] across; working in free loops of beginning ch *(Fig. 3b, page 3)*, (slip st, ch 3, work Cluster) in first ch, [skip next 2 chs, (slip st, ch 3, work Cluster) in next ch] across ending in marked ch; working in end of rows, (slip st, ch 3, work Cluster) in top of first row, skip next row, [(slip st, ch 3, work Cluster) in top of next row, skip next row] across; join with slip st to first slip st, finish off.

Design by Diana B. Husband.

Shadow

Finished Size: 46" x 65" (117 cm x 165 cm)

MATERIALS
Worsted Weight Yarn:
  Black - 24 ounces, 1,355 yards
    (680 grams, 1,239 meters)
  White - 7¹/₂ ounces, 425 yards
    (210 grams, 388.5 meters)
  Grey - 7¹/₂ ounces, 425 yards
    (210 grams, 388.5 meters)
  Crochet hook, size I (5.5 mm) **or** size needed
    for gauge

GAUGE: In pattern, one point to point
      repeat (32 sts) = 11¹/₂" (29.25 cm)
      Rows 2-9 = 4¹/₂" (11.5 cm)

Gauge Swatch: 23"w x 4"h (58.5 cm x 10 cm)
With Black, ch 67.
Work same as Afghan for 7 rows.

STITCH GUIDE

TREBLE CROCHET *(abbreviated tr)*
YO twice, insert hook in st or sp indicated, YO
and pull up a loop (4 loops on hook), (YO and
draw through 2 loops on hook) 3 times.

DC DECREASE (uses next 2 sts)
★ YO, insert hook in **next** st, YO and pull up a
loop, YO and draw through 2 loops on hook;
repeat from ★ once **more**, YO and draw
through all 3 loops on hook **(counts as
one dc)**.

RIGHT DECREASE
  (uses next ch-1 sp and next sc)
YO, insert hook in next ch-1 sp, YO and pull up
a loop, YO and draw through 2 loops on hook,
YO, insert hook in next sc, YO and pull up a
loop, YO and draw through 2 loops on hook,
YO and draw through all 3 loops on hook
(counts as one dc).

LEFT DECREASE
  (uses next sc and next ch-1 sp)
YO, insert hook in next sc, YO and pull up a
loop, YO and draw through 2 loops on hook,
YO, insert hook in next ch-1 sp, YO and pull up
a loop, YO and draw through 2 loops on hook,
YO and draw through all 3 loops on hook
(counts as one dc).

RIGHT TR DECREASE
  (uses next ch-1 sp and next sc)
First Leg: YO twice, skip next ch-1 sp, insert
hook in next sc, YO and pull up a loop, (YO and
draw through 2 loops on hook) twice (2 loops
remaining on hook).

Second Leg: YO twice, working **behind**
First Leg, insert hook in skipped ch-1 sp, YO
and pull up a loop, (YO and draw through
2 loops on hook) twice, YO and draw through
all 3 loops on hook.

LEFT TR DECREASE
  (uses next sc and next ch-1 sp)
First Leg: YO twice, skip next sc, insert hook
in next ch-1 sp, YO and pull up a loop, (YO and
draw through 2 loops on hook) twice (2 loops
remaining on hook).

Second Leg: YO twice, working **behind**
First Leg, insert hook in skipped sc, YO and pull
up a loop, (YO and draw through 2 loops on
hook) twice, YO and draw through all 3 loops
on hook.

AFGHAN
With Black, ch 131.

Row 1 (Right side)**:** Working in back ridges of
beginning ch *(Fig. 1, page 3)*, 2 dc in fourth ch
from hook **(3 skipped chs count as first dc)**, dc
in next 12 chs, dc decrease, dc in next ch,
dc decrease, dc in next 12 chs, 2 dc in next ch, dc
in next ch, ★ 2 dc in next ch, dc in next 12 chs,
dc decrease, dc in next ch, dc decrease, dc in next
12 chs, 2 dc in next ch, dc in next ch; repeat from
★ across; finish off: 129 dc.

Note: Loop a short piece of yarn around any stitch
to mark Row 1 as **right** side.

Continued on page 74.

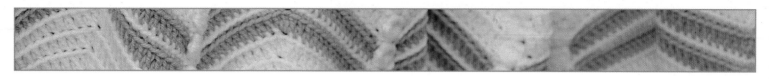

Fresh Flowers

Finished Size: 46" x 64$^1/_2$" (117 cm x 164 cm)

MATERIALS
Worsted Weight Yarn:
Off-White - 33$^1/_2$ ounces, 1,895 yards
(950 grams, 1,733 meters)
Teal - 3$^1/_2$ ounces, 200 yards
(100 grams, 183 meters)
Crochet hook, size G (4 mm) **or** size needed
for gauge

GAUGE: In pattern, one point to point
repeat = 7$^1/_2$" (19 cm)
Rows 1-11 = 6$^1/_2$" (16.5 cm)

Gauge Swatch: 14$^1/_4$"w x 4$^3/_4$"h
(36.25 cm x 12 cm)
With Off-White, ch 63.
Work same as Afghan Body for 7 rows.

STITCH GUIDE

3-DC CLUSTER (uses one st)
★ YO, insert hook in st indicated, YO and pull
up a loop, YO and draw through 2 loops on
hook; repeat from ★ 2 times **more**, YO and
draw through all 4 loops on hook.

5-DC CLUSTER (uses one st)
★ YO, insert hook in st indicated, YO and pull
up a loop, YO and draw through 2 loops on
hook; repeat from ★ 4 times **more**, YO and
draw through all 6 loops on hook.

SC DECREASE
Pull up a loop in next 2 dc, YO and draw
through all 3 loops on hook **(counts as
one sc)**.

DC DECREASE (uses next 2 sts)
★ YO, insert hook in **next** st, YO and pull up a
loop, YO and draw through 2 loops on hook;
repeat from ★ once **more**, YO and draw
through all 3 loops on hook **(counts as
one dc)**.

AFGHAN BODY
With Off-White, ch 191.

Row 1 (Right side)**:** Dc in fourth ch from hook
(3 skipped chs count as first dc) and in next
12 chs, 3 dc in next ch, dc in next 14 chs, ★ skip
next ch, work 5-dc Cluster in next ch, skip next ch,
dc in next 14 chs, 3 dc in next ch, dc in next
14 chs; repeat from ★ across; finish off: 186 dc and
5 5-dc Clusters.

Note: Loop a short piece of yarn around any stitch
to mark Row 1 as **right** side.

Work in Back Loops Only throughout **(Fig. 2,
page 3)** unless otherwise specified.

Row 2: With **right** side facing, join Off-White with
dc in first dc **(see Joining With Dc, page 3)**;
dc decrease, dc in next 6 dc, ch 5, skip next 2 dc,
dc in next 4 dc, 3 dc in next dc, dc in next 4 dc,
ch 5, ★ skip next 2 dc, dc in next 8 dc, skip next
dc, work 5-dc Cluster in **both** loops of next
5-dc Cluster, skip next dc, dc in next 8 dc, ch 5,
skip next 2 dc, dc in next 4 dc, 3 dc in next dc, dc
in next 4 dc, ch 5; repeat from ★ 4 times **more**,
skip next 2 dc, dc in next 6 dc, dc decrease, dc in
last dc; finish off: 167 sts and 12 ch-5 sps.

Row 3: With **right** side facing, join Off-White with
dc in first dc; dc decrease, dc in next 3 dc, ★ † ch 3,
sc in next ch-5 sp, ch 3, skip next 2 dc, dc in next
3 dc, 3 dc in next dc, dc in next 3 dc, ch 3, sc in
next ch-5 sp, ch 3 †, skip next 2 dc, dc in next 5 dc,
skip next dc, work 5-dc Cluster in **both** loops of next
5-dc Cluster, skip next dc, dc in next 5 dc; repeat
from ★ 4 times **more**, then repeat from † to † once,
skip next 2 dc, dc in next 3 dc, dc decrease, dc in
last dc; finish off: 131 sts and 24 ch-3 sps.

Row 4: With **right** side facing, join Off-White with
dc in first dc; dc decrease, ★ † ch 5, sc in next
ch-3 sp, work 3-dc Cluster in **both** loops of next sc,
sc in next ch-3 sp, ch 5, skip next 2 dc, dc in next
2 dc, 3 dc in next dc, dc in next 2 dc, ch 5, sc in
next ch-3 sp, work 3-dc Cluster in **both** loops of
next sc, sc in next ch-3 sp, ch 5 †, skip next 2 dc,
dc in next 2 dc, skip next dc, work 5-dc Cluster in
both loops of next 5-dc Cluster, skip next dc, dc in
next 2 dc; repeat from ★ 4 times **more**, then repeat
from † to † once, skip next 2 dc, dc decrease, dc in
last dc; finish off: 107 sts and 24 ch-5 sps.

Continued on page 73.

Row 5: With **right** side facing, join Off-White with slip st in first dc; ch 2, ★ † dc in next dc and in next 2 chs, ch 3, skip next sc, sc in **both** loops of next 3-dc Cluster, ch 3, skip next 3 chs, dc in next 2 chs and in next 3 dc, 3 dc in next dc, dc in next 3 dc and in next 2 chs, ch 3, skip next sc, sc in **both** loops of next 3-dc Cluster, ch 3 †, skip next 3 chs, dc in next 2 chs and in next dc, skip next dc, work 5-dc Cluster in **both** loops of next 5-dc Cluster, skip next dc; repeat from ★ 4 times **more**, then repeat from † to † once, skip next 3 chs, dc in next 2 chs, dc decrease; finish off: 131 sts and 24 ch-3 sps.

Row 6: With **right** side facing, join Off-White with dc in first dc; dc decrease, dc in next 2 chs, ★ † ch 2, skip next sc and next ch, dc in next 2 chs and in next 6 dc, 3 dc in next dc, dc in next 6 dc and in next 2 chs, ch 2, skip next sc and next ch †, dc in next 2 chs and next 2 dc, skip next dc, work 5-dc Cluster in **both** loops of next 5-dc Cluster, skip next dc, dc in next 2 dc and in next 2 chs; repeat from ★ 4 times **more**, then repeat from † to † once, dc in next 2 chs, dc decrease, dc in last dc; finish off: 167 sts and 12 ch-2 sps.

Row 7: With **right** side facing, join Off-White with dc in first dc; dc decrease, dc in next dc and in next 2 chs, ★ † dc in next 9 dc, 3 dc in next dc, dc in next 9 dc and in next 2 chs †, dc in next 3 dc, skip next dc, work 5-dc Cluster in **both** loops of next 5-dc Cluster, skip next dc, dc in next 3 dc and in next 2 chs; repeat from ★ 4 times **more**, then repeat from † to † once, dc in next dc, dc decrease, dc in last dc; finish off: 191 sts.

Row 8: With **right** side facing, join Teal with dc in first dc; dc decrease, dc in next 12 dc, 3 dc in next dc, ★ dc in next 14 dc, skip next 3 sts, dc in next 14 dc, 3 dc in next dc; repeat from ★ 4 times **more**, dc in next 12 dc, dc decrease, dc in last dc; finish off: 186 dc.

Row 9: With **right** side facing, join Off-White with sc in first dc *(see Joining With Sc, page 1)*; sc decrease, sc in next 12 dc, 3 sc in next dc, ★ sc in next 14 dc, working in **front** of sts on previous row *(Fig. 6, page 3)*, work 5-dc Cluster in **both** loops of skipped 5-dc Cluster one row **below**, skip next 2 sts on previous row from last sc made, sc in next 14 dc, 3 sc in next dc; repeat from ★ 4 times **more**, sc in next 12 dc, sc decrease, sc in last dc; finish off: 191 sts.

Row 10: With **right** side facing, join Teal with dc in first sc; dc decrease, dc in next 12 sc, 3 dc in next sc, ★ dc in next 14 sc, skip next 3 sts, dc in next 14 sc, 3 dc in next sc; repeat from ★ 4 times **more**, dc in next 12 sc, dc decrease, dc in last sc; finish off: 186 dc.

Row 11: Repeat Row 9: 191 sts.

Row 12: With **right** side facing, join Off-White with dc in first sc; dc decrease, dc in next 12 sc, 3 dc in next sc, ★ dc in next 14 sc, skip next sc, work 5-dc Cluster in **both** loops of next 5-dc Cluster, skip next sc, dc in next 14 sc, 3 dc in next sc; repeat from ★ 4 times **more**, dc in next 12 dc, dc decrease, dc in last dc; finish off.

Rows 13-106: Repeat Rows 2-12, 8 times; then repeat Rows 2-7 once **more**; at end of Row 106, do **not** finish off.

EDGING

Ch 1; with **right** side facing, (sc, ch 3, work 3-dc Cluster) in top of last dc made on Row 106; working in end of rows, (sc, ch 3, work 3-dc Cluster) in top of next 7 rows, skip next row, (sc, ch 3, work 3-dc Cluster) in top of next row, skip next row, [(sc, ch 3, work 3-dc Cluster) in top of next 8 rows, skip next row, (sc, ch 3, work 3-dc Cluster) in top of next row, skip next row] 8 times, (sc, ch 3, work 3-dc Cluster) in top of next 7 rows; working in free loops of beginning ch *(Fig. 3b, page 3)*, (sc, ch 3, work 3-dc Cluster) twice in first ch, skip next ch, † [(sc, ch 3, work 3-dc Cluster) in next ch, skip next 2 chs] 9 times, (sc, ch 3, work 3-dc Cluster) in next 2 ch-1 sps, skip next 2 chs †; repeat from † to † 4 times **more**, (sc, ch 3, work 3-dc Cluster) in next ch, [skip next 2 chs, (sc, ch 3, work 3-dc Cluster) in next ch] 8 times, (sc, ch 3, work 3-dc Cluster) twice in next ch; working in end of rows, (sc, ch 3, work 3-dc Cluster) in top of first 7 rows, [skip next row, (sc, ch 3, work 3-dc Cluster) in top of next row, skip next row, (sc, ch 3, work 3-dc Cluster) in top of next 8 rows] across; working in **both** loops of sts across Row 106, [skip next dc, (sc, ch 3, work 3-dc Cluster) in next dc, skip next 2 dc, (sc, ch 3, work 3-dc Cluster) in next dc] 3 times, ★ [skip next 2 dc, (sc, ch 3, work 3-dc Cluster) in next dc, skip next sc, (sc, ch 3, work 3-dc Cluster) in next dc] twice, [skip next 2 dc, (sc, ch 3, work 3-dc Cluster) in next st] 4 times, [skip next dc, (sc, ch 3, work 3-dc Cluster) in next dc, skip next 2 dc, (sc, ch 3, work 3-dc Cluster) in next dc] twice; repeat from ★ 4 times **more**, skip next 2 dc, (sc, ch 3, work 3-dc Cluster) in next dc, skip next dc, [(sc, ch 3, work 3-dc Cluster) in next dc, skip next 2 dc, (sc, ch 3, work 3-dc Cluster) in next dc, skip next dc] twice; join with slip st to first sc, finish off.

Design by Pat Gibbons.

73

Shadow

Continued from page 69.

Row 2: With **wrong** side facing, join White with sc in first st *(see Joining With Sc, page 1)*; (sc in next st, ch 2, skip next st) 6 times, (sc in next st, ch 1, skip next st) 3 times, ★ (sc in next st, ch 2, skip next st) 13 times, (sc in next st, ch 1, skip next st) 3 times; repeat from ★ 2 times **more**, (sc in next st, ch 2, skip next st) 6 times, sc in last 2 sts; finish off: 66 sc and 63 sps.

Row 3: With **wrong** side facing, join Black with dc in first sc *(see Joining With Dc, page 3)*; 2 dc in next sc, (dc in next ch-2 sp and in next sc) 6 times, work right decrease, dc in next ch-1 sp, work left decrease, (dc in next sc and in next ch-2 sp) 6 times, 2 dc in next sc, ★ dc in next ch-2 sp, 2 dc in next sc, (dc in next ch-2 sp and in next sc) 6 times, work right decrease, dc in next ch-1 sp, work left decrease, (dc in next sc and in next ch-2 sp) 6 times, 2 dc in next sc; repeat from ★ across to last sc, dc in last sc; finish off: 129 dc.

Row 4: With **wrong** side facing, join White with sc in first st; (sc in next st, ch 2, skip next st) 6 times, (sc in next st, ch 1, skip next st) 3 times, ★ (sc in next st, ch 2, skip next st) 13 times, (sc in next st, ch 1, skip next st) 3 times; repeat from ★ 2 times **more**, (sc in next st, ch 2, skip next st) 6 times, sc in last 2 sts; finish off: 66 sc and 63 sps.

Row 5: With **right** side facing, join Grey with slip st in first sc; ch 4 **(counts as first tr, now and throughout)**, tr in next sc, working **behind** tr just made, tr in same st as joining slip st, (skip next ch-2 sp, tr in next sc, working **behind** tr just made, tr in skipped ch-2 sp) 6 times, work right tr decrease, dc in next ch-1 sp, work left tr decrease, ★ (skip next sc, tr in next ch-2 sp, working **behind** tr just made, tr in skipped sc) 7 times, tr in same sp as next-to-the-last tr made and in next sc, working **behind** last tr made, tr in same sp as next-to-the-last tr made, (skip next ch-2 sp, tr in next sc, working **behind** tr just made, tr in skipped ch-2 sp) 6 times, work right tr decrease, dc in next ch-1 sp, work left tr decrease; repeat from ★ 2 times **more**, (skip next sc, tr in next ch-2 sp, working **behind** tr just made, tr in skipped sc) 6 times, skip next sc, tr in last sc, working **behind** tr just made, tr in skipped sc and in same st as next-to-the-last tr made; finish off: 129 sts.

Row 6: With **wrong** side facing, join Black with sc in first st; (sc in next st, ch 2, skip next st) 6 times, (sc in next st, ch 1, skip next st) 3 times, ★ (sc in next st, ch 2, skip next st) 13 times, (sc in next st, ch 1, skip next st) 3 times; repeat from ★ 2 times **more**, (sc in next st, ch 2, skip next st) 6 times, sc in last 2 sts; finish off: 66 sc and 63 sps.

Row 7: With **right** side facing, join White with dc in first sc; 2 dc in next sc, (dc in next ch-2 sp and in next sc) 6 times, work right decrease, dc in next ch-1 sp, work left decrease, (dc in next sc and in next ch-2 sp) 6 times, 2 dc in next sc, ★ dc in next ch-2 sp, 2 dc in next sc, (dc in next ch-2 sp and in next sc) 6 times, work right decrease, dc in next ch-1 sp, work left decrease, (dc in next sc and in next ch-2 sp) 6 times, 2 dc in next sc; repeat from ★ across to last sc, dc in last sc; finish off: 129 sts.

Row 8: Repeat Row 6.

Row 9: Repeat Row 5.

Rows 10-12: Repeat Rows 2-4.

Row 13: With **right** side facing, join Black with dc in first sc; 2 dc in next sc, (dc in next ch-2 sp and in next sc) 6 times, work right decrease, dc in next ch-1 sp, work left decrease, (dc in next sc and in next ch-2 sp) 6 times, 2 dc in next sc, ★ dc in next ch-2 sp, 2 dc in next sc, (dc in next ch-2 sp and in next sc) 6 times, work right decrease, dc in next ch-1 sp, work left decrease, (dc in next sc and in next ch-2 sp) 6 times, 2 dc in next sc; repeat from ★ across to last sc, dc in last sc; do **not** finish off: 129 sts.

Rows 14-17: Ch 3 **(counts as first dc, now and throughout)**, turn; ★ 2 dc in next dc, dc in next 12 dc, dc decrease, dc in next dc, dc decrease, dc in next 12 dc, 2 dc in next dc, dc in next dc; repeat from ★ across; at end of last row, finish off.

Rows 18-109: Repeat Rows 2-17, 5 times; then repeat Rows 2-13 once **more**; at end of Row 109, finish off.

Holding 6 strands of Black together, each 17" (43 cm) long, add fringe evenly spaced across short edges of Afghan *(Figs. 8a & b, page 4)*.

Design by Rena V. Stevens.

74

Americana

Finished Size: 51" x 70" (129.5 cm x 178 cm)

MATERIALS
Worsted Weight Yarn:
   Navy - 28 ounces, 1,635 yards
      (800 grams, 1,495 meters)
   Red - 24^1/$_2$ ounces, 1,430 yards
      (700 grams, 1,307.5 meters)
   White - 12 ounces, 700 yards
      (340 grams, 640 meters)
Crochet hook, size I (5.5 mm) **or** size needed
   for gauge

GAUGE: In pattern,
      14 sc and 16 rows = 3^1/$_2$" (9 cm);
      Rows 1-22 = 7^1/$_4$" (18.5 cm);
      from large point to large
      point (50 sts) = 8^1/$_2$" (21.5 cm)

Gauge Swatch: 3^1/$_2$" (9 cm) square
With Red, ch 15.
Row 1: Sc in back ridge of second ch from hook
(Fig. 1, page 3) and each ch across: 14 sc.
Rows 2-16: Ch 1, turn; sc in Back Loop Only of
each sc across *(Fig. 2, page 3)*.
Finish off.

AFGHAN
With Red, ch 299.

Row 1 (Right side)**:** Working in back ridges of
beginning ch *(Fig. 1, page 3)*, sc in second ch from
hook and in next 4 chs, ★ † 3 sc in next ch, sc in
next ch, skip next 2 chs, sc in next 10 chs, 3 sc in
next ch, sc in next 3 chs, skip next 2 chs, sc in next
3 chs, 3 sc in next ch, sc in next 10 chs, skip next
2 chs, sc in next ch, 3 sc in next ch, sc in next
5 chs †, skip next 2 chs, sc in next 5 chs; repeat
from ★ 4 times **more**, then repeat from † to †
once: 300 sc.

Note: Loop a short piece of yarn around any stitch
to mark Row 1 as **right** side.

Work in Back Loops Only throughout *(Fig. 2,
page 3)*.

Rows 2-4: Ch 1, turn; sc in first sc, skip next sc,
sc in next 4 sc, ★ † 3 sc in next sc, sc in next sc,
skip next 2 sc, sc in next 10 sc, 3 sc in next sc, sc
in next 3 sc, skip next 2 sc, sc in next 3 sc, 3 sc in
next sc, sc in next 10 sc, skip next 2 sc, sc in next
sc, 3 sc in next sc †, sc in next 5 sc, skip next 2 sc,
sc in next 5 sc; repeat from ★ 4 times **more**, then
repeat from † to † once, sc in next 4 sc, skip next
sc, sc in last sc; at end of Row 4, finish off.

Row 5: With **right** side facing, join White with sc
in first sc *(see Joining With Sc, page 1)*; skip
next sc, sc in next 4 sc, ★ † 3 sc in next sc, sc in
next sc, skip next 2 sc, sc in next 10 sc, 3 sc in next
sc, sc in next 3 sc, skip next 2 sc, sc in next 3 sc,
3 sc in next sc, sc in next 10 sc, skip next 2 sc, sc
in next sc, 3 sc in next sc †, sc in next 5 sc, skip
next 2 sc, sc in next 5 sc; repeat from ★ 4 times
more, then repeat from † to † once, sc in next 4 sc,
skip next sc, sc in last sc.

Rows 6-8: Ch 1, turn; sc in first sc, skip next sc,
sc in next 4 sc, ★ † 3 sc in next sc, sc in next sc,
skip next 2 sc, sc in next 10 sc, 3 sc in next sc, sc
in next 3 sc, skip next 2 sc, sc in next 3 sc, 3 sc in
next sc, sc in next 10 sc, skip next 2 sc, sc in next
sc, 3 sc in next sc †, sc in next 5 sc, skip next 2 sc,
sc in next 5 sc; repeat from ★ 4 times **more**, then
repeat from † to † once, sc in next 4 sc, skip next
sc, sc in last sc; at end of Row 8, finish off.

Rows 9-12: With Red, repeat Rows 5-8.

Row 13: With **right** side facing, join Navy with sc
in first sc; skip next sc, sc in next 4 sc, ★ † 3 sc in
next sc, sc in next sc, skip next 2 sc, sc in next
10 sc, 3 sc in next sc, sc in next 3 sc, skip next
2 sc, sc in next 3 sc, 3 sc in next sc, sc in next
10 sc, skip next 2 sc, sc in next sc, 3 sc in next
sc †, sc in next 5 sc, skip next 2 sc, sc in next 5 sc;
repeat from ★ 4 times **more**, then repeat from † to
† once, sc in next 4 sc, skip next sc, sc in last sc.

Continued on page 83.

Azalea Lane

Finished Size: 42$\frac{1}{2}$" x 59$\frac{1}{2}$"
(108 cm x 151 cm)

MATERIALS
Worsted Weight Yarn:
Ecru - 13 ounces, 735 yards
(370 grams, 672 meters)
Rose - 9$\frac{1}{2}$ ounces, 535 yards
(270 grams, 489 meters)
Green - 9$\frac{1}{2}$ ounces, 535 yards
(270 grams, 489 meters)
Lt Rose - 6 ounces, 340 yards
(170 grams, 311 meters)
Lt Green - 6 ounces, 340 yards
(170 grams, 311 meters)
Crochet hook, size G (4 mm) **or** size needed
for gauge

GAUGE: In pattern, one point to point
repeat (23 sts) = 4$\frac{1}{4}$" (10.75 cm);
Rows 2-31 = 12$\frac{1}{2}$" (31.75 cm)

Gauge Swatch: 8$\frac{1}{2}$"w x 3$\frac{1}{2}$"h
(21.5 cm x 9 cm)
With Green, ch 45.
Work same as Afghan for 8 rows.

STITCH GUIDE

DECREASE (uses next 6 sc)
★ YO, skip **next** 2 sc, insert hook in **next** sc,
YO and pull up a loop, YO and draw through
2 loops on hook; repeat from ★ once **more**,
YO and draw through all 3 loops on hook
(counts as one dc).

ENDING DECREASE (uses last 4 sc)
YO, skip next 2 sc, insert hook in next sc, YO
and pull up a loop, YO and draw through
2 loops on hook, YO, insert hook in last sc, YO
and pull up a loop, YO and draw through
2 loops on hook, YO and draw through all
3 loops on hook **(counts as one dc).**

CLUSTER (uses one sc)
★ YO, insert hook in sc indicated, YO and pull
up a loop, YO and draw through 2 loops on
hook; repeat from ★ once **more**, YO and draw
through all 3 loops on hook.

PUFF ST (uses one sp)
★ YO, insert hook in sp indicated, YO and pull
up a loop even with loop on hook; repeat from
★ 4 times **more**, YO and draw through all
11 loops on hook.

AFGHAN
With Green, ch 229.

Row 1 (Right side)**:** Working in back ridges of
beginning ch **(Fig. 1, page 3)**, sc in second ch from
hook and in next 9 chs, 3 sc in next ch, sc in next
10 chs, ★ skip next 2 chs, sc in next 10 chs, 3 sc in
next ch, sc in next 10 chs; repeat from ★ across:
230 sc.

Note: Loop a short piece of yarn around any stitch
to mark Row 1 as **right** side.

Row 2: Ch 1, turn; sc in first sc, skip next sc, sc in
next 9 sc, 3 sc in next sc, ★ sc in next 10 sc, skip
next 2 sc, sc in next 10 sc, 3 sc in next sc; repeat
from ★ across to last 11 sc, sc in next 9 sc, skip
next sc, sc in last sc.

Row 3: Ch 2, turn; skip first sc, dc in next sc, skip
next 2 sc, [(dc, ch 1, dc) in next sc, skip next 2 sc]
twice, dc in next sc, ch 1, (dc, ch 1) twice in next sc,
dc in next sc, [skip next 2 sc, (dc, ch 1, dc) in next
sc] twice, ★ decrease, skip next 2 sc, [(dc, ch 1, dc)
in next sc, skip next 2 sc] twice, dc in next sc, ch 1,
(dc, ch 1) twice in next sc, dc in next sc, [skip next
2 sc, (dc, ch 1, dc) in next sc] twice; repeat from ★
across to last 4 sc, work ending decrease: 131 dc
and 70 ch-1 sps.

Continued on page 84.

Sailboat Celebration

Finished Size: 56" x 64" (142 cm x 162.5 cm)

MATERIALS
Worsted Weight Yarn:
  Med Blue - 24 ounces, 1,355 yards
    (680 grams, 1,239 meters)
  White - 16 ounces, 905 yards
    (450 grams, 827.5 meters)
  Navy - 16 ounces, 905 yards
    (450 grams, 827.5 meters)
  Lt Blue - 8 ounces, 450 yards
    (230 grams, 411.5 meters)
  Blue - 8 ounces, 450 yards
    (230 grams, 411.5 meters)
  Dk Blue - 8 ounces, 450 yards
    (230 grams, 411.5 meters)
  Purple - 1 ounce, 55 yards
    (30 grams, 50.5 meters)
  Orange - 1 ounce, 55 yards
    (30 grams, 50.5 meters)
  Red - 1 ounce, 55 yards
    (30 grams, 50.5 meters)
  Green - 1 ounce, 55 yards
    (30 grams, 50.5 meters)
  Yellow - $^1/_2$ ounce, 30 yards
    (15 grams, 27.5 meters)
Crochet hook, size F (3.75 mm) **or** size needed
  for gauge
Yarn needle

GAUGE: Square A or B = 3" (7.5 cm)
      Sailboat Strip Block = 9$^1/_2$" (24.25 cm)
      Square C or D = 2$^1/_4$" (5.75 cm)
      Star Strip Block = 9$^1/_2$" (24.25 cm)

Gauge Swatch: 3" (7.5 cm) square
Work same as Square A.

STITCH GUIDE

> **TREBLE CROCHET *(abbreviated tr)***
> YO twice, insert hook in st or sp indicated, YO and pull up a loop (4 loops on hook), (YO and draw through 2 loops on hook) 3 times.
>
> **LONG SINGLE CROCHET**
>   **(abbreviated LSC)**
> Working **around** last 3 dc made *(Fig. 6, page 3)*, insert hook in st indicated, YO and pull up a loop even with loop on hook, YO and draw through both loops on hook.
>
> **DECREASE** (uses next 5 sts)
> † YO, insert hook in **next** st, YO and pull up a loop, YO and draw through 2 loops on hook †; repeat from † to † once **more**, skip next st, repeat from † to † twice, YO and draw through all 5 loops on hook.

SAILBOAT STRIPS
BLOCK (Make 10)
SQUARE A

Make the number of Squares indicated with the following colors: Med Blue - 30, White - 10, Purple - 2, Orange - 2, Red - 2, Green - 2, Dk Blue - 1, and Yellow - 1.

Rnd 1 (Right side)**:** Ch 5, **[**2 dc, (tr, 2 dc) 3 times**]** in fifth ch from hook; join with slip st to top of beginning ch-5: 12 sts.

Note: Loop a short piece of yarn around any stitch to mark Rnd 1 as **right** side.

Rnd 2: Ch 4 **(counts as first tr, now and throughout)**, 2 dc in same st, dc in next 2 dc, ★ (2 dc, tr, 2 dc) in next corner tr, dc in next 2 dc; repeat from ★ 2 times **more**, 2 dc in same st as first tr; join with slip st to first tr: 28 sts.

Rnd 3: Ch 4, 2 dc in same st, dc in next 6 dc, ★ (2 dc, tr, 2 dc) in next corner tr, dc in next 6 dc; repeat from ★ 2 times **more**, 2 dc in same st as first tr; join with slip st to first tr, finish off: 44 sts.

Continued on page 81.

SQUARE B

Med Blue & White - 20
Med Blue & Orange - 4
Med Blue & Green - 4
Med Blue & Purple - 4
Med Blue & Red - 4
Med Blue & Dk Blue - 2
Med Blue & Yellow - 2

Rnd 1 (Right side)**:** With Med Blue, ch 5, (2 dc, tr, 2 dc) in fifth ch from hook changing to contrasting color in last dc made *(Fig. 4c, page 3)*, do **not** cut Med Blue; working over Med Blue *(Fig. 16)*, (tr, 2 dc) twice in same ch; drop contrasting color, with Med Blue, join with slip st to top of beginning ch-5, do **not** cut contrasting color: 12 sts.

Fig. 16

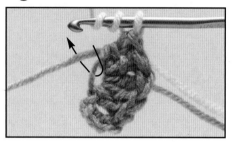

Note: Mark Rnd 1 as **right** side.

Continue to change colors in same manner and work over unused color; do **not** cut yarn until specified.

Rnd 2: Ch 4, 2 dc in same st, † dc in next 2 dc, (2 dc, tr, 2 dc) in next corner tr, dc in next 2 dc †, 2 dc in next corner tr changing to contrasting color; (tr, 2 dc) in same st, repeat from † to † once, 2 dc in same st as first tr; join with slip st to first tr changing to Med Blue: 28 sts.

Rnd 3: Ch 4, 2 dc in same st, † dc in next 6 dc, (2 dc, tr, 2 dc) in next corner tr, dc in next 6 dc †, 2 dc in next corner tr changing to contrasting color; cut Med Blue, (tr, 2 dc) in same st, repeat from † to † once, 2 dc in same st as first tr; join with slip st to first tr, finish off: 44 sts.

SAILBOAT BLOCK ASSEMBLY

Hold two Squares with **wrong** sides together. Using Placement Diagram as a guide, matching color, and working through **inside** loops only, whipstitch Squares together *(Fig. 7b, page 4)* forming 3 strips of 3 Squares **each** for Block, beginning in first corner tr and ending in next corner tr. Join strips in same manner.

PLACEMENT DIAGRAM

STRIP ASSEMBLY

With Med Blue, using Placement Diagram as a guide, and working through **inside** loops only, tack 5 Sailboat Blocks together at corner tr to form one Strip. Repeat to form second Strip.

BORDER
FIRST SIDE

Row 1: With **right** side of one Sailboat Strip facing and working in Back Loops Only *(Fig. 2, page 3)*, skip first corner tr and next 3 dc and join Navy with dc in next dc *(see Joining With Dc, page 3)*; dc in next 2 dc, work LSC in last skipped dc, skip next dc, dc in next 3 dc, work LSC in skipped dc, ★ † [skip same st as joining on same Square, dc in same st as joining on next Square and in next 2 dc, work LSC in skipped st, (skip next dc, dc in next 3 dc, work LSC in skipped dc) twice] 2 times, (2 dc, tr, 2 dc) in next corner tr, (skip next dc, dc in next 3 dc, work LSC in skipped dc) twice, [skip next dc, dc in next dc, dc in same st as joining on same Square and in same st as joining on next Square, work LSC in skipped dc, (skip next dc, dc in next 3 dc, work LSC in skipped dc) twice] 2 times †, (YO, insert hook in **next** dc, YO and pull up a loop, YO and draw through 2 loops on hook) twice, YO, skip next joining, insert hook in next dc on next Square, YO and pull up a loop, YO and draw through 2 loops on hook, YO, insert hook in next dc, YO and pull up a loop, YO and draw through 2 loops on hook, YO and draw through all 5 loops on hook, (skip next dc, dc in next 3 dc, work LSC in skipped dc) twice; repeat from ★ 3 times **more**, then repeat from † to † once, dc in same st as last dc made, leave remaining 3 sts unworked; finish off: 350 sts.

Row 2: With **right** side facing and working in both loops, skip first 3 dc and join Navy with dc in next LSC; dc in next 2 dc, work LSC in last skipped dc, (skip next dc, dc in next 3 sts, work LSC in skipped dc) 7 times, (2 dc, tr, 2 dc) in next tr, (skip next dc, dc in next 3 sts, work LSC in skipped dc) 8 times, ★ decrease, (skip next dc, dc in next 3 sts, work LSC in skipped dc) 8 times, (2 dc, tr, 2 dc) in next tr, (skip next dc, dc in next 3 dc, work LSC in skipped dc) 8 times; repeat from ★ across to last 3 sts, dc in same st as last dc made, leave remaining 3 sts unworked; finish off.

Rows 3 and 4: With Dk Blue, repeat Row 2 twice.

Rows 5 and 6: With Blue, repeat Row 2 twice.

Rows 7 and 8: With Med Blue, repeat Row 2 twice.

Rows 9 and 10: With Lt Blue, repeat Row 2 twice.

Row 11: With White, repeat Row 2.

SECOND SIDE
Rows 1-11: Working in sts on opposite side of Sailboat Strip, work same as First Side.

Repeat Border on Second Sailboat Strip.

STAR STRIP
BLOCK (Make 4)
SQUARE C (Make 16 Navy and 16 White)

Rnd 1 (Right side)**:** Ch 5, [2 dc, (tr, 2 dc) 3 times] in fifth ch from hook; join with slip st to top of beginning ch-5: 12 sts.

Rnd 2: Ch 4, 2 dc in same st, dc in next 2 dc, ★ (2 dc, tr, 2 dc) in next corner tr, dc in next 2 dc; repeat from ★ 2 times **more**, 2 dc in same st as first tr; join with slip st to first tr, finish off: 28 sts.

SQUARE D (Make 32)
With Navy, ch 4; join with slip st to form a ring.

Rnd 1 (Right side)**:** Ch 4, (2 dc, tr, 2 dc) in ring changing to White, do **not** cut Navy; working over Navy, (tr, 2 dc) twice in ring; join with slip st to first tr changing to Navy: 12 sts.

Note: Mark Rnd 1 as **right** side.

Rnd 2: Ch 4, 2 dc in same st, † dc in next 2 dc, (2 dc, tr, 2 dc) in next corner tr, dc in next 2 dc †, 2 dc in next corner tr changing to White; cut Navy, (tr, 2 dc) in same st, repeat from † to † once, 2 dc in same st as first tr; join with slip st to first tr, finish off: 28 sts.

STAR BLOCK ASSEMBLY
Hold two Squares with **wrong** sides together. Using Placement Diagram as a guide, matching color, and working through **inside** loops only, whipstitch Squares together forming 4 strips of 4 Squares **each** for Block, beginning in first corner tr and ending in next corner tr. Join strips in same manner.

STRIP ASSEMBLY
With Navy, using Placement Diagram as a guide, and working through **inside** loops only, tack Blocks together at corner tr to form one Strip.

FINISHING
STRIP JOINING
With **right** side facing and using Placement Diagram as a guide, hold one Sailboat Strip adjacent to one side of Star Strip, matching tr at outer points and decreases on inner points of last row on Strip Border to corner tr on Blocks. With Navy, working through **inside** loops only, and easing to fit, whipstitch Strips together, beginning in first corner tr and ending in next corner tr. Whipstitch remaining Sailboat Strip to opposite side of Star Strip in same manner.

Continued on page 83.

FILL-IN TRIANGLE

Row 1: With **right** side facing, using Placement Diagram as a guide, and working in **both** loops, skip first 3 dc on first Sailboat Strip Border and join White with dc in next LSC; dc in next 2 dc, work LSC in last skipped dc, (skip next dc, dc in next 3 sts, work LSC in skipped dc) 7 times, YO, insert hook in same st as last dc made, YO and pull up a loop, YO and draw through 2 loops on hook, YO, insert hook in same st as joining on same Sailboat Strip Border, YO and pull up a loop, YO and draw through 2 loops on hook, YO, skip Star Block, insert hook in same st as joining on next Sailboat Strip Border, YO and pull up a loop, YO and draw through 2 loops on hook, YO, insert hook in next dc, YO and pull up a loop, YO and draw through 2 loops on hook, YO and draw through all 5 loops on hook, dc in next 3 dc, work LSC in same st as last leg of last st made, (skip next dc, dc in next 3 sts, work LSC in skipped dc) across to last 3 sts, dc in same st as last dc made, leave remaining 3 sts unworked; finish off: 66 sts.

Row 2: With **right** side facing, skip first 3 dc and join Navy with dc in next LSC; dc in next 2 dc, work LSC in last skipped dc, (skip next dc, dc in next 3 sts, work LSC in last skipped dc) 6 times, decrease, (skip next dc, dc in next 3 sts, work LSC in skipped dc) across to last 3 sts, dc in same st as last dc made, leave remaining 3 sts unworked; finish off: 58 sts.

Row 3: With **right** side facing, skip first 3 dc and join Dk Blue with dc in next LSC; dc in next 2 dc, work LSC in last skipped dc, (skip next dc, dc in next 3 sts, work LSC in last skipped dc) 5 times, decrease, (skip next dc, dc in next 3 sts, work LSC in skipped dc) across to last 3 sts, dc in same st as last dc made, leave remaining 3 sts unworked; finish off: 50 sts.

Row 4: With **right** side facing, skip first 3 dc and join Blue with dc in next LSC; dc in next 2 dc, work LSC in last skipped dc, (skip next dc, dc in next 3 sts, work LSC in last skipped dc) 4 times, decrease, (skip next dc, dc in next 3 sts, work LSC in skipped dc) across to last 3 sts, dc in same st as last dc made, leave remaining 3 sts unworked; finish off: 42 sts.

Row 5: With **right** side facing, skip first 3 dc and join Med Blue with dc in next LSC; dc in next 2 dc, work LSC in last skipped dc, (skip next dc, dc in next 3 sts, work LSC in last skipped dc) 3 times, decrease, (skip next dc, dc in next 3 sts, work LSC in skipped dc) across to last 3 sts, dc in same st as last dc made, leave remaining 3 sts unworked; finish off: 34 sts.

Row 6: With **right** side facing, skip first 3 dc and join Lt Blue with dc in next LSC; dc in next 2 dc, work LSC in last skipped dc, (skip next dc, dc in next 3 sts, work LSC in last skipped dc) twice, decrease, (skip next dc, dc in next 3 sts, work LSC in skipped dc) across to last 3 sts, dc in same st as last dc made, leave remaining 3 sts unworked; finish off: 26 sts.

Row 7: With **right** side facing, skip first 3 dc and join White with dc in next LSC; dc in next 2 dc, work LSC in last skipped dc, skip next dc, dc in next 3 sts, work LSC in last skipped dc, decrease, (skip next dc, dc in next 3 sts, work LSC in skipped dc) twice, dc in same st as last dc made, leave remaining 3 sts unworked; finish off: 18 sts.

Row 8: With **right** side facing, skip first 3 dc and join Navy with dc in next LSC; dc in next 2 dc, work LSC in last skipped dc, decrease, skip next dc, dc in next 3 sts, work LSC in skipped dc, dc in same st as last dc made, leave remaining 3 sts unworked; do **not** finish off: 10 sts.

Row 9: Turn; slip st in first 3 sts, ch 2, decrease, leave remaining 2 sts unworked; finish off.

Repeat for second Fill-In Triangle.

Designed by Julene S. Watson.

Americana

Continued from page 75.

Rows 14-22: Ch 1, turn; sc in first sc, skip next sc, sc in next 4 sc, ★ † 3 sc in next sc, sc in next sc, skip next 2 sc, sc in next 10 sc, 3 sc in next sc, sc in next 3 sc, skip next 2 sc, sc in next 3 sc, 3 sc in next sc, sc in next 10 sc, skip next 2 sc, sc in next sc, 3 sc in next sc †, sc in next 5 sc, skip next 2 sc, sc in next 5 sc; repeat from ★ 4 times **more**, then repeat from † to † once, sc in next 4 sc, skip next sc, sc in last sc; at end of Row 22, finish off.

Rows 23-26: With Red, repeat Rows 5-8.

Rows 27-210: Repeat Rows 5-26, 8 times; then repeat Rows 5-12 once **more**.

Design by Leigh K. Nestor.

Azalea Lane

Continued from page 77.

Row 4: Ch 1, turn; sc in first dc and in next ch-1 sp, (sc in next 2 dc and in next ch-1 sp) twice, sc in next dc, 3 sc in next ch-1 sp, sc in next dc and in next ch-1 sp, (sc in next 2 dc and in next ch-1 sp) twice, ★ sc in next dc, skip next dc, sc in next dc and in next ch-1 sp, (sc in next 2 dc and in next ch-1 sp) twice, sc in next dc, 3 sc in next ch-1 sp, sc in next dc and in next ch-1 sp, (sc in next 2 dc and in next ch-1 sp) twice; repeat from ★ across to last 2 dc, skip next dc, sc in last dc; finish off: 210 sc.

Row 5: With **right** side facing, join Lt Green with sc in first sc *(see Joining With Sc, page 1)*; skip next sc, sc in next 7 sc, 2 sc in next sc, 3 sc in next sc, 2 sc in next sc, ★ sc in next 8 sc, skip next 2 sc, sc in next 8 sc, 2 sc in next sc, 3 sc in next sc, 2 sc in next sc; repeat from ★ across to last 9 sc, sc in next 7 sc, skip next sc, sc in last sc: 230 sc.

Rows 6-8: Repeat Rows 2-4.

Rows 9-12: With Lt Rose, repeat Rows 5-8.

Rows 13-16: With Rose, repeat Rows 5-8.

Row 17: With Ecru, repeat Row 5.

Rows 18-22: Ch 1, turn; sc in first sc, skip next sc, sc in next 9 sc, 3 sc in next sc, ★ sc in next 10 sc, skip next 2 sc, sc in next 10 sc, 3 sc in next sc; repeat from ★ across to last 11 sc, sc in next 9 sc, skip next sc, sc in last sc; at end of last row, finish off.

Row 23: With **right** side facing, join Green with slip st in first sc; ch 2, dc in next sc, ★ † skip next 2 sc, [work (Cluster, ch 1, Cluster) in next sc, skip next 2 sc] twice, dc in next sc, ch 1, (work Cluster, ch 1) twice in next sc, dc in next sc, [skip next 2 sc, work (Cluster, ch 1, Cluster) in next sc] twice †, decrease; repeat from ★ 8 times **more**, then repeat from † to † once, skip next 2 sc, work ending decrease; finish off: 100 Clusters, 31 dc, and 70 ch-1 sps.

Row 24: With **wrong** side facing, join Rose with sc in first dc; ★ † (work Puff St in next ch-1 sp, ch 1, sc in next 2 sts) twice, sc in next ch-1 sp and in next Cluster, (sc, work Puff St, ch 1, sc) in next ch-1 sp, sc in next Cluster and in next ch-1 sp, (sc in next 2 sts, work Puff St in next ch-1 sp, ch 1) twice †, sc in next Cluster, skip next dc, sc in next Cluster; repeat from ★ 8 times **more**, then repeat from † to † once, skip next Cluster, sc in last dc; finish off: 160 sc, 50 Puff Sts, and 50 chs.

Row 25: With **right** side facing, join Ecru with sc in first sc; skip next ch and next Puff St, sc in next 2 sc and in next ch, skip next Puff St, sc in next 4 sc, 2 sc in next sc, 3 sc in next ch, skip next Puff St, 2 sc in next sc, sc in next 4 sc and in next ch, ★ skip next Puff St, sc in next 2 sc and in next ch, skip next Puff St and next 2 sc, sc in next ch, skip next Puff St, sc in next 2 sc and in next ch, skip next Puff St, sc in next 4 sc, 2 sc in next sc, 3 sc in next ch, skip next Puff St, 2 sc in next sc, sc in next 4 sc and in next ch; repeat from ★ 8 times **more**, skip next Puff St, sc in next 2 sc, skip next ch and next Puff St, sc in last sc: 230 sc.

Rows 26-30: Ch 1, turn; sc in first sc, skip next sc, sc in next 9 sc, 3 sc in next sc, ★ sc in next 10 sc, skip next 2 sc, sc in next 10 sc, 3 sc in next sc; repeat from ★ across to last 11 sc, sc in next 9 sc, skip next sc, sc in last sc; at end of last row, finish off.

Row 31: With **right** side facing, join Green with sc in first sc; skip next sc, sc in next 9 sc, 3 sc in next sc, ★ sc in next 10 sc, skip next 2 sc, sc in next 10 sc, 3 sc in next sc; repeat from ★ across to last 11 sc, sc in next 9 sc, skip next sc, sc in last sc.

Rows 32-136: Repeat Rows 2-31, 3 times; then repeat Rows 2-16 once **more**; at end of Row 136, do **not** finish off.

Row 137: Ch 1, turn; sc in first sc, skip next sc, sc in next 7 sc, 2 sc in next sc, 3 sc in next sc, 2 sc in next sc, ★ sc in next 8 sc, skip next 2 sc, sc in next 8 sc, 2 sc in next sc, 3 sc in next sc, 2 sc in next sc; repeat from ★ across to last 9 sc, sc in next 7 sc, skip next sc, sc in last sc; finish off.

Design by Nanette M. Seale.

Vibrance

Finished Size: 45" x 56" (114.5 cm x 142 cm)

MATERIALS
Worsted Weight Yarn:
Blue - 23 ounces, 1,390 yards
(650 grams, 1,271 meters)
Green - 20 ounces, 1,210 yards
(570 grams, 1,106.5 meters)
Variegated - 11 ounces, 665 yards
(310 grams, 608 meters)
Crochet hook, size I (5.5 mm) **or** size needed
for gauge

GAUGE: In pattern, one point to point repeat
(43 sts) and 23 rows = $7^1/2$" (19 cm)

Gauge Swatch: 4" (10 cm) square
With Blue, ch 17.
Row 1: Sc in second ch from hook and in each ch
across: 16 sc.
Rows 2-16: Ch 1, turn; working in Back Loops
Only **(Fig. 2, page 3)**, sc in each sc across.
Finish off.

Afghan is reversible. You will have Loop Sts on both
sides of Afghan.

AFGHAN
With Blue, ch 263.

Row 1 (Right side)**:** Working in back ridges of
beginning ch **(Fig. 1, page 3)**, 2 sc in second ch
from hook, ★ skip next 2 chs, sc in next 20 chs,
3 sc in next ch, sc in next 20 chs; repeat from ★
across to last 3 chs, skip next 2 chs, 2 sc in last ch:
262 sc.

Note: Loop a short piece of yarn around any stitch
to mark Row 1 as **right** side.

Rows 2-10: Ch 1, turn; working in Back Loops
Only **(Fig. 2, page 3)**, 2 sc in first sc, ★ skip next
2 sc, sc in next 20 sc, 3 sc in next sc, sc in next
20 sc; repeat from ★ across to last 3 sc, skip next
2 sc, 2 sc in last sc; at end of last row, finish off.

Row 11: With **right** side facing and working in
both loops, join Green with sc in first sc **(see
Joining With Sc, page 1)**; sc in same st, ★ skip
next 2 sc, sc in next 20 sc, 3 sc in next sc, sc in
next 20 sc; repeat from ★ across to last 3 sc, skip
next 2 sc, 2 sc in last sc.

STITCH GUIDE

LOOP STITCH (abbreviated Loop St)
Insert hook in st indicated, wrap yarn around
index finger of left hand 2 times **more**, insert
hook through all 3 strands on finger following
direction indicated by arrow **(Fig. 17a)**, being
careful to hook all strands **(Fig. 17b)**, draw
through st pulling both loops to measure
approximately 1" (2.5 cm), remove finger from
loops, YO and draw through all 4 loops on hook
(Loop St made, Fig. 17c).

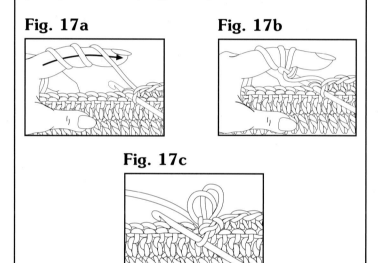

Fig. 17a   Fig. 17b

Fig. 17c

Rows 12-15: Ch 1, turn; 2 sc in first sc, ★ skip
next 2 sc, sc in next 20 sc, 3 sc in next sc, sc in
next 20 sc; repeat from ★ across to last 3 sc, skip
next 2 sc, 2 sc in last sc; at end of last row,
finish off.

Row 16: With **wrong** side facing, join Variegated
with sc in first sc; sc in same st, ★ skip next 2 sc, sc
in next 20 sc, 3 sc in next sc, sc in next 20 sc;
repeat from ★ across to last 3 sc, skip next 2 sc,
2 sc in last sc.

Row 17: Ch 1, turn; work 2 Loop Sts in first sc,
★ skip next 2 sc, work Loop St in next 20 sc, work
3 Loop Sts in next sc, work Loop St in next 20 sc;
repeat from ★ across to last 3 sc, skip next 2 sc,
work 2 Loop Sts in last sc.

Continued on page 93.

Navajo Bargello

Finished Size: 50" x 66" (127 cm x 167.5 cm)

MATERIALS

Worsted Weight Yarn:
- Ecru - 26^1/$_2$ ounces, 1,440 yards (750 grams, 1,316.5 meters)
- Dk Green - 14 ounces, 760 yards (400 grams, 695 meters)
- Green - 13 ounces, 705 yards (370 grams, 644.5 meters)
- Lt Green - 13 ounces, 705 yards (370 grams, 644.5 meters)
- Red - 13 ounces, 705 yards (370 grams, 644.5 meters)

Crochet hook, size I (5.5 mm) **or** size needed for gauge

Safety pins - 24

GAUGE: In pattern, one repeat
(61 sts) = 11^1/$_2$" (29.25 cm);
Rows 3-14 = 5^1/$_4$" (13.25 cm)

Gauge Swatch: 4"w x 4^1/$_4$"h (10 cm x 10.75 cm)
With Ecru, ch 14.
Row 1: Dc in fourth ch from hook **(3 skipped chs count as first dc)** and in each ch across: 12 dc.
Row 2: Ch 1, turn; sc in each dc across.
Row 3: Ch 3 **(counts as first dc)**, turn; dc in next sc and in each sc across.
Rows 4-12: Repeat Rows 2 and 3, 4 times; then repeat Row 2 once **more**.
Finish off.

STITCH GUIDE

CHAIN LOOP *(abbreviated Ch Loop)*
Ch 12, slip st in top of last dc made.

SC DECREASE (uses next 5 sts)
Pull up a loop in next dc, skip next 3 dc, pull up a loop in next dc, YO and draw through all 3 loops on hook.

DC DECREASE (uses next 5 sts)
† YO, insert hook in **next** st, YO and pull up a loop, YO and draw through 2 loops on hook †, skip next 3 sts, repeat from † to † once, YO and draw through all 3 loops on hook **(counts as one dc)**.

AFGHAN BODY

With Dk Green, ch 288.

Row 1 (Wrong side)**:** Slip st in twelfth ch from hook **(first Ch Loop made)**, ch 3 **(counts as first dc)**, dc in next 9 chs, dc decrease, work Ch Loop, dc in next 10 chs, ★ (2 dc, ch 2, 2 dc) in next ch, dc in next 5 chs, dc decrease, work Ch Loop, (dc in next 2 chs, 2 dc in next ch) twice, dc in next 4 chs, (2 dc in next ch, dc in next 2 chs) twice, dc decrease, work Ch Loop, dc in next 5 chs, (2 dc, ch 2, 2 dc) in next ch, dc in next 10 chs, dc decrease, work Ch Loop, dc in next 10 chs; repeat from ★ across: 265 dc and 14 Ch Loops.

Note: Loop a short piece of yarn around back of any stitch on Row 1 to mark **right** side.

Keep Ch Loops to **right** side of work throughout.

Row 2: Ch 12 **(first Ch Loop made)**, turn; 2 sc in each of first 2 dc, sc in next 6 sc, sc decrease, ★ sc in next 10 dc, (2 sc, ch 12, 2 sc) in next ch-2 sp **(Ch Loop made)**, sc in next 5 dc, sc decrease, (sc in next 2 dc, 2 sc in next dc) twice, sc in next 4 dc, (2 sc in next dc, sc in next 2 sc) twice, sc decrease, sc in next 5 dc, (2 sc, ch 12, 2 sc) in next ch-2 sp **(Ch Loop made)**, sc in next 10 dc, sc decrease; repeat from ★ across to last 8 dc, sc in next 6 dc, 2 sc in each of last 2 dc; finish off.

Row 3: With Ecru, ch 12, slip st in first ch to form first Ch Loop; with **wrong** side facing, 2 dc in each of first 2 sc, dc in next 6 sc, dc decrease, work Ch Loop, ★ dc in next 9 sc, 2 dc in next sc, (dc, ch 2, dc) in sp **before** next sc, 2 dc in next sc, dc in next 4 dc, dc decrease, work Ch Loop, (dc in next 2 sc, 2 dc in next sc) twice, dc in next 4 sc, (2 dc in next sc, dc in next 2 sc) twice, dc decrease, work Ch Loop, dc in next 4 sc, 2 dc in next sc, (dc, ch 2, dc) in sp **before** next sc, 2 dc in next sc, dc in next 9 sc, dc decrease, work Ch Loop; repeat from ★ across to last 8 sc, dc in next 6 sc, 2 dc in each of last 2 sc.

Continued on page 94.

Flower Show

Finished Size: 48" x 63" (122 cm x 160 cm)

MATERIALS
Worsted Weight Yarn:
  Ecru - 19 ounces, 1,075 yards
    (540 grams, 983 meters)
  Lt Green - 18 ounces, 1,015 yards
    (510 grams, 928 meters)
  Green - 14¹/₂ ounces, 820 yards
    (410 grams, 750 meters)
  Pink - 7¹/₂ ounces, 425 yards
    (210 grams, 388.5 meters)
Crochet hook, size H (5 mm) **or** size needed
  for gauge
Yarn needle

GAUGE: Each Square = 6" (15.25 cm)
     In pattern, one point to point
     repeat (45 sts) = 7³/₄" (19.75 cm);
     12 rows = 4" (10 cm)
     16 sc and 18 rows = 4" (10 cm)

Gauge Swatch: 5" (12.75 cm) square
Work same as Square, page 91, through Rnd 8.

STITCH GUIDE

DOUBLE TREBLE CROCHET
  (abbreviated dtr)
YO 3 times, insert hook in sp indicated, YO and
pull up a loop (5 loops on hook), (YO and draw
through 2 loops on hook) 4 times.

DC CLUSTER
★ YO, insert hook in dc indicated, YO and pull
up a loop, YO and draw through 2 loops on
hook; repeat from ★ 2 times **more**, YO and
draw through all 4 loops on hook.

TR CLUSTER
★ YO twice, insert hook in dc indicated, YO and
pull up a loop, (YO and draw through 2 loops
on hook) twice; repeat from ★ 2 times **more**,
YO and draw through all 4 loops on hook.

DECREASE
Pull up a loop in Back Loop Only of next dc and
in next corner ch-3 sp; with **right** side of next
Square facing, pull up a loop in corner ch-3 sp
and in Back Loop Only of next dc, YO and draw
through all 5 loops on hook.

BOTTOM RIPPLE
With Ecru, ch 272.

Row 1 (Wrong side)**:** 2 Sc in second ch from hook,
sc in next 21 chs, skip next 2 chs, sc in next
21 chs, ★ 3 sc in next ch, sc in next 21 chs, skip
next 2 chs, sc in next 21 chs; repeat from ★ across
to last ch, 2 sc in last ch: 271 sc.

Note: Loop a short piece of yarn around **back** of
any stitch on Row 1 to mark **right** side.

Work in Back Loops Only throughout *(Fig. 2,
page 3)*.

Rows 2-4: Ch 1, turn; 2 sc in first sc, sc in next
21 sc, skip next 2 sc, sc in next 21 sc, ★ 3 sc in
next sc, sc in next 21 sc, skip next 2 sc, sc in next
21 sc; repeat from ★ across to last sc, 2 sc in last
sc; at end of last row, finish off.

Row 5: With **wrong** side facing, join Green with sc
in first sc *(see Joining With Sc, page 1)*; sc in
same st and in next 21 sc, skip next 2 sc, sc in next
21 sc, ★ 3 sc in next sc, sc in next 21 sc, skip next
2 sc, sc in next 21 sc; repeat from ★ across to last
sc, 2 sc in last sc.

Row 6: Repeat Row 2; finish off.

Row 7: With Ecru, repeat Row 5.

Rows 8-10: Repeat Row 2-4; at end of last row,
finish off.

Row 11: With Lt Green, repeat Row 5.

Rows 12-18: Ch 1, turn; 2 sc in first sc, sc in
next 21 sc, skip next 2 sc, sc in next 21 sc, ★ 3 sc
in next sc, sc in next 21 sc, skip next 2 sc, sc in
next 21 sc; repeat from ★ across to last sc, 2 sc in
last sc; at end of last row, finish off.

Row 19: With Ecru, repeat Row 5; finish off.

Continued on page 91.

89

SQUARE (Make 17)

Rnd 1 (Right side)**:** With Pink, ch 2, 6 sc in second ch from hook; do **not** join.

Note: Mark Rnd 1 as **right** side.

Rnd 2: Working in Back Loops Only, (3 sc in next sc, 2 sc in next sc) 3 times; join with slip st to **both** loops of first sc, place marker in joining sc for st placement: 15 sc.

Rnd 3: Ch 1, working in **front** of Rnd 2 *(Fig. 6, page 3)* and in free loops of sc on Rnd 1 *(Fig. 3a, page 3)*, (slip st, ch 6) twice in first sc and in each sc around; join with slip st to first slip st: 12 loops.

Rnd 4: Ch 1, sc in marked sc on Rnd 2, ch 3, skip next 2 sc, ★ sc in next sc, ch 3, skip next 2 sc; repeat from ★ around; join with slip st to first sc: 5 ch-3 sps.

Rnd 5: (Slip st, ch 4, 10 dtr, ch 4, slip st) in first ch-3 sp, ch 1, ★ (slip st, ch 4, 10 dtr, ch 4, slip st) in next ch-3 sp, ch 1; repeat from ★ around; join with slip st to first slip st: 5 petals.

Rnd 6: Ch 8, keeping ch **behind** petals, slip st in next ch-1 sp, (ch 8, slip st in next ch-1 sp) around; finish off: 5 ch-8 sps.

Rnd 7: With **right** side facing, join Green with dc in any ch-8 sp *(see Joining With Dc, page 3)*; 11 dc in same sp and in each ch-8 sp around; join with slip st to first dc: 56 dc.

Rnd 8: Ch 1, sc in same st, ch 3, skip next dc, work (dc Cluster, ch 3, tr Cluster, ch 3, dc Cluster) in next dc, ch 3, ★ skip next dc, (sc in next dc, ch 3, skip next dc) 6 times, work (dc Cluster, ch 3, tr Cluster, ch 3, dc Cluster) in next dc, ch 3; repeat from ★ 2 times **more**, skip next dc, (sc in next dc, ch 3, skip next dc) 5 times; join with slip st to first sc, finish off: 36 sts and 36 ch-3 sps.

Rnd 9: With **right** side facing, join Ecru with dc in any tr Cluster; (dc, ch 3, 2 dc) in same st, 2 dc in each of next 9 ch-3 sps, ★ (2 dc, ch 3, 2 dc) in next tr Cluster, 2 dc in each of next 9 ch-3 sps; repeat from ★ 2 times **more**; join with slip st to first dc, finish off: 88 dc and 4 ch-3 sps.

HALF SQUARE (Make 2)

Row 1: With Pink, ch 2, 4 sc in second ch from hook.

Row 2 (Right side)**:** Ch 1, turn; working in Back Loops Only, 3 sc in first sc, 2 sc in next sc, 3 sc in next sc, 2 sc in next sc: 10 sc.

Note: Mark Row 2 as **right** side.

Row 3: Ch 1, turn; working **behind** Row 2 and in free loops of sc on Row 1, (slip st, ch 6) 3 times in first sc, (slip st, ch 6) twice in next 2 sc, (slip st, ch 6, slip st) in last sc: 8 loops.

Row 4: Ch 1, turn; working in both loops, sc in first sc on Row 2, ch 2, skip next 2 sc, sc in next sc, ch 3, skip next 2 sc, sc in next sc, ch 2, skip next 2 sc, sc in last sc; finish off: 3 sps.

Row 5: With **right** side facing, join Pink with slip st in first ch-2 sp; (ch 4, 5 dtr, ch 4, slip st) in same sp, ch 1, (slip st, ch 4, 10 dtr, ch 4, slip st) in next ch-3 sp, ch 1, (slip st, ch 4, 5 dtr, ch 4, slip st) in last ch-2 sp: 3 petals.

Row 6: Ch 4, turn; working in **front** of petals, slip st in next ch-1 sp, ch 8, slip st in next ch-1 sp, ch 4, slip st in joining slip st; finish off: 3 sps.

Row 7: With **wrong** side facing, join Green with dc in first ch-4 sp; 9 dc in same sp, 13 dc in next ch-8 sp, 10 dc in last ch-4 sp: 33 dc.

Row 8: Ch 4, turn; skip first 2 dc, work (tr Cluster, ch 3, dc Cluster) in next dc, ch 3, skip next dc, (sc in next dc, ch 3, skip next dc) 6 times, work (dc Cluster, ch 3, tr Cluster, ch 3, dc Cluster) in next dc, ch 3, skip next dc, (sc in next dc, ch 3, skip next dc) 6 times, work (dc Cluster, ch 3, tr Cluster) in next dc, ch 4, skip next dc, slip st in last dc; finish off: 19 sts and 18 ch-3 sps.

Row 9: With **right** side facing, join Ecru with dc in first tr Cluster; dc in same st, 2 dc in each of next 9 ch-3 sps, (2 dc, ch 3, 2 dc) in next tr Cluster, 2 dc in each of next 9 ch-3 sps, 2 dc in last tr Cluster; finish off: 44 dc and one ch-3 sp.

SECOND RIPPLE

You will be joining 6 Squares on Row 1.

Row 1 (Joining row)**:** With **right** side of first Square facing and working in Back Loops Only, join Ecru with sc in first dc; sc in next 21 dc, 3 sc in next corner ch-3 sp, ★ sc in next 21 dc, decrease, sc in next 21 dc, 3 sc in next corner ch-3 sp; repeat from ★ 4 times **more**, sc in next 22 dc; finish off: 277 sc.

Work in Back Loops Only throughout.

Row 2: With **wrong** side facing, join Lt Green with sc in first sc; skip next sc, sc in next 21 sc, 3 sc in next sc, sc in next 21 sc, ★ skip next 3 sts, sc in next 21 sc, 3 sc in next sc, sc in next 21 sc; repeat from ★ across to last 2 sc, skip next sc, sc in last sc: 272 sc.

Rows 3-9: Ch 1, turn; sc in first sc, skip next sc, sc in next 21 sc, 3 sc in next sc, sc in next 21 sc, ★ skip next 2 sc, sc in next 21 sc, 3 sc in next sc, sc in next 21 sc; repeat from ★ across to last 2 sc, skip next sc, sc in last sc; at end of last row, finish off.

Row 10: With **wrong** side facing, join Ecru with sc in first sc; skip next sc, sc in next 21 sc, 3 sc in next sc, sc in next 21 sc, ★ skip next 2 sc, sc in next 21 sc, 3 sc in next sc, sc in next 21 sc; repeat from ★ across to last 2 sc, skip next sc, sc in last sc.

Rows 11-13: Ch 1, turn; sc in first sc, skip next sc, sc in next 21 sc, 3 sc in next sc, sc in next 21 sc, ★ skip next 2 sc, sc in next 21 sc, 3 sc in next sc, sc in next 21 sc; repeat from ★ across to last 2 sc, skip next sc, sc in last sc; at end of last row, finish off.

Rows 14 and 15: With Green, repeat Rows 10 and 11; at end of last row, finish off.

Rows 16-19: Repeat Rows 10-13.

Row 20: With **wrong** side facing, join Lt Green with sc in first sc; skip next sc, sc in next 21 sc, 3 sc in next sc, sc in next 21 sc, ★ skip next 2 sc, sc in next 21 sc, 3 sc in next sc, sc in next 21 sc; repeat from ★ across to last 2 sc, skip next sc, sc in last sc.

Rows 21-46: Repeat Rows 3-20 once, then repeat Rows 3-10 once **more**.

Finish off.

With **right** sides facing and Ecru, whipstitch unworked edge of Squares to Row 19 of Bottom Ripple through **inside** loops *(Fig. 7b, page 4)*.

THIRD RIPPLE

You will be joining 5 Squares and 2 Half Squares on Row 1.

Row 1 (Joining row)**:** With **right** side of first Half Square facing, and working in Back Loops Only, join Ecru with sc in first dc on Row 6; sc in same st and in next 21 dc, pull up a loop in next ch-3 sp; with **right** side of next Square facing, pull up a loop in corner ch-3 sp and in next dc, YO and draw through all 4 loops on hook, sc in next 21 dc, 3 sc in next corner ch-3 sp, sc in next 21 dc, ★ decrease, sc in next 21 dc, 3 sc in next corner ch-3 sp, sc in next 21 dc; repeat from ★ 3 times **more**, pull up a loop in next dc and in next ch-3 sp; with **right** side of last Half Square facing, pull up a loop in ch-3 sp, YO and draw through all 4 loops on hook, sc in next 21 dc, 2 sc in last dc; finish off: 277 sc.

Work in Back Loops Only throughout.

Row 2: With **wrong** side facing, join Lt Green with sc in first sc; sc in same st and in next 21 sc, skip next 3 sts, ★ sc in next 21 sc, 3 sc in next sc, sc in next 21 sc, skip next 3 sts; repeat from ★ 4 times **more**, sc in next 21 sc, 2 sc in last sc: 271 sc.

Rows 3-9: Ch 1, turn; 2 sc in first sc, sc in next 21 sc, skip next 2 sc, sc in next 21 sc, ★ 3 sc in next sc, sc in next 21 sc, skip next 2 sc, sc in next 21 sc; repeat from ★ across to last sc, 2 sc in last sc; at end of last row, finish off.

Row 10: With **wrong** side facing, join Ecru with sc in first sc; sc in same st and in next 21 sc, skip next 2 sc, sc in next 21 sc, ★ 3 sc in next sc, sc in next 21 sc, skip next 2 sc, sc in next 21 sc; repeat from ★ across to last sc, 2 sc in last sc.

Rows 11-13: Ch 1, turn; 2 sc in first sc, sc in next 21 sc, skip next 2 sc, sc in next 21 sc, ★ 3 sc in next sc, sc in next 21 sc, skip next 2 sc, sc in next 21 sc; repeat from ★ across to last sc, 2 sc in last sc; at end of last row, finish off.

Rows 14 and 15: With Green, repeat Rows 10 and 11; at end of last row, finish off.

Rows 16-19: Repeat Rows 10-13.

Row 20: With **wrong** side facing, join Lt Green with sc in first sc; sc in same st and in next 21 sc, skip next 2 sc, sc in next 21 sc, ★ 3 sc in next sc, sc in next 21 sc, skip next 2 sc, sc in next 21 sc; repeat from ★ across to last sc, 2 sc in last sc.

Rows 21-46: Repeat Rows 3-20 once, then repeat Rows 3-10 once **more**.

Finish off.

With **right** sides facing and Ecru, whipstitch unworked edge of Squares to Row 46 of Second Ripple through **inside** loops only.

TOP RIPPLE

You will be joining 6 remaining Squares on Row 1.

Row 1 (Joining row)**:** With **right** side of first Square facing and working in Back Loops Only, join Ecru with sc in first dc; sc in next 21 dc, 3 sc in next corner ch-3 sp, ★ sc in next 21 dc, decrease, sc in next 21 dc, 3 sc in next corner ch-3 sp; repeat from ★ 4 times **more**, sc in next 22 dc; finish off: 277 sc.

Continued on page 93.

Row 2: With **wrong** side facing, join Lt Green with sc in first sc; skip next sc, sc in next 21 sc, 3 sc in next sc, sc in next 21 sc, ★ skip next 3 sts, sc in next 21 sc, 3 sc in next sc, sc in next 21 sc; repeat from ★ across to last 2 sc, skip next sc, sc in last sc: 272 sc.

Rows 3-9: Ch 1, turn; sc in first sc, skip next sc, sc in next 21 sc, 3 sc in next sc, sc in next 21 sc, ★ skip next 2 sc, sc in next 21 sc, 3 sc in next sc, sc in next 21 sc; repeat from ★ across to last 2 sc, skip next sc, sc in last sc; at end of last row, finish off.

Row 10: With **wrong** side facing, join Ecru with sc in first sc; skip next sc, sc in next 21 sc, 3 sc in next sc, sc in next 21 sc, ★ skip next 2 sc, sc in next 21 sc, 3 sc in next sc, sc in next 21 sc; repeat from ★ across to last 2 sc, skip next sc, sc in last sc.

Rows 11-13: Ch 1, turn; sc in first sc, skip next sc, sc in next 21 sc, 3 sc in next sc, sc in next 21 sc, ★ skip next 2 sc, sc in next 21 sc, 3 sc in next sc, sc in next 21 sc; repeat from ★ across to last 2 sc, skip next sc, sc in last sc; at end of last row, finish off.

Rows 14 and 15: With Green, repeat Rows 10 and 11; at end of last row, finish off.

Rows 16-19: Repeat Rows 10-13.

With **right** sides facing and Ecru, whipstitch unworked edge of Squares to Row 46 of Third Ripple through **inside** loops only.

EDGING
Rnd 1: With **right** side facing and working through **both** loops, join Green with sc in first sc on Row 19 of Top Ripple; sc in same st, skip next sc, sc in next 21 sc, 3 sc in next sc, sc in next 21 sc, ★ skip next 2 sc, sc in next 21 sc, 3 sc in next sc, sc in next 21 sc; repeat from ★ across to last 2 sc, skip next sc, 3 sc in last sc; † working in end of rows, sc in next 19 rows, sc in next corner sp of Square, sc in next 46 rows, work 24 sc evenly spaced across Half Square, sc in next 46 rows, sc in next corner sp of Square, sc in next 19 rows †; working in free loops *(Fig. 3b, page 3)* and in sps of beginning ch, 3 sc in ch at base of first sc, sc in next 21 chs, 3 sc in next sp, sc in next 21 chs, (skip next ch, sc in next 21 chs, 3 sc in next sp, sc in next 21 sc) across to last ch, 3 sc in last ch; repeat from † to † once, sc in same st as first sc; join with slip st to first sc: 864 sc.

Rnd 2: Ch 1, (sc, ch 3, 3 dc) in same st, skip next 2 sc, ★ (sc, ch 3, 3 dc) in next sc, skip next 2 sc; repeat from ★ around; join with slip st to first sc, finish off.

Design by Joan E. Reeves.

Vibrance
Continued from page 85.

Row 18: Ch 1, turn; 2 sc in first Loop St, ★ skip next 2 Loop Sts, sc in next 20 Loop Sts, 3 sc in next Loop St, sc in next 20 Loop Sts; repeat from ★ across to last 3 Loop Sts, skip next 2 Loop Sts, 2 sc in last Loop St; finish off.

Rows 19-23: Repeat Rows 11-15.

Row 24: With **wrong** side facing, join Blue with sc in first sc; sc in same st, ★ skip next 2 sc, sc in next 20 sc, 3 sc in next sc, sc in next 20 sc; repeat from ★ across to last 3 sc, skip next 2 sc, 2 sc in last sc.

Rows 25-33: Ch 1, turn; working in Back Loops Only, 2 sc in first sc, ★ skip next 2 sc, sc in next 20 sc, 3 sc in next sc, sc in next 20 sc; repeat from ★ across to last 3 sc, skip next 2 sc, 2 sc in last sc; at end of last row, finish off.

Row 34: With **wrong** side facing and working in both loops, join Green with sc in first sc; sc in same st, ★ skip next 2 sc, sc in next 20 sc, 3 sc in next sc, sc in next 20 sc; repeat from ★ across to last 3 sc, skip next 2 sc, 2 sc in last sc.

Rows 35-38: Ch 1, turn; 2 sc in first sc, ★ skip next 2 sc, sc in next 20 sc, 3 sc in next sc, sc in next 20 sc; repeat from ★ across to last 3 sc, skip next 2 sc, 2 sc in last sc; at end of last row, finish off.

Row 39: With **right** side facing, join Variegated with sc in first sc; sc in same st, ★ skip next 2 sc, sc in next 20 sc, 3 sc in next sc, sc in next 20 sc; repeat from ★ across to last 3 sc, skip next 2 sc, 2 sc in last sc.

Rows 40 and 41: Repeat Rows 17 and 18.

Rows 42-46: Repeat Rows 34-38.

Row 47: With **right** side facing, join Blue with sc in first sc; sc in same st, ★ skip next 2 sc, sc in next 20 sc, 3 sc in next sc, sc in next 20 sc; repeat from ★ across to last 3 sc, skip next 2 sc, 2 sc in last sc.

Rows 48-171: Repeat Rows 2-47 twice, then repeat Rows 2-33 once **more**.

Design by Joyce L. Rodriguez.

Navajo Bargello

Continued from page 87.

Row 4: Ch 12 **(first Ch Loop made)**, turn; 2 sc in each of first 2 dc, sc in next 6 sc, sc decrease, ★ sc in next 10 dc, (2 sc, ch 12, 2 sc) in next ch-2 sp **(Ch Loop made)**, sc in next 5 dc, sc decrease, (sc in next 2 dc, 2 sc in next dc) twice, sc in next 4 dc, (2 sc in next dc, sc in next 2 sc) twice, sc decrease, sc in next 5 dc, (2 sc, ch 12, 2 sc) in next ch-2 sp **(Ch Loop made)**, sc in next 10 dc, sc decrease; repeat from ★ across to last 8 dc, sc in next 6 dc, 2 sc in each of last 2 dc; finish off.

Rows 5 and 6: With Red, repeat Rows 3 and 4.

Rows 7 and 8: With Green, repeat Rows 3 and 4.

Rows 9 and 10: With Lt Green, repeat Rows 3 and 4.

Rows 11 and 12: Repeat Rows 3 and 4.

Rows 13 and 14: With Dk Green, repeat Rows 3 and 4.

Rows 15-145: Repeat Rows 3-14, 10 times; then repeat Rows 3-13 once **more**.

Row 146: Ch 1, turn; 2 sc in each of first 2 dc, sc in next 6 sc, sc decrease, ★ sc in next 10 dc, (sc, ch 2, sc) in next ch-2 sp, sc in next 5 dc, sc decrease, 2 sc in next dc, (sc in next 4 dc, 2 dc in next dc) 3 times, sc decrease, sc in next 5 dc, (sc, ch 2, sc) in next ch-2 sp, sc in next 10 dc, sc decrease; repeat from ★ across to last 8 dc, sc in next 6 dc, 2 sc in each of last 2 dc, place loop from hook onto safety pin to keep piece from unraveling while braiding Ch Loops.

Braid Ch Loops from bottom edge to top edge as follows: Beginning at outside edge, insert Ch Loop on Row 3 from **back** to **front** through Ch Loop on Row 1, (insert next Ch Loop from **back** to **front** through last Ch Loop) across; secure last Ch Loop with safety pin to Row 146 of Afghan Body. Braid remaining sections in same manner.

EDGING
TOP
Place loop from Row 146 onto hook, ch 1; working from **left** to **right** and around Ch Loop, work 2 reverse sc in first sc **(Figs. 18a-d)**, work reverse sc in each sc across and in sc decreases and ch-2 sps while working around each Ch Loop, ending with 2 reverse sc in last sc while working around last Ch Loop; finish off.

BOTTOM
With **right** side facing and working in free loops **(Fig. 3b, page 3)** and in sps across beginning ch, join Dk Green with sc in ch at base of last dc; working from **left** to **right**, work reverse sc evenly across increasing and decreasing as necessary to keep piece laying flat; finish off.

Design by Julene S. Watson.

REVERSE SINGLE CROCHET
Working from **left** to **right**, insert hook in stitch to right of hook **(Fig. 18a)**, YO and draw through, under and to left of loop on hook (2 loops on hook) **(Fig. 18b)**, YO and draw through both loops on hook **(Fig. 18c) (reverse sc made, Fig. 18d)**.

Fig. 18a

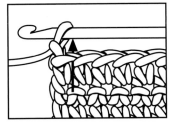

Fig. 18b

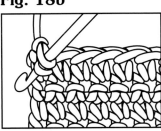

Fig. 18c

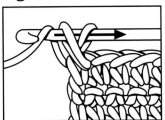

Fig. 18d

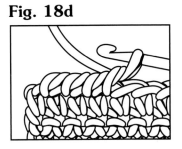

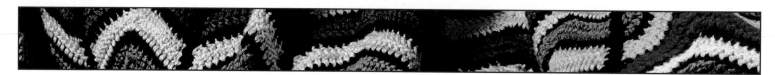

Stained Glass

Finished Size: 48" x 60^1/$_2$"
(122 cm x 153.5 cm)

MATERIALS

Worsted Weight Yarn:
Black - 23^1/$_2$ ounces, 1,370 yards
(670 grams, 1,252.5 meters)
Green - 7 ounces, 410 yards
(200 grams, 375 meters)
Lt Green - 7 ounces, 410 yards
(200 grams, 375 meters)
Purple - 7 ounces, 410 yards
(200 grams, 375 meters)
Lt Purple - 6 ounces, 350 yards
(170 grams, 320 meters)
Blue - 6 ounces, 350 yards
(170 grams, 320 meters)
Lt Blue - 6 ounces, 350 yards
(170 grams, 320 meters)
Crochet hook, size G (4 mm) **or** size needed
for gauge
Yarn needle

GAUGE: Each Panel = 6" (15.25 cm) wide
In pattern, 12 rows = 6" (15.25 cm)
Rows 1-9 = 4^3/$_4$" (12 cm)

Gauge Swatch: 5^1/$_2$"w x 4^3/$_4$"h (14 cm x 12 cm)
Work same as Panel for 9 rows.

STITCH GUIDE

SC DECREASE
Pull up a loop in next 2 sts, YO and draw
through all 3 loops on hook.

HDC DECREASE (uses next 2 dc)
★ YO, insert hook in **next** dc, YO and pull up a
loop; repeat from ★ once **more**, YO and draw
through all 3 loops on hook **(counts as
one hdc)**.

DC DECREASE (uses next 2 sts)
★ YO, insert hook in **next** st, YO and pull up a
loop, YO and draw through 2 loops on hook;
repeat from ★ once **more**, YO and draw
through all 3 loops on hook **(counts as
one dc)**.

PANEL (Make 8)

With Green, ch 24.

Row 1 (Right side)**:** Dc in third ch from hook and
in next 7 chs, dc decrease, (2 dc, ch 1, 2 dc) in next
ch, dc decrease, dc in next 7 chs, dc decrease:
22 dc and one ch-1 sp.

Note: Loop a short piece of yarn around any stitch
to mark Row 1 as **right** side and bottom edge.

Row 2: Ch 2, turn; skip first dc, dc in next 8 dc,
dc decrease, (2 dc, ch 1, 2 dc) in next ch-1 sp,
dc decrease, dc in next 7 dc, dc decrease changing
to Black *(Fig. 4a, page 3)*.

Continue to change colors in same manner.

Row 3: With Black, ch 1, turn; skip first dc, hdc in
next 8 dc, hdc decrease, (2 hdc, ch 1, 2 hdc) in next
ch-1 sp, hdc decrease, hdc in next 7 dc,
hdc decrease.

Row 4: With Lt Green, ch 2, turn; skip first hdc,
dc in next 8 hdc, dc decrease, (2 dc, ch 1, 2 dc) in
next ch-1 sp, dc decrease, dc in next 7 hdc,
dc decrease.

Row 5: Ch 2, turn; skip first dc, dc in next 8 dc,
dc decrease, (2 dc, ch 1, 2 dc) in next ch-1 sp,
dc decrease, dc in next 7 dc, dc decrease changing
to Black.

Row 6: With Black, ch 1, turn; skip first dc, hdc in
next 8 dc, hdc decrease, (2 hdc, ch 1, 2 hdc) in next
ch-1 sp, hdc decrease, hdc in next 7 dc,
hdc decrease.

Rows 7 and 8: With Purple, repeat Rows 4
and 5.

Row 9: With Black, ch 1, turn; skip first dc, hdc in
next 8 dc, hdc decrease, (2 hdc, ch 1, 2 hdc) in next
ch-1 sp, hdc decrease, hdc in next 7 dc,
hdc decrease.

Rows 10 and 11: With Lt Purple, repeat Rows 4
and 5.

Continued on page 103.

Royal Bargello

Finished Size: 43" x 68$\frac{1}{2}$" (109 cm x 174 cm)

MATERIALS
Worsted Weight Yarn:
- Purple - 10 ounces, 565 yards
  (280 grams, 516.5 meters)
- Amethyst - 8 ounces, 455 yards
  (230 grams, 416 meters)
- Dk Blue - 8 ounces, 455 yards
  (230 grams, 416 meters)
- Blue - 8 ounces, 455 yards
  (230 grams, 416 meters)
- Turquoise - 8 ounces, 455 yards
  (230 grams, 416 meters)

Crochet hook, size K (6.5 mm) **or** size needed for gauge

GAUGE: In pattern, from large point
to large point = 9$\frac{3}{4}$" (24.75 cm);
4 rows = 6" (15.25 cm)

Gauge Swatch: 13$\frac{1}{2}$"w x 6"h
(34.25 cm x 15.25 cm)
With Purple, ch 79.
Work same as Afghan for 4 rows.

STITCH GUIDE

TREBLE CROCHET *(abbreviated tr)*
YO twice, insert hook in st indicated, YO and pull up a loop (4 loops on hook), (YO and draw through 2 loops on hook) 3 times.

DOUBLE TREBLE CROCHET
(abbreviated dtr)
YO 3 times, insert hook in st indicated, YO and pull up a loop (5 loops on hook), (YO and draw through 2 loops on hook) 4 times.

SHELL
(3 Dc, tr, dtr, tr, 3 dc) in st indicated.

BEGINNING DECREASE (uses next 4 dc)
YO twice, insert hook in next dc, YO and pull up a loop, (YO and draw through 2 loops on hook) twice (2 loops on hook), ★ YO, insert hook in **next** dc, YO and pull up a loop, YO and draw through 2 loops on hook; repeat from ★ 2 times **more**, YO and draw through all 5 loops on hook.

ENDING DECREASE (uses last 5 sts)
★ YO, insert hook in **next** st, YO and pull up a loop, YO and draw through 2 loops on hook; repeat from ★ 2 times **more** (4 loops on hook), YO twice, insert hook in next st, YO and pull up a loop, (YO and draw through 2 loops on hook) twice (5 loops on hook), YO 3 times, insert hook in last st, YO and pull up a loop, (YO and draw through 2 loops on hook) 3 times, YO and draw through all 6 loops on hook.

FRONT POST DECREASE
(abbreviated FP decrease) (uses next 9 sts)
(YO, insert hook in **next** dc, YO and pull up a loop, YO and draw through 2 loops on hook) 3 times (4 loops on hook), YO twice, insert hook in next dc, YO and pull up a loop, (YO and draw through 2 loops on hook) twice, YO 4 times, insert hook from **front** to **back** around center post of next decrease *(Fig. 5, page 3)*, YO and pull up a loop, (YO and draw through 2 loops on hook) 4 times, YO twice, insert hook in next dc, YO and pull up a loop, (YO and draw through 2 loops on hook) twice (7 loops on hook), ★ YO, insert hook in **next** dc, YO and pull up a loop, YO and draw through 2 loops on hook; repeat from ★ 2 times **more**, YO and draw through all 10 loops on hook.

BACK POST DECREASE
(abbreviated BP decrease) (uses next 9 sts)
(YO, insert hook in **next** dc, YO and pull up a loop, YO and draw through 2 loops on hook) 3 times (4 loops on hook), YO twice, insert hook in next dc, YO and pull up a loop, (YO and draw through 2 loops on hook) twice, YO 4 times, insert hook from **back** to **front** around post of center leg of next decrease *(Fig. 5, page 3)*, YO and pull up a loop, (YO and draw through 2 loops on hook) 4 times, YO twice, insert hook in next dc, YO and pull up a loop, (YO and draw through 2 loops on hook) twice (7 loops on hook), ★ YO, insert hook in **next** dc, YO and pull up a loop, YO and draw through 2 loops on hook; repeat from ★ 2 times **more**, YO and draw through all 10 loops on hook.

Continued on page 104.

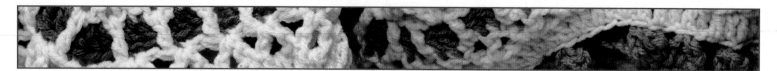

Ribbons & Lace

Finished Size: 50" x 66" (127 cm x 167.5 cm)

MATERIALS
Worsted Weight Yarn:
Ecru - 29^1/$_2$ ounces, 1,665 yards
(840 grams, 1,522.5 meters)
Purple - 3 ounces, 170 yards
(90 grams, 155.5 meters)
Dk Pink, Yellow, Pink, Blue, **and**
Green - 2^1/$_2$ ounces, 140 yards
(70 grams, 128 meters) **each** color
Crochet hook, size J (6 mm) **or** size needed
for gauge

GAUGE: In pattern, one point to point
repeat (32 sts) = 10" (25.5 cm)
Rows 1-7 = 4^1/$_2$" (11.5 cm)

Gauge Swatch: 20"w x 4^1/$_2$"h
(50.75 cm x 11.5 cm)
With Ecru, ch 67.
Work same as Afghan for 7 rows.
Finish off.

STITCH GUIDE

TREBLE CROCHET *(abbreviated tr)*
YO twice, insert hook in sp indicated, YO and
pull up a loop (4 loops on hook), (YO and draw
through 2 loops on hook) 3 times.

DECREASE *(uses next 2 sts)*
★ YO, insert hook in **next** st, YO and pull up a
loop, YO and draw through 2 loops on hook;
repeat from ★ once **more**, YO and draw
through all 3 loops on hook **(counts as
one dc)**.

V-ST
(Dc, ch 2, dc) in st indicated.

TOP PETAL
Ch 4, (2 dc, ch 3, slip st) in fourth ch from
hook.

PETAL
Ch 4, 2 dc in fourth ch from hook.

BOTTOM PETAL
Ch 4, place marker in fourth ch from hook for st
placement, YO, insert hook in fourth ch from
hook, YO and pull up a loop (3 loops on hook),
holding working yarn toward you, insert hook
from **front** to **back** in dc indicated, YO and
draw through dc and first 2 loops on hook, YO
and draw through remaining 2 loops on hook,
(dc, ch 3, slip st) in marked ch (do **not** remove
marker).

AFGHAN
With Ecru, ch 163.

Row 1 (Right side)**:** Working in back ridges of
beginning ch *(Fig. 1, page 3)*, 2 dc in fourth ch
from hook **(3 skipped chs count as first dc)**, dc
in next 12 chs, decrease, dc in next ch, decrease, dc
in next 12 chs, 2 dc in next ch, dc in next ch,
★ 2 dc in next ch, dc in next 12 chs, decrease, dc in
next ch, decrease, dc in next 12 chs, 2 dc in next
ch, dc in next ch; repeat from ★ across: 161 dc.

Note: Loop a short piece of yarn around any stitch
to mark Row 1 as **right** side.

Row 2: Ch 4 **(counts as first dc plus ch 1,
now and throughout)**, turn; dc in same st, (skip
next 2 dc, work V-St in next dc) 4 times, (skip next
3 dc, work V-St in next dc) twice, (skip next 2 dc,
work V-St in next dc) 3 times, ★ skip next 2 dc, dc
in next dc, (ch 1, dc in same st) twice, (skip next
2 dc, work V-St in next dc) 4 times, (skip next 3 dc,
work V-St in next dc) twice, (skip next 2 dc, work
V-St in next dc) 3 times; repeat from ★ across to
last 3 dc, skip next 2 dc, (dc, ch 1, dc) in last dc:
106 dc and 55 sps.

Row 3: Ch 3 **(counts as first dc, now and
throughout)**, turn; ★ 2 dc in next ch-1 sp, (dc in
next 2 dc and in next ch-2 sp) 4 times, decrease, dc
in next ch-2 sp, decrease, (dc in next ch-2 sp and in
next 2 dc) 4 times, 2 dc in next ch-1 sp, dc in next
dc; repeat from ★ across: 161 dc.

Continued on page 101.

Row 4: Ch 4, turn; dc in same st, (skip next 2 dc, work V-St in next dc) 4 times, (skip next 3 dc, work V-St in next dc) twice, (skip next 2 dc, work V-St in next dc) 3 times, ★ skip next 2 dc, dc in next dc, (ch 1, dc in same st) twice, (skip next 2 dc, work V-St in next dc) 4 times, (skip next 3 dc, work V-St in next dc) twice, (skip next 2 dc, work V-St in next dc) 3 times; repeat from ★ across to last 3 dc, skip next 2 dc, (dc, ch 1, dc) in last dc; finish off: 106 dc and 55 sps.

Row 5: With **right** side facing, join Purple with dc in first dc *(see Joining With Dc, page 3)*; dc in same st, ch 1, (skip next sp, dc in next 2 dc, ch 1) 4 times, (skip next ch-2 sp, decrease, ch 1) twice, (skip next ch-2 sp, dc in next 2 dc, ch 1) 4 times, ★ skip next ch-1 sp, 3 dc in next dc, ch 1, (skip next sp, dc in next 2 dc, ch 1) 4 times, (skip next ch-2 sp, decrease, ch 1) twice, (skip next ch-2 sp, dc in next 2 dc, ch 1) 4 times; repeat from ★ across to last ch-1 sp, skip last ch-1 sp, 2 dc in last dc; finish off.

Row 6: With **right** side facing and working in Back Loops Only *(Fig. 2, page 3)*, join Ecru with slip st in first dc; slip st in next dc, working in **front** of next ch *(Fig. 6, page 3)*, tr in ch-1 sp one row **below**, (slip st in next 2 dc, working in **front** of next ch, tr in ch-2 sp one row **below**) 4 times, (slip st in next dc, working in **front** of next ch, tr in ch-2 sp one row **below**) twice, (slip st in next 2 dc, working in **front** of next ch, tr in sp one row **below**) 4 times, ★ slip st in next 3 dc, working in **front** of next ch, tr in ch-1 sp one row **below**, (slip st in next 2 dc, working in **front** of next ch, tr in ch-2 sp one row **below**) 4 times, (slip st in next dc, working in **front** of next ch, tr in ch-2 sp one row **below**) twice, (slip st in next 2 dc, working in **front** of next ch, tr in sp one row **below**) 4 times; repeat from ★ across to last 2 dc, slip st in last 2 dc: 161 sts.

Row 7: Ch 4, turn; working in both loops, dc in same st, (skip next 2 sts, work V-St in next slip st) 4 times, (skip next 3 sts, work V-St in next st) twice, (skip next 2 sts, work V-St in next slip st) 3 times, ★ skip next 2 sts, dc in next slip st, (ch 1, dc in same st) twice, (skip next 2 sts, work V-St in next slip st) 4 times, (skip next 3 sts, work V-St in next st) twice, (skip next 2 sts, work V-St in next slip st) 3 times; repeat from ★ across to last 3 sts, skip next 2 sts, (dc, ch 1, dc) in last slip st: 106 dc and 55 sps.

Row 8: Ch 3, turn; ★ 2 dc in next ch-1 sp, (dc in next 2 dc and in next ch-2 sp) 4 times, decrease, dc in next ch-2 sp, decrease, (dc in next ch-2 sp and in next 2 dc) 4 times, 2 dc in next ch-1 sp, dc in next dc; repeat from ★ across; finish off: 161 dc.

Row 9: With Purple, work Top Petal; with **right** side of previous row facing and working from **left** to **right**, skip first 2 dc, work Bottom Petal in next dc, work 2 Petals, ★ (skip next 6 dc on previous row, work Bottom Petal in next dc, work 2 Petals) 4 times, skip next 3 dc on previous row, work Bottom Petal in next dc, work 2 Petals; repeat from ★ 3 times **more**, skip next 6 dc on previous row, work Bottom Petal in next dc, (work 2 Petals, skip next 6 dc on previous row, work Bottom Petal in next dc) 3 times, leave remaining 2 dc on previous row unworked: 74 Petals.

Row 10: Work 3 Top Petals place marker around second Top Petal worked for st placement; with **right** side facing, slip st in marked ch on first Bottom Petal, remove marker, ★ (ch 3, slip st in ch at base of next Petal) twice, work 2 Top Petals, slip st in marked ch on next Bottom Petal, remove marker; repeat from ★ across; finish off: 51 Petals.

When instructed to slip st around dc on Top Petal, insert hook from **back** to **front** around post of dc indicated *(Fig. 5, page 3)*, YO and **loosely** draw yarn around dc and through loop on hook.

Row 11: With **right** side facing, join Ecru with slip st in first dc on last Ecru row, ch 3; working around dc of Top Petals only, slip st around second dc on marked Petal, ch 6, place marker in third ch from hook for st placement, slip st around second dc on next Petal, ch 2, slip st around first dc on next Petal, ch 2, slip st around second dc on next Petal, ch 2, slip st around first dc on next Petal, ch 1, slip st around second dc on next Petal, ch 3, slip st around first dc on next Petal, ch 1, slip st around second dc on next Petal, ch 2, slip st around first dc on next Petal, ch 2, slip st around second dc on next Petal, ch 2, slip st around first dc on next Petal, ★ ch 5, slip st around second dc on next Petal, ch 2, slip st around first dc on next Petal, ch 2, slip st around second dc on next Petal, ch 2, slip st around first dc on next Petal, ch 1, slip st around second dc on next Petal, ch 3, slip st around first dc on next Petal, ch 1, slip st around second dc on next Petal, ch 2, slip st around first dc on next Petal, ch 2, slip st around second dc on next Petal, ch 2, slip st around first dc on next Petal; repeat from ★ across to last Petal, ch 2, YO 4 times, insert hook in last dc on last Ecru row, YO and pull up a loop, (YO and draw through 2 loops on hook) twice (4 loops remain on hook), insert hook from **front** to **back** around post of first dc on last Petal, YO and draw yarn around dc and through 2 loops on hook (3 loops remain on hook), (YO and draw through 2 loops on hook) twice; finish off: 161 sts.

Row 12: With **right** side facing, join Ecru with dc in marked ch; 2 dc in next ch, dc in next 12 sts, decrease, dc in next ch, decrease, dc in next 12 sts, 2 dc in next ch, ★ dc in next ch, 2 dc in next ch, dc in next 12 sts, decrease, dc in next ch, decrease, dc in next 12 sts, 2 dc in next ch; repeat from ★ across to last st, dc in last st: 161 dc.

Row 13: Ch 4, turn; dc in same st, (skip next 2 dc, work V-St in next dc) 4 times, (skip next 3 dc, work V-St in next dc) twice, (skip next 2 dc, work V-St in next dc) 3 times, ★ skip next 2 dc, dc in next dc, (ch 1, dc in same st) twice, (skip next 2 dc, work V-St in next dc) 4 times, (skip next 3 dc, work V-St in next dc) twice, (skip next 2 dc, work V-St in next dc) 3 times; repeat from ★ across to last 3 dc, skip next 2 dc, (dc, ch 1, dc) in last dc; finish off: 106 dc and 55 sps.

Row 14: With **right** side facing, join Purple with dc in first dc; dc in same st, ch 1, (skip next sp, dc in next 2 dc, ch 1) 4 times, (skip next ch-2 sp, decrease, ch 1) twice, (skip next ch-2 sp, dc in next 2 dc, ch 1) 4 times, ★ skip next ch-1 sp, 3 dc in next dc, ch 1, (skip next sp, dc in next 2 dc, ch 1) 4 times, (skip next ch-2 sp, decrease, ch 1) twice, (skip next ch-2 sp, dc in next 2 dc, ch 1) 4 times; repeat from ★ across to last ch-1 sp, skip last ch-1 sp, 2 dc in last dc; finish off.

Row 15: With **right** side facing and working in Back Loops Only, join Ecru with slip st in first dc; slip st in next dc, working in **front** of next ch, tr in ch-1 sp one row **below**, (slip st in next 2 dc, working in **front** of next ch, tr in ch-2 sp one row **below**) 4 times, (slip st in next dc, working in **front** of next ch, tr in ch-2 sp one row **below**) twice, (slip st in next 2 dc, working in **front** of next ch, tr in sp one row **below**) 4 times, ★ slip st in next 3 dc, working in **front** of next ch, tr in ch-1 sp one row **below**, (slip st in next 2 dc, working in **front** of next ch, tr in ch-2 sp one row **below**) 4 times, (slip st in next dc, working in **front** of next ch, tr in ch-2 sp one row **below**) twice, (slip st in next 2 dc, working in **front** of next ch, tr in sp one row **below**) 4 times; repeat from ★ across to last 2 dc, slip st in last 2 dc: 161 sts.

Row 16: Ch 4, turn; working in both loops, dc in same st, (skip next 2 sts, work V-St in next slip st) 4 times, (skip next 3 sts, work V-St in next st) twice, (skip next 2 sts, work V-St in next slip st) 3 times, ★ skip next 2 sts, dc in next slip st, (ch 1, dc in same st) twice, (skip next 2 sts, work V-St in next slip st) 4 times, (skip next 3 sts, work V-St in next st) twice, (skip next 2 sts, work V-St in next slip st) 3 times; repeat from ★ across to last 3 sts, skip next 2 sts, (dc, ch 1, dc) in last slip st: 106 dc and 55 sps.

Row 17: Ch 3, turn; ★ 2 dc in next ch-1 sp, (dc in next 2 dc and in next ch-2 sp) 4 times, decrease, dc in next ch-2 sp, decrease, (dc in next ch-2 sp and in next 2 dc) 4 times, 2 dc in next ch-1 sp, dc in next dc; repeat from ★ across: 161 dc.

Rows 18-20: Repeat Rows 2-4: 106 dc and 55 sps.

Row 21: With Dk Pink, repeat Row 5.

Rows 22-24: Repeat Rows 6-8: 161 dc.

Rows 25 and 26: With Dk Pink, repeat Rows 9 and 10: 51 Petals.

Rows 27-29: Repeat Rows 11-13: 106 dc and 55 sps.

Row 30: With Dk Pink, repeat Row 14.

Rows 31-33: Repeat Rows 15-17: 161 dc.

Rows 34-36: Repeat Rows 2-4: 106 dc and 55 sps.

Row 37: With Yellow, repeat Row 5.

Rows 38-40: Repeat Rows 6-8: 161 dc.

Rows 41 and 42: With Yellow, repeat Rows 9 and 10: 51 Petals.

Rows 43-45: Repeat Rows 11-13: 106 dc and 55 sps.

Row 46: With Yellow, repeat Row 14.

Rows 47-49: Repeat Rows 15-17: 161 dc.

Rows 50-52: Repeat Rows 2-4: 106 dc and 55 sps.

Row 53: With Pink, repeat Row 5.

Rows 54-56: Repeat Rows 6-8: 161 dc.

Rows 57 and 58: With Pink, repeat Rows 9 and 10: 51 Petals.

Rows 59-61: Repeat Rows 11-13: 106 dc and 55 sps.

Row 62: With Pink, repeat Row 14.

Rows 63-65: Repeat Rows 15-17: 161 dc.

Rows 66-68: Repeat Rows 2-4: 106 dc and 55 sps.

Row 69: With Blue, repeat Row 5.

Rows 70-72: Repeat Rows 6-8: 161 dc.

Rows 73 and 74: With Blue, repeat Rows 9 and 10: 51 Petals.

Rows 75-77: Repeat Rows 11-13: 106 dc and 55 sps.

Row 78: With Blue, repeat Row 14.

Continued on page 103.

Rows 79-81: Repeat Rows 15-17: 161 dc.

Rows 82-84: Repeat Rows 2-4: 106 dc and 55 sps.

Row 85: With Green, repeat Row 5.

Rows 86-88: Repeat Rows 6-8: 161 dc.

Rows 89 and 90: With Green, repeat Rows 9 and 10: 51 Petals.

Rows 91-93: Repeat Rows 11-13: 106 dc and 55 sps.

Row 94: With Green, repeat Row 14.

Rows 95-97: Repeat Rows 15-17: 161 dc.

Rows 98-115: Repeat Rows 2-17 once, then repeat Rows 2 and 3 once **more**.

Finish off.

Design by Rena V. Stevens.

Stained Glass
Continued from page 95.

Row 12: With Black, ch 1, turn; skip first dc, hdc in next 8 dc, hdc decrease, (2 hdc, ch 1, 2 hdc) in next ch-1 sp, hdc decrease, hdc in next 7 dc, hdc decrease.

Rows 13 and 14: With Blue, repeat Rows 4 and 5.

Row 15: With Black, ch 1, turn; skip first dc, hdc in next 8 dc, hdc decrease, (2 hdc, ch 1, 2 hdc) in next ch-1 sp, hdc decrease, hdc in next 7 dc, hdc decrease.

Rows 16 and 17: With Lt Blue, repeat Rows 4 and 5.

Row 18: With Black, ch 1, turn; skip first dc, hdc in next 8 dc, hdc decrease, (2 hdc, ch 1, 2 hdc) in next ch-1 sp, hdc decrease, hdc in next 7 dc, hdc decrease.

Rows 19 and 20: With Green, repeat Rows 4 and 5.

Rows 21-116: Repeat Rows 3-20, 5 times; then repeat Rows 3-8 once **more**; do **not** finish off.

BORDER
With Black, ch 1, turn; 3 sc in first dc, sc in next 8 dc, sc decrease, 3 sc in next ch-1 sp, sc decrease, sc in next 8 dc, 3 sc in last dc; working in end of rows, 2 sc in each of first 2 rows, (sc in next row, 2 sc in each of next 2 rows) across; working in free loops of beginning ch *(Fig. 3b, page 3)*, 3 sc in first ch, sc in next 10 chs, skip next ch, sc in next 10 chs, 3 sc in next ch; working in end of rows, 2 sc in each of first 2 rows, (sc in next row, 2 sc in each of next 2 rows) across; join with slip st to first sc, finish off: 441 sc.

ASSEMBLY
Having bottom edges at same end and working through **both** loops, whipstitch long edge of Panels together with Black *(Fig. 7a, page 4)*, beginning in center sc of first corner 3-sc group and ending in center sc of next corner 3-sc group.

EDGING
With **right** side facing and working across top edge, join Black with sc in center sc of 3-sc group in first corner; 2 sc in same st, sc in next 9 sc, sc decrease, 3 sc in next sc, sc decrease, sc in next 9 sc, ★ pull up a loop in same st as joining on same Panel **and** in same st as joining on next Panel, YO and draw through all 3 loops on hook, sc in next 9 sc, sc decrease, 3 sc in next sc, sc decrease, sc in next 9 sc; repeat from ★ across to center sc of next corner 3-sc group, 3 sc in center sc; sc in each sc across to center sc of next corner 3-sc group, 3 sc in center sc, sc in next 9 sc, sc decrease twice, sc in next 9 sc, (3 sc in next joining, sc in next 9 sc, sc decrease twice, sc in next 9 sc) across to center sc of next corner 3-sc group, 3 sc in center sc; sc in each sc across; join with slip st to first sc, finish off.

Design by Sandra Tolene.

103

AFGHAN

With Purple, ch 247.

Row 1: YO twice, insert hook in sixth ch from hook, YO and pull up a loop, (YO and draw through 2 loops on hook) twice, (YO, insert hook in **next** ch, YO and pull up a loop, YO and draw through 2 loops on hook) 3 times, YO and draw through all 5 loops on hook **(beginning decrease made)**, dc in next 3 chs, skip next ch, work Shell in next ch, skip next ch, dc in next 3 chs, ★ † [(YO, insert hook in **next** ch, YO and pull up a loop, YO and draw through 2 loops on hook) 3 times (4 loops on hook), YO twice, insert hook in next ch, YO and pull up a loop, (YO and draw through 2 loops on hook) twice, YO 3 times, insert hook in next ch, YO and pull up a loop, (YO and draw through 2 loops on hook) 3 times, YO twice, insert hook in next ch, YO and pull up a loop, (YO and draw through 2 loops on hook) twice (7 loops on hook), (YO, insert hook in **next** ch, YO and pull up a loop, YO and draw through 2 loops on hook) 3 times, YO and draw through all 10 loops on hook **(decrease made)]** †, dc in next 13 chs, skip next ch, work Shell in next ch, skip next ch, dc in next 13 chs, repeat from † to † once, dc in next 3 chs, skip next ch, work Shell in next ch, skip next ch, dc in next 3 chs; repeat from ★ across to last 5 chs, work ending decrease: 225 sts.

Row 2 (Right side)**:** Ch 5, turn; skip first st, work beginning decrease, dc in next 3 sts, work Shell in Back Loop Only of next dtr *(Fig. 2, page 3)*, dc in **both** loops of next 3 sts, ★ work FP decrease, dc in next 13 sts, work Shell in Back Loop Only of next dtr, dc in **both** loops of next 13 sts, work FP decrease, dc in next 3 sts, work Shell in Back Loop Only of next dtr, dc in **both** loops of next 3 sts; repeat from ★ across to last 5 sts, work ending decrease; finish off.

Note: Loop a short piece of yarn around any stitch to mark Row 2 as **right** side.

Row 3: With **wrong** side facing, join Amethyst with slip st in first st; ch 5, work beginning decrease, dc in next 3 sts, work Shell in Back Loop Only of next dtr, dc in **both** loops of next 3 sts, ★ work BP decrease, dc in next 13 sts, work Shell in Back Loop Only of next dtr, dc in **both** loops of next 13 sts, work BP decrease, dc in next 3 sts, work Shell in Back Loop Only of next dtr, dc in **both** loops of next 3 sts; repeat from ★ across to last 5 sts, work ending decrease.

Row 4: Ch 5, turn; skip first st, work beginning decrease, dc in next 3 sts, work Shell in Back Loop Only of next dtr, dc in **both** loops of next 3 sts, ★ work FP decrease, dc in next 13 sts, work Shell in Back Loop Only of next dtr, dc in **both** loops of next 13 sts, work FP decrease, dc in next 3 sts, work Shell in Back Loop Only of next dtr, dc in **both** loops of next 3 sts; repeat from ★ across to last 5 sts, work ending decrease; finish off.

Rows 5 and 6: With Dk Blue, repeat Rows 3 and 4.

Rows 7 and 8: With Blue, repeat Rows 3 and 4.

Rows 9 and 10: With Turquoise, repeat Rows 3 and 4.

Rows 11 and 12: With Purple, repeat Rows 3 and 4.

Rows 13-42: Repeat Rows 3-12, 3 times.

Design by Rena V. Stevens.

Baby Love

Finished Size: 35" x 46½" (89 cm x 118 cm)

MATERIALS
Worsted Weight Yarn:
    White - 11½ ounces, 650 yards
      (330 grams, 594.5 meters)
    Yellow - 4 ounces, 225 yards
      (110 grams, 205.5 meters)
    Pink - 3½ ounces, 200 yards
      (100 grams, 183 meters)
    Green - 3½ ounces, 200 yards
      (100 grams, 183 meters)
    Variegated - 3½ ounces, 200 yards
      (100 grams, 183 meters)
    Teal - 3½ ounces, 200 yards
      (100 grams, 183 meters)
  Crochet hook, size J (6 mm) **or** size needed
    for gauge

GAUGE: In pattern, one point to point
        repeat (12 sts) = 3½" (9 cm);
        8 rows = 4½" (11.5 cm)

Gauge Swatch: 7"w x 4½"h
                 (17.75 cm x 11.5 cm)
With Yellow, ch 27.
Work same as Afghan for 8 rows.

STITCH GUIDE

> **SC DECREASE** (uses next 2 dc)
> Pull up a loop in next 2 dc, YO and draw
> through all 3 loops on hook.
>
> **DC DECREASE** (uses next 2 sts)
> ★ YO, insert hook in **next** st, YO and pull up a
> loop, YO and draw through 2 loops on hook;
> repeat from ★ once **more**, YO and draw
> through all 3 loops on hook **(counts as
> one dc)**.

AFGHAN
With Yellow, ch 123.

Row 1 (Right side)**:** Dc in fourth ch from hook
(3 skipped chs count as first dc) and in next
3 chs, dc decrease twice, dc in next 3 chs, ★ 2 dc in
each of next 2 chs, dc in next 3 chs, dc decrease
twice, dc in next 3 chs; repeat from ★ across to last
ch, 2 dc in last ch; finish off: 120 sts.

Note: Loop a short piece of yarn around any stitch
to mark Row 1 as **right** side.

Work in Back Loops Only throughout **(Fig. 2,
page 3)**.

Row 2: With **wrong** side facing, join White with sc
in first dc **(see Joining With Sc, page 1)**; sc in
same st and in next 3 dc, sc decrease twice, sc in
next 3 dc, ★ 2 sc in each of next 2 dc, sc in next
3 dc, sc decrease twice, sc in next 3 dc; repeat from
★ across to last dc, 2 sc in last dc; finish off.

Row 3: With **right** side facing, join Pink with dc in
first sc **(see Joining With Dc, page 3)**; dc in same
st and in next 3 sc, dc decrease twice, dc in next
3 sc, ★ 2 dc in each of next 2 sc, dc in next 3 sc,
dc decrease twice, dc in next 3 sc; repeat from ★
across to last sc, 2 dc in last sc; finish off.

Row 4: Repeat Row 2.

Row 5: With Green, repeat Row 3.

Row 6: Repeat Row 2.

Row 7: With Variegated, repeat Row 3.

Row 8: Repeat Row 2.

Row 9: With Teal, repeat Row 3.

Row 10: Repeat Row 2.

Row 11: With Yellow, repeat Row 3.

Rows 12-81: Repeat Rows 2-11, 7 times.

Holding 2 strands of White together, each 17"
(43 cm) long, add fringe in each st across short
edges of Afghan **(Figs. 8a & b, page 4)**.

Design by Tina Prystup.

Mountain Flowers

Finished Size: 42" x 64" (106.5 cm x 162.5 cm)

MATERIALS

Worsted Weight Yarn:
 Lt Green - 9 ounces, 510 yards
  (260 grams, 466.5 meters)
 Green - 9 ounces, 510 yards
  (260 grams, 466.5 meters)
 Dk Green - 9 ounces, 510 yards
  (260 grams, 466.5 meters)
 Ecru - 7 ounces, 395 yards
  (200 grams, 361 meters)
Crochet hook, size J (6 mm) **or** size needed
 for gauge

GAUGE: In pattern, one point to point
   repeat (44 sts) = $10^1/_2$" (26.75 cm)

Gauge Swatch: 21"w x $3^1/_2$"h (53.25 cm x 9 cm)
With Lt Green, ch 90.
Work same as Afghan for 4 rows.
Finish off.

STITCH GUIDE

DECREASE (uses next 2 sts)
★ YO, insert hook in **next** st, YO and pull up a loop, YO and draw through 2 loops on hook; repeat from ★ once **more**, YO and draw through all 3 loops on hook **(counts as one dc)**.

DOUBLE DECREASE (uses next 5 sts)
★ YO, insert hook in **next** st, YO and pull up a loop, YO and draw through 2 loops on hook; repeat from ★ 4 times **more**, YO and draw through all 6 loops on hook **(counts as one dc)**.

ENDING DECREASE (uses last 3 sts)
★ YO, insert hook in **next** st, YO and pull up a loop, YO and draw through 2 loops on hook; repeat from ★ 2 times **more**, YO and draw through all 4 loops on hook **(counts as one dc)**.

TOP PETAL
Ch 4, (2 dc, ch 3, slip st) in fourth ch from hook.

PETAL
Ch 4, 2 dc in fourth ch from hook.

BOTTOM PETAL
Ch 4, place marker in fourth ch from hook for st placement, YO, insert hook in fourth ch from hook, YO and pull up a loop (3 loops on hook), holding working yarn toward you, insert hook from **front** to **back** in dc indicated, YO and draw through dc and first 2 loops on hook, YO and draw through remaining 2 loops on hook, (dc, ch 3, slip st) in marked ch (do **not** remove marker).

AFGHAN

With Lt Green, ch 178.

Row 1 (Right side)**:** Working in back ridges of beginning ch *(Fig. 1, page 3)*, [YO, insert hook in third ch from hook, YO and pull up a loop, YO and draw through 2 loops on hook, YO, insert hook in next ch, YO and pull up a loop, YO and draw through 2 loops on hook, YO and draw through all 3 loops on hook **(decrease made)]**, dc in next 19 chs, 5 dc in next ch, dc in next 19 chs, ★ double decrease, dc in next 19 chs, 5 dc in next ch, dc in next 19 chs; repeat from ★ 2 times **more**, work ending decrease: 177 dc.

Note: Loop a short piece of yarn around any stitch to mark Row 1 as **right** side.

Rows 2 and 3: Ch 2, turn; working in Back Loops Only *(Fig. 2, page 3)*, decrease, dc in next 19 dc, 5 dc in next dc, dc in next 19 dc, ★ double decrease, dc in next 19 dc, 5 dc in next dc, dc in next 19 dc; repeat from ★ 2 times **more**, work ending decrease; at end of Row 3, finish off.

Row 4: With **wrong** side facing and working in Back Loops Only, join Green with slip st in first dc; ch 2, decrease, dc in next 19 dc, 5 dc in next dc, dc in next 19 dc, ★ double decrease, dc in next 19 dc, 5 dc in next dc, dc in next 19 dc; repeat from ★ 2 times **more**, work ending decrease.

Rows 5 and 6: Repeat Rows 2 and 3.

Continued on page 113.

107

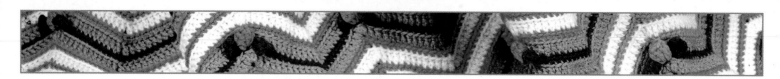

Budding Beauty

Finished Size: 47" x 58^1/$_2$"
          (119.5 cm x 148.5 cm)

MATERIALS
Worsted Weight Yarn:
  Green - 14 ounces, 790 yards
    (400 grams, 722.5 meters)
  Ecru - 13^1/$_2$ ounces, 765 yards
    (380 grams, 699.5 meters)
  Dk Green - 6 ounces, 340 yards
    (170 grams, 311 meters)
  Purple, Blue, **and** Pink -
    4^1/$_2$ ounces, 255 yards
      (130 grams, 233 meters) **each** color
Crochet hook, size G (4 mm) **or** size needed
  for gauge

GAUGE: In pattern, one point to point
          repeat (27 sts) = 5^1/$_4$" (13.25 cm);
          8 rows = 3^3/$_4$" (9.5 cm)

Gauge Swatch: 10^1/$_2$"w x 3^3/$_4$"h
              (26.75 cm x 9.5 cm)
With Green, ch 55.
Work same as Afghan for 8 rows.

STITCH GUIDE

LEAF (uses one dc)
Sc in next dc, ch 3, ★ YO, insert hook in **same**
dc, YO and pull up a loop, YO and draw
through 2 loops on hook; repeat from ★ once
more, YO and draw through all 3 loops on
hook, ch 2, slip st in top of st just made, ch 3,
slip st in same dc.

POPCORN
6 Dc in free loop of dc 2 rows **below** next dc,
drop loop from hook, insert hook in first dc of
6-dc group, hook dropped loop and draw
through, ch 1 to close.

DC DECREASE (uses next 2 sts)
★ YO, insert hook in **next** st, YO and pull up a
loop, YO and draw through 2 loops on hook;
repeat from ★ once **more**, YO and draw
through all 3 loops on hook **(counts as
one dc)**.

AFGHAN
With Green, ch 251.

Row 1 (Right side)**:** Working in back ridges of
beginning ch **(Fig. 1, page 3)**, dc in fourth ch from
hook **(3 skipped chs count as first dc)** and in
next 10 chs, 3 dc in next ch, dc in next 12 chs,
★ skip next 3 chs, dc in next 12 chs, 3 dc in next
ch, dc in next 12 chs; repeat from ★ across;
finish off: 243 dc.

Note: Loop a short piece of yarn around any stitch
to mark Row 1 as **right** side.

Work in Back Loops Only throughout **(Fig. 2,
page 3)**.

Row 2: With **right** side facing, join Dk Green with
sc in first dc **(see Joining With Sc, page 1)**; skip
next dc, sc in next 10 dc, work Leaf, 3 sc in next
dc, work Leaf, ★ sc in next 11 dc, skip next 2 dc, sc
in next 11 dc, work Leaf, 3 sc in next dc, work
Leaf; repeat from ★ across to last 12 dc, sc in next
10 dc, skip next dc, sc in last dc; finish off: 225 sc
and 18 Leaves.

Row 3: With **right** side facing and keeping Leaves
to **right** side of work, join Green with dc in first sc
(see Joining With Dc, page 3); dc decrease, dc in
next 7 sc, 2 dc in next sc, skip next Leaf, dc in next
sc, 3 dc in next sc, dc in next sc, skip next Leaf,
2 dc in next sc, ★ dc in next 9 sc, skip next 2 sc, dc
in next 9 sc, 2 dc in next sc, skip next Leaf, dc in
next sc, 3 dc in next sc, dc in next sc, skip next
Leaf, 2 dc in next sc; repeat from ★ across to last
10 sc, dc in next 7 sc, dc decrease, dc in last sc;
finish off: 243 dc.

Row 4: With **right** side facing, join Purple with sc
in first dc; skip next dc, sc in next 10 dc, 2 sc in
next dc, work Popcorn, skip dc **behind** Popcorn,
2 sc in next dc, ★ sc in next 11 dc, skip next 2 dc,
sc in next 11 dc, 2 sc in next dc, work Popcorn,
skip dc **behind** Popcorn, 2 sc in next dc; repeat
from ★ across to last 12 dc, sc in next 10 dc, skip
next dc, sc in last dc; finish off: 234 sc and
9 Popcorns.

Continued on page 114.

Fantasy Garden

Finished Size: 45¹/₂" x 64"
(115.5 cm x 162.5 cm)

MATERIALS
Worsted Weight Yarn:
 Black - 30 ounces, 1,695 yards
  (850 grams, 1,550 meters)
 Teal - 14 ounces, 790 yards
  (400 grams, 722.5 meters)
 Variegated - 14 ounces, 810 yards
  (400 grams, 740.5 meters)
Crochet hook, size I (5.5 mm) **or** size needed
 for gauge

GAUGE: In pattern, one point to point
 repeat (17 sts) = 3¹/₂" (9 cm);
 10 rows = 4" (10 cm)

Gauge Swatch: 7"w x 3"h (17.75 cm x 7.5 cm)
With Black, ch 33.
Work same as Afghan for 10 rows.
Finish off.

STITCH GUIDE

FRONT POST CLUSTER
(abbreviated FP Cluster)
★ YO 3 times, insert hook from **front** to **back**
around post of sc indicated *(Fig. 5, page 3)*,
YO and pull up a loop, (YO and draw through
2 loops on hook) 3 times; repeat from ★ 2 times
more, YO and draw through all 4 loops on
hook.

AFGHAN
With Black, ch 220.

Row 1 (Right side)**:** Working in back ridges of
beginning ch *(Fig. 1, page 3)*, sc in second ch from
hook and in next 6 chs, 3 sc in next ch, sc in next
7 chs, ★ skip next 2 chs, sc in next 7 chs, 3 sc in
next ch, sc in next 7 chs; repeat from ★ across:
221 sc.

Note: Loop a short piece of yarn around any stitch
to mark Row 1 as **right** side.

Work in Back Loops Only *(Fig. 2, page 3)*
throughout unless otherwise specified.

Rows 2-4: Ch 1, turn; sc in first sc, skip next sc,
sc in next 6 sc, 3 sc in next sc, ★ sc in next 7 sc,
skip next 2 sc, sc in next 7 sc, 3 sc in next sc;
repeat from ★ across to last 8 sc, sc in next 6 sc,
skip next sc, sc in last sc; at end of Row 4,
finish off.

Row 5: With **right** side facing, join Teal with sc in
first sc *(see Joining With Sc, page 1)*; skip next
sc, sc in next 2 sc, work FP Cluster around sc
3 rows **below** (sc **before** next 3-sc group), skip next
sc on previous row from last sc made, sc in next
3 sc, 3 sc in next sc, sc in next 3 sc, work
FP Cluster around sc 3 rows **below** (sc **after** same
3-sc group), ★ skip next sc on previous row from
last sc made, sc in next 3 sc, skip next 2 sc, sc in
next 3 sc, work FP Cluster around sc 3 rows **below**
(sc **before** next 3-sc group), skip next sc on
previous row from last sc made, sc in next 3 sc, 3 sc
in next sc, sc in next 3 sc, work FP Cluster around
sc 3 rows **below** (sc **after** same 3-sc group); repeat
from ★ across to last 5 sc on previous row, skip
next sc from last sc made, sc in next 2 sc, skip next
sc, sc in last sc.

Row 6: Ch 1, turn; sc in first sc, skip next sc, sc in
next 6 sts, 3 sc in next sc, ★ sc in next 7 sts, skip
next 2 sc, sc in next 7 sts, 3 sc in next sc; repeat
from ★ across to last 8 sts, sc in next 6 sts, skip
next sc, sc in last sc; finish off.

Row 7: With **right** side facing, join Variegated with
sc in first sc; skip next sc, sc in next 6 sc, 3 sc in
next sc, ★ sc in next 7 sc, skip next 2 sc, sc in next
7 sc, 3 sc in next sc; repeat from ★ across to last
8 sc, sc in next 6 sc, skip next sc, sc in last sc.

Row 8: Ch 1, turn; sc in first sc, skip next sc, sc in
next 6 sc, 3 sc in next sc, ★ sc in next 7 sc, skip
next 2 sc, sc in next 7 sc, 3 sc in next sc; repeat
from ★ across to last 8 sc, sc in next 6 sc, skip next
sc, sc in last sc; finish off.

Continued on page 113.

111

Row 9: With **right** side facing, join Black with sc in first sc; skip next sc, sc in next 2 sc, work FP Cluster around sc 3 rows **below** (sc **before** next 3-sc group), skip next sc on previous row from last sc made, sc in next 3 sc, 3 sc in next sc, sc in next 3 sc, work FP Cluster around sc 3 rows **below** (sc **after** same 3-sc group), ★ skip next sc on previous row from last sc made, sc in next 3 sc, skip next 2 sc, sc in next 3 sc, work FP Cluster around sc 3 rows **below** (sc **before** next 3-sc group), skip next sc on previous row from last sc made, sc in next 3 sc, 3 sc in next sc, sc in next 3 sc, work FP Cluster around sc 3 rows **below** (sc **after** same 3-sc group); repeat from ★ across to last 5 sc on previous row, skip next sc from last sc made, sc in next 2 sc, skip next sc, sc in last sc.

Rows 10-12: Ch 1, turn; sc in first sc, skip next sc, sc in next 6 sts, 3 sc in next sc, ★ sc in next 7 sts, skip next 2 sc, sc in next 7 sts, 3 sc in next sc; repeat from ★ across to last 8 sts, sc in next 6 sts, skip next sc, sc in last sc; at end of last row, finish off.

Rows 13 and 14: With Variegated, repeat Rows 5 and 6.

Rows 15 and 16: With Teal, repeat Rows 7 and 8.

Rows 17-20: With Black, repeat Rows 9-12.

Rows 21-156: Repeat Rows 5-20, 8 times; then repeat Rows 5-12 once **more**.

Design by Leigh K. Nestor.

Mountain Flowers
Continued from page 107.

Row 7: With **right** side facing and working in Back Loops Only, join Dk Green with slip st in first dc; ch 2, decrease, dc in next 19 dc, 5 dc in next dc, dc in next 19 dc, ★ double decrease, dc in next 19 dc, 5 dc in next dc, dc in next 19 dc; repeat from ★ 2 times **more**, work ending decrease.

Rows 8 and 9: Repeat Rows 2 and 3.

Row 10: With **right** side of previous row facing, working from **left** to **right** and in **both** loops, and using Ecru, work Bottom Petal in first dc; work 2 Petals, (skip next 7 dc on previous row, work Bottom Petal in next dc, work 2 Petals) twice, (skip next 5 dc on previous row, work Bottom Petal in next dc, work 2 Petals) twice, ★ (skip next 7 dc on previous row, work Bottom Petal in next dc, work 2 Petals) 4 times, (skip next 5 dc on previous row, work Bottom Petal in next dc, work 2 Petals) twice; repeat from ★ 2 times **more**, skip next 7 dc on previous row, work Bottom Petal in next dc, work 2 Petals, skip next 7 dc on previous row, work Bottom Petal in last dc: 73 Petals.

Row 11: Work Top Petal, do **not** turn; working from **right** to **left**, slip st in marked ch on first Bottom Petal, remove marker, (ch 3, slip st in ch at base of next Petal) twice, ★ work 2 Top Petals, slip st in marked ch on next Bottom Petal, remove marker, (ch 3, slip st in ch at base of next Petal) twice; repeat from ★ across to last Bottom Petal, work Top Petal, slip st in marked ch on last Bottom Petal, remove marker; finish off: 48 Petals.

When instructed to slip st around dc on Top Petal, insert hook from **back** to **front** around post of dc indicated *(Fig. 5, page 3)*, YO and **loosely** draw yarn around dc and through loop on hook.

Row 12: With **right** side facing, join Dk Green with slip st around first dc of first Top Petal; slip st around next dc, ★ † (ch 3, slip st around second dc of next Top Petal, ch 2, slip st around first dc of next Top Petal) twice, ch 5, slip st around second dc of next Top Petal, ch 1, slip st around first dc of next Top Petal, ch 5 †, slip st around second dc of next Top Petal, (ch 2, slip st around first dc of next Top Petal, ch 3, slip st around second dc of next Top Petal) twice, ch 1, slip st around first dc of next Top Petal; repeat from ★ 2 times **more**, then repeat from † to † once, (slip st around second dc of next Top Petal, ch 2, slip st around first dc of next Top Petal, ch 3) twice, slip st around first dc of last Top Petal and around next dc; finish off: 177 sts.

113

Row 13: With **right** side facing, join Dk Green with slip st in first slip st; ch 2, decrease, dc in next 19 sts, 5 dc in next ch, dc in next 19 sts, ★ double decrease, dc in next 19 sts, 5 dc in next ch, dc in next 19 sts; repeat from ★ 2 times **more**, work ending decrease.

Rows 14-18: Repeat Rows 2-6.

Rows 19-21: With Lt Green, repeat Rows 7-9.

Rows 22 and 23: Repeat Rows 10 and 11.

Rows 24 and 25: With Lt Green, repeat Rows 12 and 13.

Rows 26-69: Repeat Rows 2-25 once, then repeat Rows 2-21 once **more**.

Design by Rena V. Stevens.

Budding Beauty

Continued from page 109.

Row 5: With **right** side facing, join Ecru with dc in first sc; dc decrease, dc in next 10 sc, 3 dc in next st, ★ dc in next 12 sc, skip next 2 sc, dc in next 12 sc, 3 dc in next st; repeat from ★ across to last 13 sc, dc in next 10 sc, dc decrease, dc in last sc; finish off: 243 dc.

Row 6: With **right** side facing, join Purple with sc in first dc; skip next dc, sc in next 11 dc, 3 sc in next dc, ★ sc in next 12 dc, skip next 2 dc, sc in next 12 dc, 3 sc in next dc; repeat from ★ across to last 13 dc, sc in next 11 dc, skip next dc, sc in last dc; finish off.

Rows 7 and 8: Repeat Rows 5 and 6.

Row 9: With Green, repeat Row 5.

Rows 10 and 11: Repeat Rows 2 and 3.

Row 12: With **right** side facing, join Blue with sc in first dc; skip next dc, sc in next 10 dc, 2 sc in next dc, work Popcorn, skip dc **behind** Popcorn, 2 sc in next dc, ★ sc in next 11 dc, skip next 2 dc, sc in next 11 dc, 2 sc in next dc, work Popcorn, skip dc **behind** Popcorn, 2 sc in next dc; repeat from ★ across to last 12 dc, sc in next 10 dc, skip next dc, sc in last dc; finish off: 234 sc and 9 Popcorns.

Row 13: With **right** side facing, join Ecru with dc in first sc; dc decrease, dc in next 10 sc, 3 dc in next st, ★ dc in next 12 sc, skip next 2 sc, dc in next 12 sc, 3 dc in next st; repeat from ★ across to last 13 sc, dc in next 10 sc, dc decrease, dc in last sc; finish off: 243 dc.

Row 14: With **right** side facing, join Blue with sc in first dc; skip next dc, sc in next 11 dc, 3 sc in next dc, ★ sc in next 12 dc, skip next 2 dc, sc in next 12 dc, 3 sc in next dc; repeat from ★ across to last 13 dc, sc in next 11 dc, skip next dc, sc in last dc; finish off.

Rows 15 and 16: Repeat Rows 13 and 14.

Row 17: With Green, repeat Row 5.

Rows 18 and 19: Repeat Rows 2 and 3.

Row 20: With **right** side facing, join Pink with sc in first dc; skip next dc, sc in next 10 dc, 2 sc in next dc, work Popcorn, skip dc **behind** Popcorn, 2 sc in next dc, ★ sc in next 11 dc, skip next 2 dc, sc in next 11 dc, 2 sc in next dc, work Popcorn, skip dc **behind** Popcorn, 2 sc in next dc; repeat from ★ across to last 12 dc, sc in next 10 dc, skip next dc, sc in last dc; finish off: 234 sc and 9 Popcorns.

Row 21: With **right** side facing, join Ecru with dc in first sc; dc decrease, dc in next 10 sc, 3 dc in next st, ★ dc in next 12 sc, skip next 2 sc, dc in next 12 sc, 3 dc in next st; repeat from ★ across to last 13 sc, dc in next 10 sc, dc decrease, dc in last sc; finish off: 243 dc.

Row 22: With **right** side facing, join Pink with sc in first dc; skip next dc, sc in next 11 dc, 3 sc in next dc, ★ sc in next 12 dc, skip next 2 dc, sc in next 12 dc, 3 sc in next dc; repeat from ★ across to last 13 dc, sc in next 11 dc, skip next dc, sc in last dc; finish off.

Rows 23 and 24: Repeat Rows 21 and 22.

Row 25: With Green, repeat Row 5.

Rows 26-121: Repeat Rows 2-25, 4 times.

Row 122: With **right** side facing, join Dk Green with sc in first dc; skip next dc, sc in next 11 dc, 3 sc in next dc, ★ sc in next 12 dc, skip next 2 dc, sc in next 12 dc, 3 sc in next dc; repeat from ★ across to last 13 dc, sc in next 11 dc, skip next dc, sc in last dc; finish off.

Row 123: With Green, repeat Row 5.

Design by Pat Gibbons.

Refreshing Ripple

Finished Size: 45" x 62¹/₂" (114.5 cm x 159 cm)

MATERIALS
Worsted Weight Yarn:
  White - 18 ounces, 1,020 yards
    (510 grams, 932.5 meters)
  Teal - 10¹/₂ ounces, 595 yards
    (300 grams, 544 meters)
  Lt Teal - 5¹/₄ ounces, 295 yards
    (150 grams, 269.5 meters)
Crochet hook, size I (5.5 mm) **or** size needed
  for gauge

GAUGE: In pattern, one point to point
      repeat (11 sts) = 2¹/₄" (5.75 cm);
      9 rows = 3" (7.5 cm)

Gauge Swatch: 4¹/₂"w x 3¹/₄"h
                (11.5 cm x 8.25 cm)
With White, ch 24.
Work same as Afghan through Row 9.

AFGHAN
With White, ch 222.

Row 1 (Right side)**:** Working in back ridges of
beginning ch *(Fig. 1, page 3)*, 2 sc in second ch
from hook, (ch 1, skip next ch, sc in next ch) twice,
skip next 2 chs, (sc in next ch, ch 1, skip next ch)
twice, ★ 3 sc in next ch, (ch 1, skip next ch, sc in
next ch) twice, skip next 2 chs, (sc in next ch, ch 1,
skip next ch) twice; repeat from ★ across to last sc,
2 sc in last sc: 141 sc and 80 ch-1 sps.

Note: Loop a short piece of yarn around any stitch
to mark Row 1 as **right** side.

Rows 2-9: Ch 1, turn; 2 sc in first sc, ch 1, sc in
next ch-1 sp, ch 1, sc in next 2 ch-1 sps, ch 1, sc in
next ch-1 sp, ch 1, ★ skip next sc, 3 sc in next sc,
ch 1, sc in next ch-1 sp, ch 1, sc in next 2 ch-1 sps,
ch 1, sc in next ch-1 sp, ch 1; repeat from ★ across
to last 2 sc, skip next sc, 2 sc in last sc; at end of
last row, finish off.

Row 10: With **wrong** side facing, join Teal with sc
in first sc *(see Joining With Sc, page 1)*; sc in
same st, ch 1, sc in next ch-1 sp, ch 1, sc in next
2 ch-1 sps, ch 1, sc in next ch-1 sp, ch 1, ★ skip
next sc, 3 sc in next sc, ch 1, sc in next ch-1 sp,
ch 1, sc in next 2 ch-1 sps, ch 1, sc in next ch-1 sp,
ch 1; repeat from ★ across to last 2 sc, skip next sc,
2 sc in last sc; finish off.

Row 11: With **right** side facing, join Lt Teal with
sc in first sc; sc in same st, ch 1, sc in next ch-1 sp,
ch 1, sc in next 2 ch-1 sps, ch 1, sc in next ch-1 sp,
ch 1, ★ skip next sc, 3 sc in next sc, ch 1, sc in
next ch-1 sp, ch 1, sc in next 2 ch-1 sps, ch 1, sc in
next ch-1 sp, ch 1; repeat from ★ across to last
2 sc, skip next sc, 2 sc in last sc; finish off.

Row 12: With **wrong** side facing, join Teal with sc
in first sc; sc in same st, ch 1, sc in next ch-1 sp,
ch 1, sc in next 2 ch-1 sps, ch 1, sc in next ch-1 sp,
ch 1, ★ skip next sc, 3 sc in next sc, ch 1, sc in
next ch-1 sp, ch 1, sc in next 2 ch-1 sps, ch 1, sc in
next ch-1 sp, ch 1; repeat from ★ across to last
2 sc, skip next sc, 2 sc in last sc; finish off.

Row 13: With **right** side facing, join White with sc
in first sc; sc in same st, ch 1, sc in next ch-1 sp,
ch 1, sc in next 2 ch-1 sps, ch 1, sc in next ch-1 sp,
ch 1, ★ skip next sc, 3 sc in next sc, ch 1, sc in
next ch-1 sp, ch 1, sc in next 2 ch-1 sps, ch 1, sc in
next ch-1 sp, ch 1; repeat from ★ across to last
2 sc, skip next sc, 2 sc in last sc; do **not** finish off.

Rows 14 and 15: Ch 1, turn; 2 sc in first sc,
ch 1, sc in next ch-1 sp, ch 1, sc in next 2 ch-1 sps,
ch 1, sc in next ch-1 sp, ch 1, ★ skip next sc, 3 sc
in next sc, ch 1, sc in next ch-1 sp, ch 1, sc in next
2 ch-1 sps, ch 1, sc in next ch-1 sp, ch 1; repeat
from ★ across to last 2 sc, skip next sc, 2 sc in last
sc; at end of last row, finish off.

Rows 16-19: Repeat Rows 10-13.

Rows 20-171: Repeat Rows 2-19, 8 times; then
repeat Rows 2-9 once **more**.

Design by Kathleen Stuart.

Majestic

Finished Size: 62" x 76" (157.5 cm x 193 cm)

MATERIALS

Worsted Weight Yarn:
Purple - $24^1/2$ ounces, 1,385 yards
(700 grams, 1,266.5 meters)
Lt Purple - $19^1/2$ ounces, 1,100 yards
(550 grams, 1,006 meters)
Dk Purple - $19^1/2$ ounces, 1,100 yards
(550 grams, 1,006 meters)
Peach - $5^1/2$ ounces, 310 yards
(160 grams, 283.5 meters)
Dk Peach - $5^1/2$ ounces, 310 yards
(160 grams, 283.5 meters)
Lt Peach - 5 ounces, 285 yards
(140 grams, 260.5 meters)
Off-White - 5 ounces, 285 yards
(140 grams, 260.5 meters)
Crochet hook, size N (9 mm) **or** size needed
for gauge

Afghan is worked holding two strands of yarn
together throughout.

GAUGE: In pattern, one point to point repeat
(68 sts) = $26^1/2$" (67.25 cm);
5 rows = $5^3/4$" (14.5 cm)
8 dc and 5 rows = 4" (10 cm)

Gauge Swatch: 4" (10 cm) square
Holding 2 strands of Lt Purple together, ch 10.
Row 1: Dc in fourth ch from hook **(3 skipped
chs count as first dc)** and in each ch across: 8 dc.
Rows 2-5: Ch 3 **(counts as first dc)**, turn; dc in
next dc and in each dc across.
Finish off.

STITCH GUIDE

DC DECREASE (uses next 2 dc)
★ YO, insert hook in **next** dc, YO and pull up a
loop, YO and draw through 2 loops on hook;
repeat from ★ once **more**, YO and draw
through all 3 loops on hook **(counts as
one dc)**.

DOUBLE DECREASE (uses next 5 sts)
† YO, insert hook in **next** st, YO and pull up a
loop, YO and draw through 2 loops on hook †;
repeat from † to † once **more**, skip next st,
repeat from † to † twice, YO and draw through
all 5 loops on hook **(counts as one dc)**.

AFGHAN

Holding two strands of Lt Purple together, ch 159.

Row 1 (Right side)**:** Working in back ridges of
beginning ch **(Fig. 1, page 3)**, dc in fourth ch from
hook and in next 8 chs, 5 dc in next ch, dc in next
10 chs, ★ double decrease, dc in next 5 chs, 5 dc in
next ch, dc in next 10 chs, double decrease, dc in
next 10 chs, 5 dc in next ch, dc in next 5 chs,
double decrease, dc in next 10 chs, 5 dc in next ch,
dc in next 10 chs; repeat from ★ once **more**:
160 dc.

Note: Loop a short piece of yarn around any stitch
to mark Row 1 as **right** side.

Rows 2 and 3: Ch 2, turn; dc in next dc,
dc decrease, dc in next 8 dc, 5 dc in next dc, ★ dc
in next 10 dc, double decrease, dc in next 5 dc,
5 dc in next dc, dc in next 10 dc, double decrease,
dc in next 10 dc, 5 dc in next dc, dc in next 5 dc,
double decrease, dc in next 10 dc, 5 dc in next dc;
repeat from ★ once **more**, dc in next 8 dc,
dc decrease, dc in next dc, leave last st unworked.

Continued on page 123.

Playful Waves

Finished Size: 47" x 64" (119.5 cm x 162.5 cm)

MATERIALS
Worsted Weight Yarn:
  Dk Blue - 12 ounces, 680 yards
    (340 grams, 622 meters)
  Blue - 8 ounces, 450 yards
    (230 grams, 411.5 meters)
  Lt Blue - 5^1/$_2$ ounces, 310 yards
    (160 grams, 283.5 meters)
  White - 4 ounces, 225 yards
    (110 grams, 205.5 meters)
Crochet hook, size J (6 mm) **or** size needed
  for gauge

GAUGE: In pattern, one large point to large point
    repeat (48 sts) = 14" (35.5 cm);
    4 rows = 4^1/$_2$" (11.5 cm)

Gauge Swatch: 19"w x 4^1/$_2$"h (48.25 x 11.5 cm)
With Dk Blue, ch 67.
Work same as Afghan for 4 rows.

STITCH GUIDE

TREBLE CROCHET *(abbreviated tr)*
YO twice, insert hook in st indicated, YO and
pull up a loop (4 loops on hook), (YO and draw
through 2 loops on hook) 3 times.

DECREASE (uses next 2 sts)
★ YO twice, insert hook in **next** st, YO and pull
up a loop, (YO and draw through 2 loops on
hook) twice; repeat from ★ once **more**, YO and
draw through all 3 loops on hook **(counts as
one tr)**.

RIGHT DECREASE
  (uses next tr and next ch-1 sp)
YO twice, insert hook in next tr, YO and pull up
a loop, (YO and draw through 2 loops on hook)
twice, YO twice, insert hook in next ch-1 sp,
YO and pull up a loop, (YO and draw through
2 loops on hook) twice, YO and draw through
all 3 loops on hook **(counts as one tr)**.

LEFT DECREASE
  (uses next ch-1 sp and next tr)
YO twice, insert hook in next ch-1 sp, YO and
pull up a loop, (YO and draw through 2 loops
on hook) twice, YO twice, insert hook in next tr,
YO and pull up a loop, (YO and draw through
2 loops on hook) twice, YO and draw through
all 3 loops on hook **(counts as one tr)**.

AFGHAN
With Dk Blue, ch 163.

Row 1 (Right side): Working in back ridges of
beginning ch *(Fig. 1, page 3)*, tr in fourth ch from
hook, decrease twice, ch 1, (tr in next ch, ch 1) 5
times, ★ decrease 6 times, tr in next 7 chs, ch 1, (tr
in next ch, ch 1) 5 times, tr in next 7 chs,
decrease 6 times, ch 1, (tr in next ch, ch 1) 5 times;
repeat from ★ across to last 6 chs, decrease 3 times:
119 tr and 42 ch-1 sps.

Note: Loop a short piece of yarn around any stitch
to mark Row 1 as **right** side.

Rows 2-4: Ch 3, turn; working in **both** loops,
skip first tr, tr in next tr, work right decrease twice,
ch 1, tr in next tr, ch 1, (tr in next ch-1 sp, ch 1, tr
in next tr, ch 1) twice, work left decrease twice,
★ decrease 4 times, tr in next 4 tr and in next
ch-1 sp, tr in next tr and in next ch-1 sp, (ch 1, tr in
next tr, ch 1, tr in next ch-1 sp) 3 times, tr in next tr
and in next ch-1 sp, tr in next 4 tr,
decrease 4 times, work right decrease twice, ch 1, tr
in next tr, ch 1, (tr in next ch-1 sp, ch 1, tr in next
tr, ch 1) twice, work left decrease twice; repeat from
★ across to last 2 tr, decrease; at end of Row 4,
finish off.

Row 5: With **right** side facing, join Blue with slip st
in first tr; ch 3, tr in next tr, work
right decrease twice, ch 1, tr in next tr, ch 1, (tr in
next ch-1 sp, ch 1, tr in next tr, ch 1) twice, work
left decrease twice, ★ decrease 4 times, tr in next 4 tr
and in next ch-1 sp, tr in next tr and in next ch-1 sp,
(ch 1, tr in next tr, ch 1, tr in next ch-1 sp) 3 times,
tr in next tr and in next ch-1 sp, tr in next 4 tr,
decrease 4 times, work right decrease twice, ch 1, tr
in next tr, ch 1, (tr in next ch-1 sp, ch 1, tr in next tr,
ch 1) twice, work left decrease twice; repeat from ★
across to last 2 tr, decrease.

 Continued on page 124.

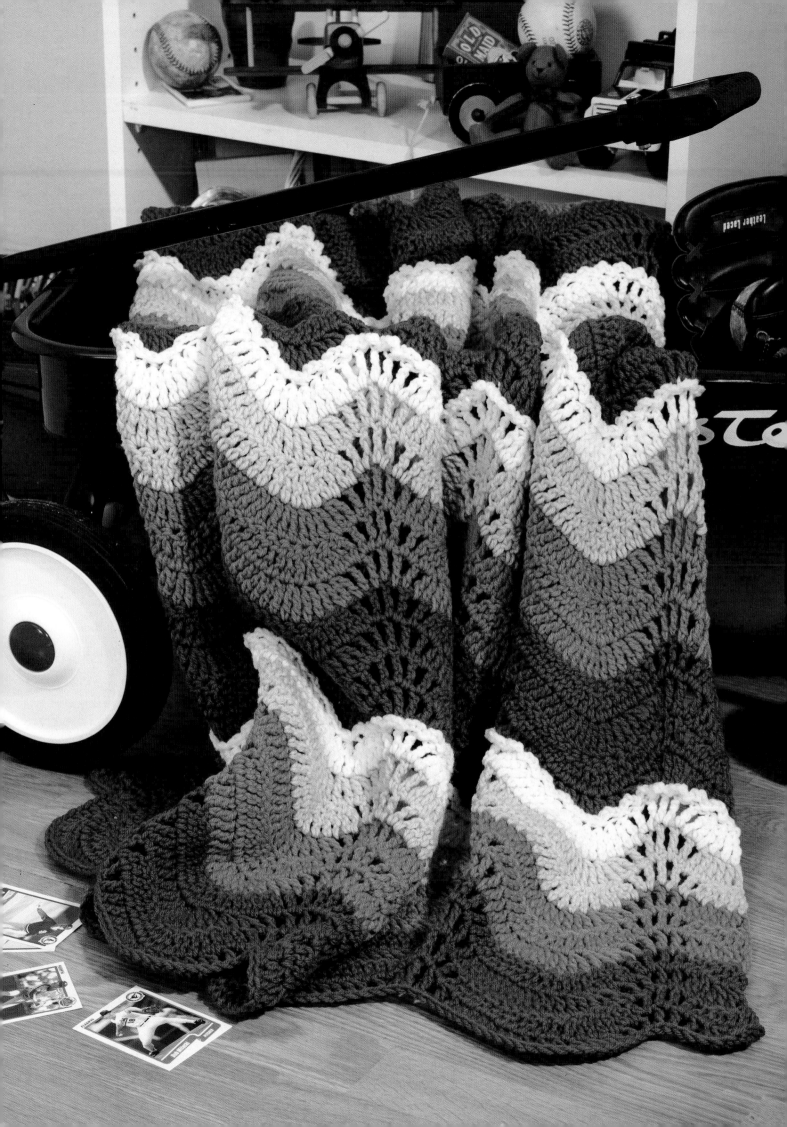

Simple Comfort

Finished Size: 45" x 62¹/₂" (114.5 cm x 159 cm)

MATERIALS
Worsted Weight Yarn:
  Off-White - 14 ounces, 790 yards
    (400 grams, 722.5 meters)
  Teal - 13¹/₂ ounces, 765 yards
    (380 grams, 699.5 meters)
  Dk Teal - 13¹/₂ ounces, 765 yards
    (380 grams, 699.5 meters)
Crochet hook, size H (5 mm) **or** size needed
  for gauge

GAUGE: In pattern, one point to point
  repeat (14 sts) = 4¹/₂" (11.5 cm);
  6 rows = 4¹/₄" (10.75 cm)

Gauge Swatch: 9¹/₂"w x 3"h
              (24.25 cm x 7.5 cm)
With Off-White, ch 32.
Work same as Afghan Body for 4 rows.

STITCH GUIDE

TREBLE CROCHET *(abbreviated tr)*
YO twice, insert hook in dc indicated, YO and
pull up a loop (4 loops on hook), (YO and draw
through 2 loops on hook) 3 times.

**FRONT POST DOUBLE TREBLE
CROCHET** *(abbreviated FPdtr)*
YO 3 times, insert hook from **front** to **back**
around post of st indicated *(Fig. 5, page 3)*,
YO and pull up a loop (5 loops on hook), (YO
and draw through 2 loops on hook) 4 times.

DC DECREASE (uses next 3 tr)
YO, insert hook in next tr, YO and pull up a
loop (3 loops on hook), YO and draw through
2 loops on hook, YO, skip next tr, insert hook
in next tr, YO and pull up a loop, YO and draw
through 2 loops on hook, YO and draw through
all 3 loops on hook **(counts as one dc)**.

ENDING DC DECREASE (uses last 2 sts)
★ YO, insert hook in **next** st, YO and pull up a
loop, YO and draw through 2 loops on hook;
repeat from ★ once **more**, YO and draw
through all 3 loops on hook **(counts as one
dc)**.

TR DECREASE (uses next 3 sts)
YO twice, insert hook in next dc, YO and pull
up a loop (4 loops on hook), (YO and draw
through 2 loops on hook) twice, YO twice, skip
next st, insert hook in next dc, YO and pull up a
loop, (YO and draw through 2 loops on hook)
twice, YO and draw through all 3 loops on hook
(counts as one tr).

ENDING TR DECREASE (uses last 2 dc)
★ YO twice, insert hook in **next** dc, YO and
pull up a loop, (YO and draw through 2 loops
on hook) twice; repeat from ★ once **more**, YO
and draw through all 3 loops on hook **(counts
as one tr)**.

AFGHAN BODY
With Off-White, ch 160.

Row 1 (Right side)**:** Dc in third ch from hook and
in next 5 chs, 3 dc in next ch, dc in next 5 chs,
★ YO, insert hook in next ch, YO and pull up a
loop, YO and draw through 2 loops on hook, (YO,
skip next ch, insert hook in **next** ch, YO and pull up
a loop, YO and draw through 2 loops on hook)
twice, YO and draw through all 4 loops on hook, dc
in next 5 chs, 3 dc in next ch, dc in next 5 chs;
repeat from ★ across to last 2 chs, work ending
dc decrease: 141 sts.

Note: Loop a short piece of yarn around any stitch
to mark Row 1 as **right** side.

Row 2: Ch 3, turn; tr in next 6 dc, (tr, ch 1, tr) in
next dc, tr in next 5 dc, ★ tr decrease, tr in next
5 dc, (tr, ch 1, tr) in next dc, tr in next 5 dc; repeat
from ★ across to last 2 dc, work ending tr decrease;
finish off: 131 tr and 10 ch-1 sps.

Continued on page 123.

Row 3: With **right** side facing, join Teal with slip st in first tr; ch 2, dc in next 6 tr, work FPdtr around first dc of 3-dc group one row **below** next ch-1 sp, dc in next ch-1 sp on previous row, work FPdtr around third dc of same 3-dc group one row **below**, dc in next 5 tr on previous row, ★ dc decrease, dc in next 5 tr, work FPdtr around first dc of next 3-dc group one row **below** next ch-1 sp, dc in next ch-1 sp on previous row, work FPdtr around third dc of same 3-dc group one row **below**, dc in next 5 tr on previous row; repeat from ★ across to last 2 tr, work ending dc decrease: 121 dc and 20 FPdtr.

Row 4: Ch 3, turn; tr in next 6 sts, (tr, ch 1, tr) in next dc, tr in next 5 sts, ★ tr decrease, tr in next 5 sts, (tr, ch 1, tr) in next dc, tr in next 5 sts; repeat from ★ across to last 2 dc, work ending tr decrease; finish off: 131 tr and 10 ch-1 sps.

Row 5: With **right** side facing, join Dk Teal with slip st in first tr; ch 2, dc in next 6 tr, work FPdtr around next FPdtr one row **below** next ch-1 sp, dc in next ch-1 sp on previous row, work FPdtr around next FPdtr one row **below**, dc in next 5 tr on previous row, ★ dc decrease, dc in next 5 tr, work FPdtr around next FPdtr one row **below** next ch-1 sp, dc in next ch-1 sp on previous row, work FPdtr around next FPdtr one row **below**, dc in next 5 tr on previous row; repeat from ★ across to last 2 tr, work ending dc decrease: 121 dc and 20 FPdtr.

Row 6: Ch 3, turn; tr in next 6 sts, (tr, ch 1, tr) in next dc, tr in next 5 sts, ★ tr decrease, tr in next 5 sts, (tr, ch 1, tr) in next dc, tr in next 5 sts; repeat from ★ across to last 2 dc, work ending tr decrease; finish off: 131 tr and 10 ch-1 sps.

Rows 7 and 8: With Off-White, repeat Rows 5 and 6.

Rows 9 and 10: With Teal, repeat Rows 5 and 6.

Rows 11-86: Repeat Rows 5-10, 12 times; then repeat Rows 5-8 once **more**; at end of Row 86, do **not** finish off.

TRIM
TOP
Ch 1, turn; sc in first 7 tr, (sc, ch 3, sc) in next ch-1 sp, ★ sc in next 6 tr, skip next tr, sc in next 6 tr, (sc, ch 3, sc) in next ch-1 sp; repeat from ★ across to last 7 tr, sc in last 7 tr; finish off.

BOTTOM
With **right** side facing and working in free loops *(Fig. 3b, page 3)* and in sps across beginning ch, join Off-White with sc in first ch *(see Joining With Sc, page 1)*; sc in next 6 chs, ★ skip next ch, sc in next 6 chs and in next sp, (sc, ch 3, sc) in next ch, sc in next sp and in next 6 chs; repeat from ★ across to last 8 chs, skip next ch, sc in next 7 chs; finish off.

Design by Leanna Moon.

Majestic
Continued from page 117.

Row 4: Cut one strand of Lt Purple; holding one strand of Lt Purple and one strand of Purple together, ch 2, turn; dc in next dc, dc decrease, dc in next 8 dc, 5 dc in next dc, ★ dc in next 10 dc, double decrease, dc in next 5 dc, 5 dc in next dc, dc in next 10 dc, double decrease, dc in next 10 dc, 5 dc in next dc, dc in next 5 dc, double decrease, dc in next 10 dc, 5 dc in next dc; repeat from ★ once **more**, dc in next 8 dc, dc decrease, dc in next dc, leave last dc unworked.

Rows 5 and 6: Repeat Rows 2 and 3.

Row 7: Cut Lt Purple; holding two strands of Purple together, repeat Row 4.

Rows 8 and 9: Repeat Rows 2 and 3.

Row 10: Cut one strand of Purple; holding one strand of Purple and one strand of Dk Purple together, repeat Row 4.

Rows 11 and 12: Repeat Rows 2 and 3.

Row 13: Cut Purple; holding two strands of Dk Purple together, repeat Row 4.

Rows 14 and 15: Repeat Rows 2 and 3; at end of last row, finish off.

Row 16: With **wrong** side facing and holding two strands of Lt Peach together, join with slip st in first dc; ch 2, dc in next dc, dc decrease, dc in next 8 dc, 5 dc in next dc, ★ dc in next 10 dc, double decrease, dc in next 5 dc, 5 dc in next dc, dc in next 10 dc, double decrease, dc in next 10 dc, 5 dc in next dc, dc in next 5 dc, double decrease, dc in next 10 dc, 5 dc in next dc; repeat from ★ once **more**, dc in next 8 dc, dc decrease, dc in next dc, leave last dc unworked.

Row 17: Cut one strand of Lt Peach; holding one strand of Lt Peach and one strand of Peach together, repeat Row 4.

Row 18: Cut Lt Peach; holding two strands of Peach together, repeat Row 4.

Row 19: Cut one strand of Peach; holding one strand of Peach and one strand of Dk Peach together, repeat Row 4.

Row 20: Cut Peach; holding two strands of Dk Peach together, repeat Row 4.

Row 21: Cut one strand of Dk Peach; holding one strand of Dk Peach and one strand of Off-White together, repeat Row 4.

Row 22: Cut Dk Peach; holding two strands of Off-White together, repeat Row 4; finish off.

Row 23: With **right** side facing and holding two strands of Lt Purple together, join with slip st in first dc; ch 2, dc in next dc, dc decrease, dc in next 8 dc, 5 dc in next dc, ★ dc in next 10 dc, double decrease, dc in next 5 dc, 5 dc in next dc, dc in next 10 dc, double decrease, dc in next 10 dc, 5 dc in next dc, dc in next 5 dc, double decrease, dc in next 10 dc, 5 dc in next dc; repeat from ★ once **more**, dc in next 8 dc, dc decrease, dc in next dc, leave last dc unworked.

Rows 24-59: Repeat Rows 2-23 once, then repeat Rows 2-15 once **more**.

Design by Julene S. Watson.

Playful Waves

Continued from page 119.

Rows 6 and 7: Repeat Rows 2 and 3; at end of Row 7, finish off.

Row 8: With **wrong** side facing, join Lt Blue with slip st in first tr; ch 3, tr in next tr, work right decrease twice, ch 1, tr in next tr, ch 1, (tr in next ch-1 sp, ch 1, tr in next tr, ch 1) twice, work left decrease twice, ★ decrease 4 times, tr in next 4 tr and in next ch-1 sp, tr in next tr and in next ch-1 sp, (ch 1, tr in next tr, ch 1, tr in next ch-1 sp) 3 times, tr in next tr and in next ch-1 sp, tr in next 4 tr, decrease 4 times, work right decrease twice, ch 1, tr in next tr, ch 1, (tr in next ch-1 sp, ch 1, tr in next tr, ch 1) twice, work left decrease twice; repeat from ★ across to last 2 tr, decrease.

Row 9: Repeat Row 2; finish off.

Row 10: With **wrong** side facing, join White with slip st in first tr; ch 3, tr in next tr, work right decrease twice, ch 1, tr in next tr, ch 1, (tr in next ch-1 sp, ch 1, tr in next tr, ch 1) twice, work left decrease twice, ★ decrease 4 times, tr in next 4 tr and in next ch-1 sp, tr in next tr and in next ch-1 sp, (ch 1, tr in next tr, ch 1, tr in next ch-1 sp) 3 times, tr in next tr and in next ch-1 sp, tr in next 4 tr, decrease 4 times, work right decrease twice, ch 1, tr in next tr, ch 1, (tr in next ch-1 sp, ch 1, tr in next tr, ch 1) twice, work left decrease twice; repeat from ★ across to last 2 tr, decrease.

Row 11: Turn; working in sts and in chs, and working in Front Loops Only *(Fig. 2, page 3)*, slip st in first tr, ch 1, slip st in next tr, (ch 3, skip next tr, slip st in next st) 7 times, ★ (ch 1, skip next tr, slip st in next tr) twice, (ch 3, skip next tr, slip st in next st) 13 times, (ch 1, skip next tr, slip st in next tr) twice, (ch 3, skip next tr, slip st in next st) 7 times; repeat from ★ across to last tr, ch 1, slip st in last tr; finish off.

Row 12: With **right** side facing and working in Back Loops Only of skipped tr *(Fig. 2, page 3)* and in free loops of sts on Row 10 *(Fig. 3a, page 3)*, join Dk Blue with slip st in first tr; ch 3, tr in next tr, decrease twice, ch 1, (tr in next st, ch 1) 5 times, ★ decrease 6 times, tr in next 7 sts, ch 1, (tr in next st, ch 1) 5 times, tr in next 7 sts, decrease 6 times, ch 1, (tr in next st, ch 1) 5 times; repeat from ★ across to last 6 sts, decrease 3 times.

Rows 13-59: Repeat Rows 2-12, 4 times; then repeat Rows 2-4 once **more**.

Design by Rena V. Stevens.

YARN INFORMATION

Each Afghan in this leaflet was made using Worsted Weight Yarn.
Any brand of Worsted Weight Yarn may be used. It is best to refer to the
yardage/meters when determining how many balls or skeins to purchase.
Remember, to arrive at the finished size, it is the GAUGE/TENSION
that is most important, not the brand of yarn.

For your convenience, listed below are the specific yarns
used to create our photography models.

WINE ON THE VINE

Red Heart® Super Saver®
Variegated - #997 Sage Mary
Dk Plum - #533 Dk Plum
Dk Green - #633 Dk Sage
Tan - #334 Buff

SNOWMAN RIDGE

Red Heart® Super Saver®
White - #311 White
Blue - #347 Lt Periwinkle
Dk Blue - #385 Royal
Variegated - #968 Starbrights

EMBOSSED RIPPLE

Red Heart® Soft
Off-White - #7313 New Aran
Blue - #7883 Country Blue

ROMANTIC MELODY

Red Heart® Super Saver®
Ecru - #313 Aran
Rose - #374 Country Rose

HUGS & KISSES

Red Heart® Soft
Ecru - #7313 New Aran
Lt Rose - #7772 Lt Country Rose
Rose - #7775 Country Rose
Dk Rose - #7760 Cranberry

PATRIOTIC PARADE

Red Heart® Super Saver®
Blue - #387 Soft Navy
Red - #376 Burgundy
Ecru - #313 Aran

WAVES OF BLUE

Red Heart® Soft®
White - #7001 White
Dk Blue - #7855 Navy
Blue - #7847 Royal Blue

Red Heart® Super Saver®
Lt Blue - #384 Skipper Blue

EVERGREEN FOREST

Red Heart® Super Saver®
Ecru - #313 Aran
Green - #389 Hunter Green

LULLABY

Red Heart® Classic®
Blue - #815 Pale Blue
Pink - #719 Lily Pink
White - #1 White

WAVES OF GRAIN

Red Heart® Soft
Ecru - #7313 New Aran
Tan - #7335 Camel

DAISY BORDER

Red Heart® Super Saver®
Variegated - #305 Aspen Print
Ecru - #313 Aran
Green - #631 Lt Sage
Brown - #336 Warm Brown
Yellow - #320 Cornmeal

BLUE SKIES

Red Heart® Super Saver®
White - #311 White
Lt Blue - #381 Lt Blue
Blue - #885 Delft Blue
Dk Blue - #886 Blue

IMPRESSIVE PLAID

Red Heart® Super Saver®
Black - #312 Black
Red - #319 Cherry Red
Grey - #400 Grey Heather

RUFFLED INTRIGUE

Red Heart® Super Saver®
Purple - #579 Pale Plum
Lt Purple - #531 Lt Plum
White - #316 Soft White

AMERICAN WAVES

Red Heart® Classic®
Red - #914 Country Red

Red Heart® Super Saver®
White - #311 White
Blue - #387 Soft Navy

LADY'S CHOICE

Red Heart® Classic®
Lt Green - #631 Lt Sage
Ecru - #111 Eggshell
Red - #760 New Berry
Green - #632 Med Sage

AZTEC SUN

Red Heart® Classic®
Red - #902 Jockey Red
Yellow - #230 Yellow
Orange - #253 Tangerine

CANDY STRIPE

Red Heart® Classic®
White - #1 White
Pink - #719 Lily Pink
Blue - #818 Blue Jewel
Yellow - #261 Maize
Green - #681 Mist Green

RIPPLING RIBBONS

Caron® Simply Soft
Blue - #2626 Country Blue
Dk Blue - #2628 Dk Country Blue
Cream - #2603 Fisherman

ROSEBUD

Red Heart® Soft
Green - #7675 Dk Yellow Green
Pink - #7772 Lt Country Rose
Lt Green - #7672 Lt Yellow Green

GRANNY'S RIPPLE

Red Heart® Super Saver®
Dk Purple - #533 Dk Plum
Lt Purple - #531 Lt Plum
Purple - #579 Pale Plum
Yellow - #320 Cornmeal